PEARSON

ALWAYS LEARNING

Financial Risk Manager (FRM®) Exam Part I

Foundations of Risk Management

Sixth Custom Edition for
Global Association of Risk Professionals
2016

 GARP | Global Association
of Risk Professionals

Grateful acknowledgment is made to the following sources for permission to reprint material copyrighted or controlled by them:

"Risk Management: A Helicopter View," "Typology of Risk Exposures," "Corporate Risk Management: A Primer," and "Corporate Governance and Risk Management," by Michael Crouhy, Dan Galai, and Robert Mark, reprinted from *The Essentials of Risk Management,* Second Edition (2014), by permission of The McGraw-Hill Companies.

"What is ERM?" by James Lam, reprinted from *Enterprise Risk Management: From Incentives to Controls*, Second Edition (2014), by permission of John Wiley & Sons, Inc.

"Risk-Taking and Risk Management by Banks," by René Stulz, reprinted from the *Journal of Applied Corporate Finance* 27, No. 1 (2015), by permission of John Wiley & Sons, Inc.

"Financial Disasters," by Steve Allen, reprinted from *Financial Risk Management: A Practitioner's Guide to Managing Market and Credit Risk*, Second Edition (2013), by permission of John Wiley & Sons, Inc.

"The Credit Crisis of 2007," by John Hull, reprinted from *Risk Management and Financial Institutions*, Third Edition (2012), by permission of John Wiley & Sons, Inc.

"Risk Management Failures: What are they and when do they happen?" by René Stulz, reprinted from the *Journal of Applied Corporate Finance* 20, No. 4 (October 2008), by permission of the author.

"The Standard Capital Asset Pricing Model," by Edwin J. Elton et al., reprinted from *Modern Portfolio Theory and Investment Analysis*, Ninth Edition (2014), by permission of John Wiley & Sons, Inc.

"Applying the CAPM to Performance Measurement: Single-Index Performance Measurement Indicators," by Noel Amenc and Veronique Le Sourd, reprinted from *Portfolio Theory and Performance Analysis* (2003), by permission of John Wiley & Sons, Inc.

"Arbitrage Pricing Theory and Multifactor Models of Risk and Return," by Zvi Bodie, Alex Kane, and Alan J. Marcus, reprinted from *Investments*, Tenth Edition (2013), by permission of The McGraw-Hill Companies.

"Information Risk and Data Quality Management," by David Loshin, reprinted from *Risk Management in Finance: Six Sigma and Other Next-Generation Techniques*, edited by Anthony Tarantino and Deborah Cernauskas (2009), by permission of John Wiley & Sons, Inc.

"Principles for Effective Data Aggregation and Risk Reporting," reprinted from *Basel Committee on Banking Supervision Publication* (January 2013), by permission of the Basel Committee on Banking Supervision.

Learning Objectives provided by the Global Association of Risk Professionals.

All trademarks, service marks, registered trademarks, and registered service marks are the property of their respective owners and are used herein for identification purposes only.

Pearson Learning Solutions, 330 Hudson Street, New York, New York 10013
A Pearson Education Company
www.pearsoned.com

Printed in the United States of America

3 16

000200010272005411

AM/KE

ISBN 10: 1-323-30853-9
ISBN 13: 978-1-323-30853-0

Contents

2016 FRM Committee Members

Dr. René Stulz (Chairman)
Ohio State University

Richard Apostolik
Global Association of Risk Professionals

Richard Brandt
Citibank

Dr. Christopher Donohue
Global Association of Risk Professionals

Hervé Geny
London Stock Exchange

Keith Isaac, FRM®
TD Bank

Steve Lerit, CFA
UBS Wealth Management

William May
Global Association of Risk Professionals

Michelle McCarthy
Nuveen Investments

Dr. Victor Ng
Goldman Sachs & Co

Dr. Elliot Noma
Garrett Asset Management

Dr. Matthew Pritsker
Federal Reserve Bank of Boston

Liu Ruixia
Industrial and Commercial Bank of China

Dr. Til Schuermann
Oliver Wyman

Nick Strange
Bank of England, Prudential Regulation Authority

Serge Sverdlov
Redmond Analytics

Alan Weindorf
Visa

Risk Management: A Helicopter View[1]

Learning Objectives

Candidates, after completing this reading, should be able to:

- Explain the concept of risk and compare risk management with risk taking.
- Describe the risk management process and identify problems and challenges which can arise in the risk management process.
- Evaluate and apply tools and procedures used to measure and manage risk, including quantitative measures, qualitative assessment, and enterprise risk management.

- Distinguish between expected loss and unexpected loss, and provide examples of each.
- Interpret the relationship between risk and reward and explain how conflicts of interest can impact risk management.
- Describe and differentiate between the key classes of risks, explain how each type of risk can arise, and assess the potential impact of each type of risk on an organization.

Excerpt is Chapter 1 and Appendix 1.1 of The Essentials of Risk Management, *Second Edition, by Michel Crouhy, Dan Galai, and Robert Mark.*

---

[1] We acknowledge the coauthorship of Rob Jameson in this chapter.

The future cannot be predicted. It is uncertain, and no one has ever been successful in consistently forecasting the stock market, interest rates, exchange rates, or commodity prices—or credit, operational, and systemic events with major financial implications. However, the financial risk that arises from uncertainty can be managed. Indeed, much of what distinguishes modern economies from those of the past is the new ability to identify risk, to measure it, to appreciate its consequences, and then to take action accordingly, such as transferring or mitigating the risk. One of the most important aspects of modern risk management is the ability, in many instances, to price risks and ensure that risks undertaken in business activities are correctly rewarded.

This simple sequence of activities, shown in more detail in Figure 1-1, is often used to define risk management as a formal discipline. But it's a sequence that rarely runs smoothly in practice. Sometimes simply identifying a risk is the critical problem; at other times arranging an efficient economic transfer of the risk is the skill that makes one risk manager stand out from another. (In Chapter 2 we discuss the risk management process from the perspective of a corporation.)

To the unwary, Figure 1-1 might suggest that risk management is a continual process of corporate risk reduction. But we mustn't think of the modern attempt to master risk in defensive terms alone. Risk management is really about how firms actively select the type and level of risk that it is appropriate for them to assume. Most business decisions are about sacrificing current resources for future uncertain returns.

In this sense, *risk management* and *risk taking* aren't opposites, but two sides of the same coin. Together they drive all our modern economies. The capacity to make forward-looking choices about risk in relation to reward, and to evaluate performance, lies at the heart of the management process of all enduringly successful corporations.

Yet the rise of financial risk management as a formal discipline has been a bumpy affair, especially over the last 15 years. On the one hand, we have had some extraordinary successes in risk management mechanisms (e.g., the lack of financial institution bankruptcies in the downturn in credit quality in 2001-2002) and we have seen an extraordinary growth in new institutions that earn their keep by taking and managing risk (e.g., hedge funds). On the other hand, the spectacular failure to control risk in the run-up to the 2007-2009 financial crisis revealed

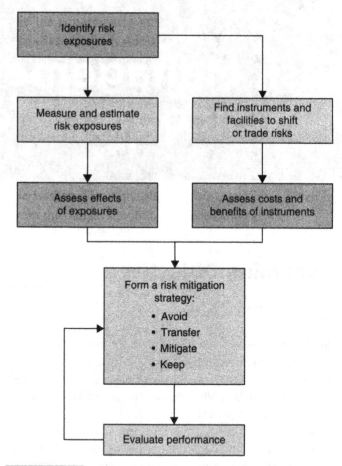

FIGURE 1-1 The risk management process.

fundamental weaknesses in the risk management process of many banks and the banking system as a whole.

As a result, risk management is now widely acknowledged as one of the most powerful forces in the world's financial markets, in both a positive and a negative sense. A striking example is the development of a huge market for credit derivatives, which allows institutions to obtain insurance to protect themselves against credit default and the widening of credit spreads (or, alternatively, to get paid for assuming credit risk as an investment). Credit derivatives can be used to redistribute part or all of an institution's credit risk exposures to banks, hedge funds, or other institutional investors. However, the misuse of credit derivatives also helped to destabilize institutions during the 2007-2009 crisis and to fuel fears of a systemic meltdown.

Back in 2002, Alan Greenspan, then chairman of the U.S. Federal Reserve Board, made some optimistic remarks about the power of risk management to improve the world, but the conditionality attached to his observations proved to be rather important:

> The development of our paradigms for containing risk has emphasized dispersion of risk to those willing, and presumably able, to bear it. If risk is properly dispersed, shocks to the overall economic system will be better absorbed and less likely to create cascading failures that could threaten financial stability.[2]

In the financial crisis of 2007–2009, risk turned out to have been concentrated rather than dispersed, and this is far from the only embarrassing failure of risk management in recent decades. Other catastrophes range from the near failure of the giant hedge fund Long-Term Capital Management (LTCM) in 1998 to the string of financial scandals associated with the millennial boom in the equity and technology markets (from Enron, WorldCom, Global Crossing, and Qwest in the United States to Parmalat in Europe and Satyam in Asia).

Unfortunately, risk management has not consistently been able to prevent market disruptions or to prevent business accounting scandals resulting from breakdowns in corporate governance. In the case of the former problem, there are serious concerns that derivative markets make it easier to take on large amounts of risk, and that the "herd behavior" of risk managers after a crisis gets underway (e.g., selling risky asset classes when risk measures reach a certain level) actually increases market volatility.

Sophisticated financial engineering played a significant role in obscuring the true economic condition and risk-taking of financial companies in the run-up to the 2007–2009 crisis, and also helped to cover up the condition of many nonfinancial corporations during the equity markets' millennial boom and bust. Alongside simpler accounting mistakes and ruses, financial engineering can lead to the violent implosion of firms (and industries) after years of false success, rather than the firms' simply fading away or being taken over at an earlier point.

Part of the reason for risk management's mixed record here lies with the double-edged nature of risk management technologies. Every financial instrument that allows a company to transfer risk also allows other corporations to assume that risk as a counterparty in the same market—wisely or not. Most important, every risk management mechanism that allows us to change the shape of cash flows, such as deferring a negative outcome into the future, may work to the short-term benefit of one group of stakeholders in a firm (e.g., managers) at the same time that it is destroying long-term value for another group (e.g., shareholders or pensioners). In a world that is increasingly driven by risk management concepts and technologies, we need to look more carefully at the increasingly fluid and complex nature of risk itself, and at how to determine whether any change in a corporation's risk profile serves the interests of stakeholders. We need to make sure we are at least as literate in the language of risk as we are in the language of reward.

. . .

WHAT IS RISK?

We're all faced with risk in our everyday lives. And although risk is an abstract term, our natural human understanding of the trade-offs between risk and reward is pretty sophisticated. For example, in our personal lives, we intuitively understand the difference between a cost that's already been budgeted for (in risk parlance, a predictable or expected loss) and an unexpected cost (at its worst, a catastrophic loss of a magnitude well beyond losses seen in the course of normal daily life).

In particular, we understand that risk is not synonymous with the *size* of a cost or of a loss. After all, some of the costs we expect in daily life are very large indeed if we think in terms of our annual budgets: food, fixed mortgage payments, college fees, and so on. These costs are big, but they are not a threat to our ambitions because they are reasonably predictable and are already allowed for in our plans.

The real *risk* is that these costs will suddenly rise in an entirely unexpected way, or that some other cost will appear from nowhere and steal the money we've set aside for our expected outlays. The risk lies in how *variable* our costs and revenues really are. In particular, we care about how likely it is that we'll encounter a loss big enough to upset our plans (one that we have not defused through some piece of personal risk management such as taking out a fixed-rate mortgage, setting aside savings for a rainy day, and so on).

---

[2] Remarks by Chairman Alan Greenspan before the Council on Foreign Relations, Washington, D.C., November 19, 2002.

This day-to-day analogy makes it easier to understand the difference between the risk management concepts of *expected loss* (or expected costs) and *unexpected loss* (or unexpected cost). Understanding this difference is the key to understanding modern risk management concepts such as economic capital attribution and risk-adjusted pricing. (However, this is not the only way to define risk.)

One of the key differences between our intuitive conception of risk and a more formal treatment of it is the use of statistics to define the extent and potential cost of any exposure. To develop a number for unexpected loss, a bank risk manager first identifies the risk factors that seem to drive volatility in any outcome (Box 1-1) and then uses statistical analysis to calculate the probabilities of various outcomes for the position or portfolio under consideration. This probability distribution can be used in various ways. For example, the risk manager might pinpoint the area of the distribution (i.e., the extent of loss) that the institution would find worrying, given the probability of this loss occurring (e.g., is it a 1 in 10 or a 1 in 10,000 chance?).

The distribution can also be related to the institution's stated "risk appetite" for its various activities. For example, as we discuss in Chapter 3, the senior risk committee at the bank might have set boundaries on the amount of risk that the institution is willing to take by specifying the maximum loss it is willing to tolerate at a given level of confidence, such as, "We are willing to countenance a 1 percent chance of a $50 million loss from our trading desks on any given day."

Since the 2007–2009 financial crisis, risk managers have tried to move away from an overdependence on historical-statistical treatments of risk. For example, they have laid more emphasis on scenario analysis and stress testing, which examine the impact or outcomes of a given adverse scenario or stress on a firm (or portfolio). The scenario may be chosen not on the basis of statistical analysis, but instead simply because it is both plausible and suitably severe—essentially, a judgment call. However, it can be difficult and perhaps unwise to remove statistical approaches from the picture entirely. For example, in the more sophisticated forms of scenario analysis, the firm will need to examine how a change in a given macroeconomic factor (e.g., unemployment rate) leads to a change in a given risk factor (e.g., the probability of default of a corporation). Making this link almost inevitably means looking back to the

BOX 1-1 Risk Factors and the Modeling of Risk

In order to measure risk, the risk analyst first seeks to identify the key factors that seem likely to cause volatility in the returns from the position or portfolio under consideration. For example, in the case of an equity investment, the risk factor will be the volatility of the stock price (categorized in the appendix to this chapter as a market risk), which can be estimated in various ways.

In this case, we identified a single risk factor. But the number of risk factors that are considered in a risk analysis—and included in any risk modeling—varies considerably depending on both the problem and the sophistication of the approach. For example, in the recent past, bank risk analysts might have analyzed the risk of an interest-rate position in terms of the effect of a single risk factor—e.g., the yield to maturity of government bonds, assuming that the yields for all maturities are perfectly correlated. But this one-factor model approach ignored the risk that the dynamic of the term structure of interest rates is driven by more factors—e.g., the forward rates. Nowadays, leading banks analyze their interest-rate exposures using at least two or three factors.

Further, the risk manager must also measure the influence of the risk factors on each other, the statistical measure of which is the "covariance." Disentangling the effects of multiple risk factors and quantifying the influence of each is a fairly complicated undertaking, especially when covariance alters over time (i.e., is *stochastic,* in the modeler's terminology). There is often a distinct difference in the behavior and relationship of risk factors during normal business conditions and during stressful conditions such as financial crises.

Under ordinary market conditions, the behavior of risk factors is relatively less difficult to predict because it does not change significantly in the short and medium term: future behavior can be extrapolated, to some extent, from past performance. However, during stressful conditions, the behavior of risk factors becomes far more unpredictable, and past behavior may offer little help in predicting future behavior. It's at this point that statistically measurable risk threatens to turn into the kind of unmeasurable uncertainty that we discuss in Box 1-2.

past to examine the nature of the statistical relationship between macroeconomic factors and risk factors, though a degree of judgment must also be factored into the analysis.

The use of statistical, economic, and stress testing concepts can make risk management sound pretty technical. But the risk manager is simply doing more formally what we all do when we ask ourselves in our personal lives, "How bad, within reason, might this problem get?" The statistical models can also help in pricing risk, or pricing the instruments that help to eliminate or mitigate the risks.

What does our distinction between expected loss and unexpected loss mean in terms of running a financial business, such as a specific banking business line? Well, the *expected* credit loss for a credit card portfolio, for example, refers to how much the bank expects to lose, on average, as a result of fraud and defaults by cardholders over a period of time, say one year. In the case of large and well-diversified portfolios (i.e., most consumer credit portfolios), expected loss accounts for almost all losses that are incurred in normal times. Because it is, by definition, predictable, expected loss is generally viewed as one of the costs of doing business, and ideally it is priced into the products and services offered to the customer. For credit cards, the expected loss is recovered by charging the businesses a certain commission (2 to 4 percent) and by charging a spread to the customer on any borrowed money, over and above the bank's funding cost (i.e., the rate the bank pays to raise funds in the money markets and elsewhere). The bank recovers mundane operating costs, such as the salaries it pays tellers, in much the same way.

The level of loss associated with a large standard credit card portfolio is relatively predictable because the portfolio is made up of numerous bite-sized exposures and the fortunes of most customers, most of the time, are not closely tied to one another. On the whole, you are not much more likely to lose your job today because your neighbor lost hers last week. There are some important exceptions to this, of course. During a prolonged and severe recession, your fortunes may become much more correlated with those of your neighbor, particularly if you work in the same industry and live in a particularly vulnerable region. Even in the relatively good times, the fortunes of small local banks, as well as their card portfolios, are somewhat driven by socioeconomic characteristics.

A corporate loan portfolio, however, tends to be much "lumpier" than a retail portfolio (i.e., there are more big loans). Furthermore, if we look at industry data on commercial loan losses over a period of decades, it's much

more apparent that in some years losses spike upward to *unexpected* loss levels, driven by risk factors that suddenly begin to act together. For example, the default rate for a bank that lends too heavily to the technology sector will be driven not just by the health of individual borrowers, but by the business cycle of the technology sector as a whole. When the technology sector shines, making loans will look risk-free for an extended period; when the economic rain comes, it will soak any banker that has allowed lending to become too concentrated among similar or interrelated borrowers. So, correlation risk—the tendency for things to go wrong together—is a major factor when evaluating the risk of this kind of portfolio.

The tendency for things to go wrong together isn't confined to the clustering of defaults among a portfolio of commercial borrowers. Whole classes of risk factors can begin to move together, too. In the world of credit risk, real estate-linked loans are a famous example of this: they are often secured with real estate collateral, which tends to lose value at exactly the same time that the default rate for property developers and owners rises. In this case, the "recovery-rate risk" on any defaulted loan is itself closely correlated with the "default-rate risk." The two risk factors acting together can sometimes force losses abruptly skyward.

In fact, anywhere in the world that we see risks (and not just credit risks) that are lumpy (i.e., in large blocks, such as very large loans) and that are driven by risk factors that under certain circumstances can become linked together (i.e., that are correlated), we can predict that at certain times high "unexpected losses" will be realized. We can try to estimate how bad this problem is by looking at the historical severity of these events in relation to any risk factors that we define and then examining the prevalence of these risk factors (e.g., the type and concentration of real estate collateral) in the particular portfolio under examination.

Our general point immediately explains why bankers became so excited about new credit risk transfer technologies such as credit derivatives. These bankers weren't looking to reduce predictable levels of loss. Instead, the new instruments seemed to offer ways to put a cap on the problem of high unexpected losses and all the capital costs and uncertainty that these bring.

The conception of risk as unexpected loss underpins two key concepts that we'll deal with in more detail later in this book: value-at-risk (VaR) and economic capital. VaR, is a statistical measure that defines a particular level of loss in terms of its chances of occurrence (the "confidence level" of the analysis, in risk management jargon). For example, we might say that our options position has a one-day VaR of $1 million at the 99% confidence level, meaning that our risk analysis shows that there is only a 1 percent probability of a loss that is greater than $1 million on any given trading day.

In effect, we're saying that if we have $1 million in liquid reserves, there's little chance that the options position will lead to insolvency. Furthermore, because we can estimate the cost of holding liquid reserves, our risk analysis gives us a pretty good idea of the cost of taking this risk.

Under the risk paradigm we've just described, risk management becomes not the process of controlling and reducing expected losses (which is essentially a budgeting, pricing, and business efficiency concern), but the process of understanding, costing, and efficiently managing unexpected levels of variability in the financial outcomes for a business. Under this paradigm, even a conservative business can take on a significant amount of risk quite rationally, in light of

- Its confidence in the way it assesses and measures the unexpected loss levels associated with its various activities
- The accumulation of sufficient capital or the deployment of other risk management techniques to protect against potential unexpected loss levels
- Appropriate returns from the risky activities, once the costs of risk capital and risk management are taken into account
- Clear communication with stakeholders about the company's target risk profile (i.e., its solvency standard once risk-taking and risk mitigation are accounted for)

This takes us back to our assertion that risk management is not just a defensive activity. The more accurately a business understands and can measure its risks against potential rewards, its business goals, and its ability to withstand unexpected but plausible scenarios, the more risk-adjusted reward the business can aggressively capture in the marketplace without driving itself to destruction.

As Box 1-2 discusses, it's important in any risk analysis to acknowledge that some factors that might create volatility in outcomes simply can't be measured—even though they may be very important. The presence of this kind of risk factor introduces an uncertainty that needs to be

made transparent, and perhaps explored using worst-case scenario analysis. Furthermore, even when statistical analysis of risk *can* be conducted, it's vital to make explicit the robustness of the underlying model, data, and risk parameter estimation.

THE CONFLICT OF RISK AND REWARD

In financial markets, as well as in many commercial activities, if one wants to achieve a higher rate of return on average, one often has to assume more risk. But the transparency of the trade-off between risk and return is highly variable.

In some cases, relatively efficient markets for risky assets help to make clear the returns that investors demand for assuming risk.

Even in the bond markets, the "price" of credit risk implied by these numbers for a particular counterparty is not quite transparent. Though bond prices are a pretty good guide to relative risk, various additional factors, such as liquidity risk and tax effects, confuse the price signal. Moreover, investors' appetite for assuming certain kinds of risk varies over time. Sometimes the differential in yield between a risky and a risk-free bond narrows to such an extent that commentators talk of an "irrational" price of credit. That was the case during the period from early 2005 to mid–2007, until the eruption of the subprime crisis. With the eruption of the crisis, credit spreads moved up dramatically, and reached a peak following the collapse of Lehman Brothers in September 2008.

However, in the case of risks that are not associated with any kind of market-traded financial instrument, the problem of making transparent the relationship between risk and reward is even more profound. A key objective of risk management is to tackle this issue and make clear the potential for large losses in the future arising from activities that generate an apparently attractive stream of profits in the short run.

Ideally, discussions about this kind of trade-off between future profits and opaque risks would be undertaken within corporations on a basis that is rational for the firm as a whole. But organizations with a poor risk management and risk governance culture sometimes allow powerful business leaders to exaggerate the potential returns while diminishing the perceived potential risks. When rewards are not properly adjusted for economic

Risk, Uncertainty . . . and Transparency about the Difference

In this chapter, we discuss risk as if it were synonymous with uncertainty. In fact, since the 1920s and a famous dissertation by Chicago economist Frank Knight,[1] thinkers about risk have made an important distinction between the two: variability that can be quantified in terms of probabilities is best thought of as "risk," while variability that cannot be quantified at all is best thought of simply as "uncertainty."

In a speech some years ago,[2] Mervyn King, then governor of the Bank of England, usefully pointed up the distinction using the example of the pensions and insurance industries. Over the last century, these industries have used statistical analysis to develop products (life insurance, pensions, annuities, and so on) that are important to us all in looking after the financial well-being of our families. These products act to "collectivize" the financial effects of any one individual's life events among any given generation.

Robust statistical tools have been vital in this collectivization of risk within a generation, but the insurance and investment industries have not found a way to put a robust number on key risks that arise *between* generations, such as how much longer future generations might live and what this might mean for life insurance, pensions, and so on. Some aspects of the future remain not just risky, but uncertain. Statistical science can help us to only a limited degree in understanding how sudden advances in medical science or the onset of a new disease such as AIDS might drive longevity up or down.

As King pointed out in his speech, "No amount of complex demographic modeling can substitute for good

judgment about those unknowns." Indeed, attempts to forecast changes in longevity over the last 20 years have all fallen wide of the mark (usually proving too conservative).[3]

As this example helps make clear, one of the most important things that a risk manager can do when communicating a risk analysis is to be clear about the degree to which the results depend on statistically measurable risk, and the degree to which they depend on factors that are entirely uncertain at the time of the analysis—a distinction that may not be obvious to the reader of a complex risk report at first glance.

In his speech, King set out two principles of risk communication for public policy makers that could equally well apply to senior risk committees at corporations looking at the results of complex risk calculations:

> First, information must be provided objectively and placed in context *so* that risks can be assessed and understood. Second, experts and policy makers must be open about the extent of our knowledge and our ignorance. Transparency about what *we* know and what *we* don't know, far from undermining credibility, helps to build trust and confidence.

---

[1] Frank H. Knight, *Risk, Uncertainty and Profit,* Boston, MA: Hart, Schaffner & Marx; Houghton Mifflin Company, 1921.

[2] Mervyn King, "What Fates Impose: Facing Up to Uncertainty," Eighth British Academy Annual Lecture, December 2004.

---

[3] We can't measure uncertainties, but we can still assess and manage them through worst-case scenarios, risk transfer, and so on. Indeed, a market is emerging that may help institutions to manage the financial risks of increased longevity. In 2003, reinsurance companies and banks began to issue financial instruments with returns linked to the aggregate longevity of specified populations, though the market for instruments that can help to manage longevity risk is still relatively immature.

---

risk, it's tempting for the self-interested to play down the potential for unexpected losses to spike somewhere in the economic cycle and to willfully misunderstand how risk factors sometimes come together to give rise to severe correlation risks. Management itself might be tempted to leave gaps in risk measurement that, if mended, would disturb the reported profitability of a business franchise. (The run-up to the 2007–2009 financial crisis provided many examples of such behavior.)

This kind of risk management failure can be hugely exacerbated by the compensation incentive schemes of the companies involved. In many firms across a broad swathe

of industries, bonuses are paid today on profits that may later turn out to be illusory, while the cost of any associated risks is pushed, largely unacknowledged, into the future.

We can see this general process in the banking industry in every credit cycle as banks loosen rules about the granting of credit in the favorable part of the cycle, only to stamp on the credit brakes as things turn sour. The same dynamic happens whenever firms lack the discipline or means to adjust their present performance measures for an activity to take account of any risks incurred. For example, it is particularly easy for trading institutions to move revenues forward through either a "mark-to-market" or a "market-to-model" process. This process employs estimates of the value the market puts on an asset to record profits on the income statement before cash is actually generated; meanwhile, the implied cost of any risk can be artificially reduced by applying poor or deliberately distorted risk measurement techniques.

This collision between conflicts of interest and the opaque nature of risk is not limited solely to risk measurement and management at the level of the individual firm. Decisions about risk and return can become seriously distorted across whole financial industries when poor industry practices and regulatory rules allow this to happen—famous examples being the U.S. savings and loan crisis in the 1980s and early 1990s and the more recent subprime crisis. History shows that industry regulators can also be drawn into the deception. When the stakes are high enough, regulators all around the world have colluded with local banking industries to allow firms to misrecord and misvalue risky assets on their balance sheets, out of fear that forcing firms to state their true condition will prompt mass insolvencies and a financial crisis.

Perhaps, in these cases, regulators think they are doing the right thing in safeguarding the financial system, or perhaps they are just desperate to postpone any pain beyond their term of office (or that of their political masters). For our purposes, it's enough to point out that the *combination* of poor standards of risk measurement with a conflict of interest is extraordinarily potent at many levels—both inside the company and outside.

THE DANGER OF NAMES

So far, we've been discussing risk in terms of its expected and unexpected nature. We can also divide up our risk portfolio according to the *type* of risk that we are running. In this book, we follow the latest regulatory approach in the global banking industry to highlight three major broad risk categories that are controllable and manageable:

Market risk is the risk of losses arising from changes in market risk factors. Market risk can arise from changes in interest rates, foreign exchange rates, or equity and commodity price factors.[3]

---

[3] The definition and breakdown of market risk into these four broad categories is consistent with the accounting standards of IFRS and GAPP in the United States.

Credit risk is the risk of loss following a change in the factors that drive the credit quality of an asset. These include adverse effects arising from credit grade migration, including default, and the dynamics of recovery rates.

Operational risk refers to financial loss resulting from a host of potential operational breakdowns that we can think in terms of risk of loss resulting from inadequate or failed internal processes, people, and systems, or from external events (e.g., frauds, inadequate computer systems, a failure in controls, a mistake in operations, a guideline that has been circumvented, or a natural disaster).

Understanding the various types of risk is important, beyond the banking industry, because each category demands a different (but related) set of risk management skills. The categories are often used to define and organize the risk management functions and risk management activities of a corporation. We've added an appendix to this chapter that offers a longer and more detailed family tree of the various types of risks faced by corporations, including key additional risks such as liquidity risk and strategic risk. This risk taxonomy can be applied to any corporation engaged in major financial transactions, project financing, and providing customers with credit facilities.

The history of science, as well as the history of management, tells us that classification schemes like this are as *valuable* as they are *dangerous*. Giving a name to something allows us to talk about it, control it, and assign responsibility for it. Classification is an important part of the effort to make an otherwise ill-defined risk measurable, manageable, and transferable. Yet the classification of risk is also fraught with danger because as soon as we define risk in terms of categories, we create the potential for missed risks and gaps in responsibilities—for being blindsided by risk as it flows across our arbitrary dividing lines.

For example, a sharp peak in market prices will create a market risk for an institution. Yet the real threat might be that a counterparty to the bank that is also affected by the spike in market prices will default (credit risk), or that some weakness in the bank's systems will be exposed by high trading volumes (operational risk). If we think of price volatility in terms of market risk alone, we are missing an important factor.

We can see the same thing happening from an organizational perspective. While categorizing risks helps us to organize risk management, it fosters the creation of "silos" of expertise that are separated from one another in terms of personnel, risk terminology, risk measures, reporting lines, systems and data, and so on. The management of risk within these silos may be quite efficient in terms of a particular risk, such as market or credit risk, or the risks run by a particular business unit. But if executives and risk managers can't communicate with one another across risk silos, they probably won't be able to work together efficiently to manage the risks that are most important to the institution as a whole.

Some of the most exciting recent advances in risk management are really attempts to break down this natural organizational tendency toward silo risk management. In the past, risk measurement tools such as VaR and economic capital have evolved, in part, to facilitate integrated measurement and management of the various risks (market, credit, and operational) and business lines. More recently, the trend toward worst-case scenario analysis is really an attempt to look at the effect of macroeconomic scenarios on a firm across its business lines and, often, across various types of risk (market, credit, and so on).

We can also see in many industries a much more broadly framed trend toward what consultants have labeled *enterprise-wide risk management,* or ERM. ERM is a concept with many definitions. Basically, though, ERM is a deliberate attempt to break through the tendency of firms to operate in risk management silos and to ignore enterprise-wide risks, and an attempt to take risk into consideration in business decisions much more explicitly than has been done in the past. There are many potential ERM tools, including conceptual tools that facilitate enterprise-wide risk measurement (such as economic capital and enterprise-wide stress testing), monitoring tools that facilitate enterprise-wide risk identification, and organizational tools such as senior risk committees with a mandate to look at all enterprise-wide risks. Through an ERM program, a firm limits its exposures to a risk level agreed upon by the board and provides its management and board of directors with reasonable assurances regarding the achievement of the organization's objectives.

As a trend, ERM is clearly in tune with a parallel drive toward the unification of risk, capital, and balance sheet management in financial institutions. Over the last 10 years, it has become increasingly difficult to distinguish risk management tools from capital management tools, since risk, according to the unexpected loss risk paradigm we outlined earlier, increasingly drives the allocation of capital in risk-intensive businesses such as banking and insurance. Similarly, it has become difficult to distinguish capital management tools from balance sheet management tools, since risk/reward relationships increasingly drive the structure of the balance sheet.

A survey in 2011 by management consultant Deloitte found that the adoption of ERM has increased sharply over the last few years: "Fifty-two percent of institutions reported having an ERM program (or equivalent), up from 36 percent in 2008. Large institutions are more likely to face complex and interconnected risks, and among institutions with total assets of $100 billion or more, 91 percent reported either having an ERM program in place or [being] in the process of implementing one."[4] But we shouldn't get too carried away here. ERM is a goal, but most institutions are a long way from fully achieving the goal.

NUMBERS ARE DANGEROUS, TOO

Once we've put boundaries around our risks by naming and classifying them, we can also try to attach meaningful *numbers* to them. Even if our numbers are only judgmental rankings of risks within a risk class (Risk No. 1, Risk Rating 3, and so on), they can help us make more rational in-class comparative decisions. More ambitiously, if we can assign absolute numbers to some risk factor (a 0.02 percent chance of default versus a 0.002 percent chance of default), then we can weigh one decision against another with some precision. And if we can put an absolute cost or price on a risk (ideally using data from markets where risks are traded or from some internal "cost of risk" calculation based on economic capital), then we can make truly rational economic decisions about assuming, managing, and transferring risks. At this point, risk management decisions become fungible with many other kinds of management decision in the running of an enterprise.

But while assigning numbers to risk is incredibly useful for risk management and risk transfer, it's also potentially dangerous. Only some kinds of numbers are truly comparable, but all kinds of numbers tempt us to make comparisons. For example, using the face value or "notional amount" of a bond to indicate the risk of a bond is a flawed approach. A million-dollar position in a par value

---

[4] Deloitte, *Global Risk Management Survey,* seventh edition, 2011, p. 14.

10-year Treasury bond does not represent at all the same amount of risk as a million-dollar position in a 4-year par value Treasury bond.

Introducing sophisticated models to describe risk is one way to defuse this problem, but this has its own dangers. Professionals in the financial markets invented the VaR framework as a way of measuring and comparing risk across many different markets. The VaR measure works well as a risk measure only for markets operating under normal conditions and only over a short period, such as one trading day. Potentially, it's a very poor and misleading measure of risk in abnormal markets, over longer time periods, or for illiquid portfolios.

Also, VaR, like all risk measures, depends for its integrity on a robust control environment. In recent rogue-trading cases, hundreds of millions of dollars of losses have been suffered by trading desks that had orders not to assume VaR exposures of more than a few million dollars. The reason for the discrepancy is nearly always that the trading desks have found some way of circumventing trading controls and suppressing risk measures. For example, a trader might falsify transaction details entered into the trade reporting system and use fictitious trades to (supposedly) balance out the risk of real trades, or tamper with the inputs to risk models, such as the volatility estimates that determine the valuation and risk estimation for an options portfolio.

The likelihood of this kind of problem increases sharply when those around the trader (back-office staff, business line managers, even risk managers) don't properly understand the critical significance of routine tasks, such as an independent check on volatility estimates, for the integrity of key risk measures. Meanwhile, those reading the risk reports (senior executives, board members) often don't seem to realize that unless they've asked key questions about the integrity of controls, they might as well tear up the risk report.

As we try to base our risk evaluations on past data and experience, we should recall that all statistical estimation is subject to estimation errors, and these can be substantial when the economic environment changes. In addition we must remember that human psychology interferes with risk assessment. Professor Daniel Kahneman, the Nobel laureate in Economics, warns us that people tend to misassess extreme probabilities (very small ones as well as very large ones). Kahneman also points out that people tend to be risk-averse in the domain of gains and risk-seeking in the domain of losses.[5]

While the specialist risk manager's job is an increasingly important one, a broad understanding of risk management must also become part of the wider culture of the firm.

THE RISK MANAGER'S JOB

There are many aspects of the risk manager's role that are open to confusion. First and foremost, a risk manager is not a prophet! The role of the risk manager is not to try to read a crystal ball, but to uncover the sources of risk and make them visible to key decision makers and stakeholders in terms of probability. For example, the risk manager's role is not to produce a point estimate of the U.S. dollar/euro exchange rate at the end of the year; but to produce a distribution estimate of the potential exchange rate at year-end and explain what this might mean for the firm (given its financial positions). These distribution estimates can then be used to help make risk management decisions, and also to produce risk-adjusted metrics such as risk-adjusted return on capital (RAROC).

As this suggests, the risk manager's role is not just defensive—firms need to generate and apply information about balancing risk and reward if they are to compete effectively in the longer term. Implementing the appropriate policies, methodologies, and infrastructure to risk-adjust numbers and improve forward-looking business decisions is an increasingly important element of the modern risk manager's job.

But the risk manager's role in this regard is rarely easy—these risk and profitability analyses aren't always accepted or welcomed in the wider firm when they deliver bad news. Sometimes the difficulty is political (business leaders want growth, not caution), sometimes it is technical (no one has found a best-practice way to measure certain types of risk, such as reputation or franchise risk), and sometimes it is systemic (it's hard not to jump over a cliff on a business idea if all your competitors are doing that too).

---

[5] Daniel Kahneman, *Thinking, Fast and Slow*, Farrar, Straus and Giroux, 2011.

This is why defining the role and reporting lines of risk managers within the wider organization is so critical. It's all very well for the risk manager to identify a risk and measure its potential impact—but if risk is not made transparent to key stakeholders, or those charged with oversight on their behalf, then the risk manager has failed. We discuss these corporate governance issues in more detail in Chapter 3.

Perhaps the trickiest balancing act over the last few years has been trying to find the right relationship between business leaders and the specialist risk management functions within an institution. The relationship should be close, but not too close. There should be extensive interaction, but not dominance. There should be understanding, but not collusion. We can still see the tensions in this relationship across any number of activities in risk-taking organizations—between the credit analyst and those charged with business development in commercial loans, between the trader on the desk and the market risk management team, and so on. Where the balance of power lies will depend significantly on the attitude of senior managers and on the tone set by the board. It will also depend on whether the institution has invested in the analytical and organizational tools that support balanced, risk-adjusted decisions.

As the risk manager's role is extended, we must increasingly ask difficult questions: "What are the risk management standards of practice" and "Who is checking up on the risk managers?" Out in the financial markets, the answer is hopefully the regulators. Inside a corporation, the answer includes the institution's audit function, which is charged with reviewing risk management's actions and its compliance with an agreed-upon set of policies and procedures (Chapter 3). But the more general answer is that risk managers will find it difficult to make the right kind of impact if the firm as a whole lacks a healthy risk culture, including a good understanding of risk management practices, concepts, and tools.

THE PAST, THE FUTURE—AND THIS BOOK'S MISSION

We can now understand better why the discipline of risk management has had such a bumpy ride across many industries over the last decade (see Box 1-3). The reasons lie partly in the fundamentally elusive and opaque nature of risk—if it's not unexpected or uncertain, it's not risk! As

---

BOX 1-3 Ups and Downs in Risk Management

Ups

- Dramatic explosion in the adoption of sophisticated risk management processes, driven by an expanding skill base and falling cost of risk technologies
- Increase in the skill levels and associated compensation of risk management personnel as sophisticated risk techniques have been adopted to measure risk exposures
- Birth of new risk management markets in credit, commodities, weather derivatives, and so on, representing some of the most innovative and potentially lucrative financial markets in the world
- Birth of global risk management industry associations as well as a dramatic rise in the number of global risk management personnel
- Extension of the risk measurement frontier out from traditional measured risks such as market risk toward credit and operational risks
- Cross fertilization of risk management techniques across diverse industries from banking to insurance, energy, chemicals, and aerospace
- Ascent of risk managers in the corporate hierarchy to become chief risk officers, to become members of the top executive team (e.g., part of the management committee), and to report to both the CEO and the board of the company

Downs

- The financial crisis of 2007–2009 revealed significant weaknesses in managing systemic and cyclical risks.
- Firms have been tempted to over-rely on historical-statistical measures of risk—a weakness that improved stress testing seeks to address.
- Risk managers continue to find it a challenge to balance their fiduciary responsibilities against the cost of offending powerful business heads.
- Risk managers do not generate revenue and therefore have not yet achieved the same status as the heads of successful revenue-generating businesses.
- It's proving difficult to make truly unified measurements of different kinds of risk and to understand the destructive power of risk interactions (e.g., credit and liquidity risk).
- Quantifying risk exposure for the whole organization can be hugely complicated and may descend into a "box ticking" exercise.
- The growing power of risk managers could be a negative force in business if risk management is interpreted as risk avoidance; it's possible to be too risk-averse.

we've seen, "risk" changes shape according to perspective, market circumstances, risk appetite, and even the classification schemes that we use.

The reasons also lie partly in the relative immaturity of financial risk management. Practices, personnel, markets, and instruments have been evolving and interacting with one another continually over the last couple of decades to set the stage for the next risk management triumph— and disaster. Rather than being a set of specific activities, computer systems, rules, or policies, risk management is better thought of as a set of concepts that allow us to see and manage risk in a particular and dynamic way.

Perhaps the biggest task in risk management is no longer to build specialized mathematical measures of risk (although this endeavor certainly continues). Perhaps it is to put down deeper risk management roots in each organization. We need to build a wider risk culture and risk literacy, in which all the key staff members engaged in a risky enterprise understand how they can affect the risk profile of the organization—from the back office to the boardroom, and from the bottom to the top of the house. That's really what this book is about. We hope it offers both nonmathematicians as well as mathematicians an understanding of the latest concepts in risk management so that they can see the strengths and question the weaknesses of a given decision.

Nonmathematicians must feel able to contribute to the ongoing evolution of risk management practice. Along the way, we can also hope to give those of our readers who are risk analysts and mathematicians a broader sense of how their analytics fit into an overall risk program, and a stronger sense that their role is to convey not just the results of any risk analysis, but also its meaning (and any broader lessons from an enterprise-wide risk management perspective).

APPENDIX

Typology of Risk Exposures

In Chapter 1 we defined risk as the volatility of returns leading to "unexpected losses" with higher volatility indicating higher risk. The volatility of returns is directly or indirectly influenced by numerous variables, which we called risk factors, and by the interaction between these risk factors. But how do we consider the universe of risk factors in a systematic way?

Risk factors can be broadly grouped together into the following major categories: market risk, credit risk, liquidity risk, operational risk, legal and regulatory risk, business risk, strategic risk, and reputation risk (Figure 1-2).[6] These categories can then be further decomposed into more specific categories, as we show in Figure 1-3 for market risk and credit risk. Market risk and credit risk are referred to as financial risks.

In this figure, we've subdivided market risk into equity price risk, interest rate risk, foreign exchange risk, and commodity price risk in a manner that is in line with our detailed discussion in this appendix. Then we've divided interest rate risk into trading risk and the special case of gap risk; the latter relates to the risk that arises in the balance sheet of an institution as a result of the different sensitivities of assets and liabilities to changes of interest rates.

In theory, the more all-encompassing the categorization and the more detailed the decomposition, the more closely the company's risk will be captured.

In practice, this process is limited by the level of model complexity that can be handled by the available technology and by the cost and availability of internal and market data.

Let's take a closer look at the risk categories in Figure 1-2.

MARKET RISK

Market risk is the risk that changes in financial market prices and rates will reduce the value of a security or a portfolio. Price risk can be decomposed into a general market risk component (the risk that the market as a whole will fall in value) and a specific market risk component, unique to the particular financial transaction under consideration. In trading activities, risk arises both from open (unhedged) positions and from imperfect correlations between market positions that are intended to offset one another.

Market risk is given many different names in different contexts. For example, in the case of a fund, the fund may be marketed as tracking the performance of a certain benchmark. In this case, market risk is important to the

---

[6] Board of Governors of the Federal Reserve System, Trading and Capital Markets Activities Manual, Washington D.C., April 2007.

FIGURE 1-2 Typology of risks.

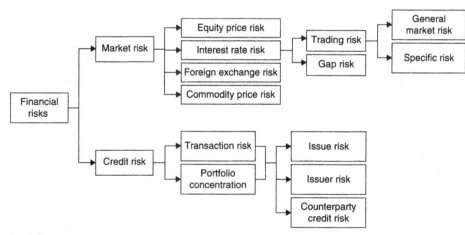

FIGURE 1-3 Schematic presentation, by categories, of financial risks.

extent that it creates a risk of tracking error. *Basis risk* is a term used in the risk management industry to describe the chance of a breakdown in the relationship between the price of a product, on the one hand, and the price of the instrument used to hedge that price exposure, on the other. Again, it is really just a context-specific form of market risk.

There are four major types of market risk: interest rate risk, equity price risk, foreign exchange risk, and commodity price risk.[7]

---

[7] These four categories of market risk are, in general, consistent with accounting standards.

Interest Rate Risk

The simplest form of interest rate risk is the risk that the value of a fixed-income security will fall as a result of an increase in market interest rates. But in complex portfolios of interest-rate-sensitive assets, many different kinds of exposure can arise from differences in the maturities and reset dates of instruments and cash flows that are asset-like (i.e., "longs") and those that are liability-like (i.e., "shorts").

In particular, "curve" risk can arise in portfolios in which long and short positions of different maturities are effectively hedged against a *parallel shift* in yields, but not against a change in the *shape of the yield curve*. Meanwhile, even when offsetting positions have the same maturity, basis risk can arise if the rates of the positions are imperfectly correlated. For example, three-month Eurodollar instruments and three-month Treasury bills both naturally pay three-month interest rates. However, these rates are not perfectly correlated with each other, and spreads between their yields may vary over time. As a result, a three-month Treasury bill funded by three-month Eurodollar deposits represents an imperfect offset or hedged position (often referred to as *basis risk*).

Equity Price Risk

This is the risk associated with volatility in stock prices. The general market risk of equity refers to the sensitivity of an instrument or portfolio value to a change in the level of broad stock market indices. The specific or idiosyncratic risk of equity refers to that portion of a stock's price volatility determined by characteristics specific to the firm, such as its line of business, the quality of its management, or a breakdown in its production process. According to portfolio theory, general market risk cannot be eliminated through portfolio diversification, while specific risk can be diversified away.

Foreign Exchange Risk

Foreign exchange risk arises from open or imperfectly hedged positions in particular foreign currency denominated assets and liabilities leading to fluctuations in profits or values as measured in a local currency. These positions may arise as a natural consequence of business operations, rather than from any conscious desire to take a trading position in a currency. Foreign exchange volatility can sweep away the return from expensive cross-border investments and at the same time place a firm at a competitive disadvantage in relation to its foreign competitors.[8] It may also generate huge operating losses and, through the uncertainty it causes, inhibit investment. The major drivers of foreign exchange risk are imperfect correlations in the movement of currency prices and fluctuations in international interest rates. Although it is important to acknowledge exchange rates as a distinct market risk factor, the valuation of foreign exchange transactions requires knowledge of the behavior of domestic and foreign interest rates, as well as of spot exchange rates.[9]

Commodity Price Risk

The price risk of commodities differs considerably from interest rate and foreign exchange risk, since most commodities are traded in markets in which the concentration of supply is in the hands of a few suppliers who can magnify price volatility. For most commodities, the number of market players having direct exposure to the particular commodity is quite limited, hence affecting trading liquidity which in turn can generate high levels of price volatility. Other fundamentals affecting a commodity price include the ease and cost of storage, which varies considerably across the commodity markets (e.g., from gold to electricity to wheat). As a result of these factors, commodity prices generally have higher volatilities and larger price discontinuities (i.e., moments when prices leap from

one level to another) than most traded financial securities. Commodities can be classified according to their characteristics as follows: hard commodities, or nonperishable commodities, the markets for which are further divided into precious metals (e.g., gold, silver, and platinum), which have a high price/weight value, and base metals (e.g., copper, zinc, and tin); soft commodities, or commodities with a short shelf life that are hard to store, mainly agricultural products (e.g., grains, coffee, and sugar); and energy commodities, which consist of oil, gas, electricity, and other energy products.

CREDIT RISK

Credit risk is the risk of an economic loss from the failure of a counterparty to fulfill its contractual obligations, or from the *increased risk* of default during the term of the transaction.[10] For example, credit risk in the loan portfolio of a bank materializes when a borrower fails to make a payment, either of the periodic interest charge or the periodic reimbursement of principal on the loan as contracted with the bank. Credit risk can be further decomposed into four main types: default risk, bankruptcy risk, downgrade risk, and settlement risk. Box 1-4 gives ISDA's definition of a credit event that may trigger a payout under a credit derivatives contract.[11]

Default risk corresponds to the debtor's incapacity or refusal to meet his/her debt obligations, whether interest or principal payments on the loan contracted, by more than a reasonable relief period from the due date, which is usually 60 days in the banking industry.

Bankruptcy risk is the risk of actually taking over the collateralized, or escrowed, assets of a defaulted borrower or counterparty. In the case of a bankrupt company, debt holders are taking over the control of the company from the shareholders.

---

[8] A famous example is Caterpillar, a U.S. heavy equipment firm, which in 1987 began a $2 billion capital investment program. A full cost reduction of 19 percent was eventually expected in 1993. During the same period the Japanese yen weakened against the U.S. dollar by 30 percent, which placed Caterpillar at a competitive disadvantage vis-à-vis its major competitor, Komatsu of Japan, even after adjusting for productivity gains.

[9] This is because of the interest rate parity condition, which describes the price of a futures contract on a foreign currency as equal to the spot exchange rate adjusted by the difference between the local interest rate and the foreign interest rate.

---

[10] In the following we use indifferently the term "borrower" or "counterparty" for a debtor. In practice, we refer to issuer risk, or borrower risk, when credit risk involves a funded transaction such as a bond or a bank loan. In derivatives markets, counterparty credit risk is the credit risk of a counterparty for an unfunded derivatives transaction such as a swap or an option.

[11] ISDA is the International Swap and Derivatives Association.

Downgrade risk is the risk that the perceived creditworthiness of the borrower or counterparty might deteriorate. In general, deteriorated creditworthiness translates into a downgrade action by the rating agencies, such as Standard and Poor's (S&P), Moody's, or Fitch in the United States, and an increase in the risk premium, or credit spread of the borrower. A major deterioration in the creditworthiness of a borrower might be the precursor of default.

Settlement risk is the risk due to the exchange of cash flows when a transaction is settled. Failure to perform on settlement can be caused by a counterparty default, liquidity constraints, or operational issues. This risk is greatest when payments occur in different time zones, especially for foreign exchange transactions, such as currency swaps, where notional amounts are exchanged in different currencies.[12]

Credit risk is an issue only when the position is an asset—i.e., when it exhibits a positive replacement value. In that situation, if the counterparty defaults, the firm loses either all of the market value of the position or, more commonly, the part of the value that it cannot recover following the credit event. The value it is likely to recover is called the *recovery value*, or *recovery rate* when expressed as a percentage; the amount it is expected to lose is called the *loss given default (LGD)*.

Unlike the potential loss given default on coupon bonds or loans, the LGD on derivative positions is usually much lower than the nominal amount of the deal, and in many cases is only a fraction of this amount. This is because the economic value of a derivative instrument is related to its replacement or market value rather than its nominal or face value. However, the credit exposures induced by the replacement values of derivative instruments are dynamic: they can be negative at one point in time, and yet become positive at a later point in time after market conditions have changed. Therefore, firms must examine not only the current exposure, measured by the current replacement value, but also the distribution of potential future exposures up to the termination of the deal.

Credit Risk at the Portfolio Level

The first factor affecting the amount of credit risk in a portfolio is clearly the credit standing of specific obligors. The critical issue, then, is to charge the appropriate interest rate, or spread, to each borrower so that the lender is compensated for the risk it undertakes, and to set aside the right amount of risk capital.

The second factor is "concentration risk," or the extent to which the obligors are diversified in terms of exposures, geography, and industry. This leads us to the third important factor that affects the risk of the portfolio: the state of the economy. During the good times of economic growth, the frequency of default falls sharply compared to periods of recession. Conversely, the default rate rises again as the economy enters a downturn. Downturns in the credit cycle often uncover the hidden tendency of customers to default together, with banks being affected to the degree that they have allowed their portfolios to become concentrated in various ways (e.g., customer, region, and industry concentrations). Credit portfolio models are an attempt to discover the degree of correlation/concentration risk in a bank portfolio.

The quality of the portfolio can also be affected by the maturities of the loans, as longer loans are generally considered riskier than short-term loans. Banks that build portfolios that are not concentrated in particular maturities—"time diversification"—can reduce this kind of portfolio maturity risk. This also helps reduce liquidity risk, or the risk that the bank will run into difficulties when it tries to refinance large amounts of its assets at the same time.

LIQUIDITY RISK

Liquidity risk comprises both "funding liquidity risk" and "trading liquidity risk" (see Figure 1-4). Funding liquidity risk relates to a firm's ability to raise the necessary cash to roll over its debt; to meet the cash, margin, and collateral requirements of counterparties; and to satisfy capital withdrawals. Funding liquidity risk can be managed through holding cash and cash equivalents, setting credit lines in place, and monitoring buying power. (Buying power refers to the amount a trading counterparty can borrow against assets under stressed market conditions.)

Trading liquidity risk, often simply called liquidity risk, is the risk that an institution will not be able to execute a transaction at the prevailing market price because there is, temporarily, no appetite for the deal on the other side of the market. If the transaction cannot be postponed, its execution may lead to a substantial loss on the position. Funding liquidity risk is also related to the size of the transaction and its immediacy. The faster and/or larger

---

[12] Settlement failures due to operational problems result only in payment delays and have only minor economic consequences. In some cases, however, the loss can be quite substantial and amount to the full amount of the payment due. A famous example of settlement risk is the 1974 failure of Herstatt Bank, a small regional German bank. The day it went bankrupt, Herstatt had received payments in Deutsche marks from a number of counterparties but defaulted before payments were made in U.S. dollars on the other legs of maturing spot and forward transactions.

Bilateral netting is one of the mechanisms that reduce settlement risk. In a netting agreement, only the net balance outstanding in each currency is paid instead of making payments on the gross amounts to each other. Currently, around 55 percent of FX transactions are settled through the CLS bank, which provides a payment-versus-payment (PVP) service that virtually eliminates the principal risk associated with settling FX trades (Basel Committee on Payment and Settlement Systems, *Progress in Reducing Foreign Exchange Settlement Risk*, Bank for International Settlements, Basel, Switzerland, May 2008).

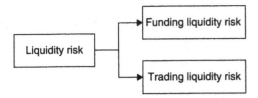

FIGURE 1-4 The dimensions of liquidity risk.

the transaction, the greater the potential for loss. This risk is generally very hard to quantify. (In current implementations of the market value-at-risk, or VaR, approach, liquidity risk is accounted for only in the sense that one of the parameters of a VaR model is the period of time, or holding period, thought necessary to liquidate the relevant positions.) Trading liquidity risk may reduce an institution's ability to manage and hedge market risk as well as its capacity to satisfy any shortfall in funding by liquidating its assets. Box 1-5 discusses valuation problems faced in a marked-to-market world in times of low asset liquidity.

OPERATIONAL RISK

Operational risk refers to potential losses resulting from a range of operational weaknesses including inadequate systems, management failure, faulty controls, fraud, and human errors; in the banking industry, operational risk is also often taken to include the risk of natural and man-made catastrophes (e.g., earthquakes, terrorism) and other nonfinancial risks. Many of the large losses from derivative trading over the last decade are the direct consequence of operational failures. Derivative trading is more prone to operational risk than cash transactions because derivatives, by their nature, are leveraged transactions. The valuation process required for complex derivatives also creates considerable operational risk. Very tight controls are an absolute necessity if a firm is to avoid large losses.

Human factor risk is a special form of operational risk. It relates to the losses that may result from human errors such as pushing the wrong button on a computer, inadvertently destroying a file, or entering the wrong value for the parameter input of a model. Operational risk also includes fraud—for example, when a trader or other employee intentionally falsifies and misrepresents the risks incurred in a transaction. *Technology risk*, principally computer systems risk, also falls into the operational risk category.

LEGAL AND REGULATORY RISK

Legal and regulatory risk arises for a whole variety of reasons; it is closely related to operational risk as well as to reputation risk (discussed below). For example, a counterparty might lack the legal or regulatory authority to engage in a risky transaction. Legal and regulatory risks are classified as operational risks under Basel II Capital Accord.

In the derivative markets, legal risks often only become apparent when a counterparty, or an investor, loses money on a transaction and decides to sue the provider firm to avoid meeting its obligations.

Another aspect of regulatory risk is the potential impact of a change in tax law on the market value of a position. For example, when the British government changed the tax code to remove a particular tax benefit during the summer of 1997, one major investment bank suffered huge losses.

BUSINESS RISK

Business risk refers to the classic risks of the world of business, such as uncertainty about the demand for products, or the price that can be charged for those products, or the cost of producing and delivering products. We offer a recent example of business risk in Box 1-6.

In the world of manufacturing, business risk is largely managed through core tasks of management, including strategic decisions—e.g., choices about channel, products, suppliers, how products are marketed, inventory policies, and so on. There is, of course, a very large, general business literature that deals with these issues, so for the most part we skirt around the problem of business risk in this book.

However, there remains the question of how business risk should be addressed within formal risk management frameworks of the kind that we describe in this book and that have become prevalent in the financial industries. Although business risks should surely be assessed and monitored, it is not obvious how to do this in a way that complements the banking industry's treatment of classic credit and market risks. There is also room for debate over whether business risks need to be supported by capital in the same explicit way. In the Basel II Capital Accord, "business risk" was excluded from the regulators' definition of

BOX 1-5 Valuation Problems in a Marked-to-Market World in Times of Low Liquidity

Financial instruments are held in the:

- "trading book," where they are measured at fair value through profit and loss, or
- "banking book," as assets available for sale (AFS), where they are subject to amortized cost accounting (also referred to as accrual accounting).

Any change in the fair value of a trading book instrument has a direct impact on a firm's income statement in the period in which the change occurs. Changes in the fair value of financial assets classified as AFS are recorded directly in equity without affecting profit and loss until the financial assets are sold, at which point the cumulative change in fair value is charged or credited to the income statement.

In contrast, unless held for sale, loans are typically measured at amortized cost using the effective interest method, less "allowance" or "provision" for impairment losses. Loans held for sale may be reported in trading or AFS portfolios or, in the United States, in held-for-sale portfolios at the lower of cost or fair value.

Instruments subject to fair value accounting are valued with reference to prices obtained from active markets, when these are available for identical or similar instruments. When market liquidity dries up—e.g., during a market crisis—price discovery based on market prices becomes much more difficult. Other valuation techniques may become necessary, such as applying a model to estimate a value.[1] Where liquid market prices are unavailable, other approaches inevitably carry with them a range of uncertainties and can give a false impression of precision.

Fair value/mark-to-market accounting has generally proven highly valuable in promoting transparency and market discipline and is an effective and reliable accounting method for securities in liquid markets. However, it can create serious, self-reinforcing challenges that make valuation more difficult and increase uncertainties around those valuations when there is no or severely limited liquidity in secondary markets. Three main criticisms of fair value accounting have been expressed:[2]

- First, unrealized losses recognized under fair value accounting may reverse over time. Market prices may deviate from fundamental values because of market illiquidity or because prices are bubble prices.
- Second, market illiquidity may render fair values difficult to measure, yielding overstated and unreliable reported losses.
- Third, firms reporting unrealized losses under fair value accounting may trigger unhelpful feedback effects—i.e., trigger further deterioration of market prices through the destabilizing downward spiral of forced liquidations, write-downs, and higher risk and liquidity premiums.

---

[1] The accounting standard for fair value (FAS 157) creates a hierarchy of inputs into fair value measurements, from most to least reliable:

- Level 1 inputs are unadjusted quoted market prices in active liquid markets for identical products.
- Level 2 inputs are other directly or indirectly observable market data. There are two broad subclasses of these inputs. The first and generally preferable subclass is quoted market prices in active markets for similar instruments. The second subclass is other observable market inputs such as yield curves, exchange rates, empirical correlations, and so on. These inputs yield mark-to-model measurements that are disciplined by market information, but that can only be as reliable as the models and the inputs that have been employed.
- Level 3 inputs are unobservable, firm-supplied estimates, such as forecasts of home price depreciation and the resulting severity of credit losses on mortgage-related positions.

---

[2] Looking at the pros and cons of fair value accounting, fair value accounting still seems better than the alternative of accrual accounting. Accrual accounting suppresses the reporting of losses and reduces the incentives for voluntary disclosure. This means that it can discourage the actions that may be necessary to resolve a crisis. The savings and loan crisis in the United States provides the best illustration. The crisis began when interest rates rose during the first oil crisis/recession in 1973–1975, causing thrifts' fixed mortgage assets to experience large economic losses that were not recognized under amortized cost accounting. This nonrecognition of economic losses allowed bank regulators and policy makers to permit the crisis to continue for 15 years, effectively encouraging thrifts to invest in risky assets, exploit deposit insurance, and in some cases even commit fraud—activities that significantly worsened the ultimate cost of the crisis.

Nonbanking Example of Business Risk: How Palm Tumbled from High-Tech Stardom

Palm was a pioneer in "handheld computers" in the early 1990s. In December 2000 annual sales were up 165 percent from the previous year. In March 2001 the first sign of slowing sales hit the firm. The top management of Palm decided that the appropriate response was to quickly launch their newest model of handheld computers, the m500 line.

The CEO, Carl Yankowski, received assurances from his management that the m500 line could be out in two weeks. Palm unveiled the m500 line on March 19. Sales of Palm's existing devices slowed further as customers decided to wait for the new model. The problem was that the waiting time wasn't two weeks. Palm didn't leave enough time for the testing of the m500 before sending the design to be manufactured. Production of the m500 line kept hitting snags. Palm wasn't able to ship the new model in volume until May, more than six weeks after the announcement.

Inventory of the older product began to pile up, leading to a huge $300 million write-off of excess inventory and a net loss of $392 million for the fiscal quarter that ended June 1, compared with a profit of $12.4 million a year earlier. The firm's stock price plummeted and, as a consequence, an acquisition that was key to Palm's strategy collapsed—the deal was for $264 million in Palm's stock. The company cut 250 workers, lost key employees, and halted the construction of new headquarters.

Palm's rivals such as RIM (BlackBerry) and Microsoft increased their efforts to capitalize on Palm's mistakes.

operational risk, even though some researchers believe it to be a greater source of volatility in bank revenue than the operational event/failure risk that the regulators *have* included within bank minimum capital requirements.

Business risk is affected by such factors as the quality of the firm's strategy and/or its reputation, as well as other factors. Therefore, it is common practice to view strategic and reputation risks as components of business risk, and the risk literature sometimes refers to a complex of business/strategic/reputation risk. In this typology we differentiate these three components. In Chapter 2 we further discuss business risk management issues in nonbank corporations.

STRATEGIC RISK

Strategic risk refers to the risk of significant investments for which there is a high uncertainty about success and profitability. It can also be related to a change in the strategy of a company vis-à-vis its competitors. If the venture is not successful, then the firm will usually suffer a major write-off and its reputation among investors will be damaged. Box 1-7 gives an example of strategic risk.

Banks, for example, suffer from a range of business and strategic risks (see Box 1-8). Some of these risks are very similar to the kind of risk seen in nonfinancial companies, while others are driven by market or credit variables, even though they are not conventionally thought of as market risks or credit risks.

REPUTATION RISK

From a risk management perspective, reputation risk can be divided into two main classes: the belief that an enterprise can and will fulfill its promises to counterparties and creditors; and the belief that the enterprise is a fair dealer and follows ethical practices.

The importance of the first form of reputation risk is apparent throughout the history of banking and was a dramatic feature of the 2007–2009 crisis. In particular, the trust that is so important in the banking sector was shattered after the Lehman Brothers collapse in September 2008. At a time of crisis, when rumors spread fast, the belief in a bank's soundness can be everything.

The second main form of reputation risk, for fair dealing, is also vitally important and took on a new dimension around the turn of the millennium following accounting scandals that defrauded the shareholders, bondholders, and employees of many major corporations during the late 1990s boom in the equity markets. Investigations into the mutual funds and insurance industry by New York Attorney General Eliot Spitzer made clear just how important a reputation for fair dealing is, with both customers and regulators.

In a survey released in August 2004 by Pricewaterhouse-Coopers (PwC) and the Economist Intelligence Unit (EIU), 34 percent of the 134 international bank respondents believed that reputation risk is the biggest risk to corporate market value and shareholder value faced by banks, while market and credit risk scored only 25 percent each.

BOX 1-7 Nonbanking Example of Strategic Risk: How Nokia, Chasing the Top End of the Market, Got Hit in the Middle Twice

Part 1: First Strategic Mistake

In 1999 Nokia launched a huge and costly effort to explore the new market for cell phones that allowed users to get on the Internet, watch movies, and play video games. Nokia spent hundreds of millions of dollars launching a string of "smartphones," allocating 80 percent of its research and development budget ($3.6 billion a year) to software, much of it designed to give phones computer-like capabilities. Nokia was also racing to thwart the threat of Microsoft's coming "first to market" with similar software for smartphones (which would set the standards for this new market).

Retrospectively, it appears that Nokia focused on the wrong battle and picked the wrong competitor to worry about. Smartphones proved too bulky and too expensive for many consumers, and remained (at the time) a tiny presence in the market.

Moreover, in concentrating on smartphones, Nokia neglected one of the hottest growth sectors in cell phones—i.e., cheaper midrange models with sharp color screens and cameras—giving competitors, such as Samsung Electronics and archrival Motorola, a rare opportunity to steal market share. The bet that phones would one day converge with computers was premature.

Nokia's global market share plunged to 29 percent from 35 percent by mid-2003. In 2003 Nokia sold 5.5 million smartphones, far short of Nokia's target of 10 million. In the first quarter of 2004, Nokia's sales fell 2 percent in a global cell phone market that grew 40 percent from the year before, as measured by the number of units sold.

Part 2: Second Strategic Mistake

In the half-dozen years leading up to 2013, Nokia failed to successfully adjust its strategy to capitalize on the smartphone revolution. The firm faced significant competition in the smartphone market, including Apple and competitors that have adopted Google's Android. Ironically, given Nokia's earlier concern that Microsoft would introduce first-to-market software for smartphones, Nokia's strategy in early 2013 was to deploy Microsoft Windows (in lieu of their own Symbian operating system) in order to make their product more attractive. Nokia might succeed in its strategy, or Nokia could be acquired; the company has extensive cash holdings, significant strategic value (say, for Microsoft), and patents that could potentially be worth billions.[1] However, Nokia has destroyed significant shareholder value: its share price has dropped by a factor of 10 and is less than its cash holding per share, while its credit rating has been downgraded to junk status.

---

[1] As this book went to press in September 2013 Microsoft announced that it had purchased Nokia's devices and services business and licenced Nokia's patents.

BOX 1-8 Examples of Business and Strategic Risk in Banking

Retail Banking

- The advent of new business models puts pressure on existing business strategies.
- A major acquisition turns out to be much less profitable than forecasted.

Mortgage Banking

- A sharp rise in interest rates triggers a sharp fall in mortgage origination volume.
- A decline in demand for new housing in a certain location leads to a decline in mortgage origination volume.

Wealth Management

- Falling or uncertain stock markets lead to lower investment fund sales.

Capital Markets Activities

- Relative size of the bank may limit its ability to win large loan underwritings.
- Higher exposure to capital markets creates earnings volatility.

Credit Cards

- Increased competition can lead banks to offer credit cards to new market segments (e.g., subprime customers whose payment behavior is not well understood).
- Competitors with sophisticated credit risk management systems may begin to steal genuinely profitable market share, leaving competitors that cannot differentiate between customers unwittingly offering business to relatively risky customers.

No doubt this was partly because, at the time, corporate scandals like Enron, Worldcom, and others were still fresh in bankers' minds. However, more recently, concern about reputation risk has become prominent again with the rapid growth of public and social networks. Anybody can spread a rumor over the Internet, and the viral spread of news, the use of talkbacks on digital news pages, and the growth of blogs can all create headaches for corporations trying to maintain their reputation.

Reputation risk poses a special threat to financial institutions because the nature of their business requires the confidence of customers, creditors, regulators, and the general market place. The development of a wide array of structured finance products, including financial derivatives for market and credit risk, asset-backed securities with customized cash flows, and specialized financial conduits that manage pools of purchased assets, has put pressure on the interpretation of accounting and tax rules and, in turn, has given rise to significant concerns about the legality and appropriateness of certain transactions. Involvement in such transactions may damage an institution's reputation and franchise value.

Financial institutions are also under increasing pressure to demonstrate their ethical, social, and environmental responsibility. As a defensive mechanism, 10 international banks from seven countries announced in June 2003 the adoption of the "Equator Principles," a voluntary set of guidelines developed by the banks for managing social and environmental issues related to the financing of projects in emerging countries. The Equator Principles are based on the policy and guidelines of the World Bank and International Finance Corporation (IFC) and require the borrower to conduct an environmental assessment for high-risk projects to address issues such as sustainable development and use of renewable natural resources, protection of human health, pollution prevention and waste minimization, socioeconomic impact, and so on.

SYSTEMIC RISK

Systemic risk, in financial terms, concerns the potential for the failure of one institution to create a chain reaction or domino effect on other institutions and consequently threaten the stability of financial markets and even the global economy.

Systemic risk may be triggered by losses at an institution. However, simply the perception of increased risk may lead to panic about the soundness of an institution, or to a more general "flight to quality" away from risky assets and toward assets perceived to be less risky. This may cause serious market disruptions to propagate across otherwise healthy segments of the market. In turn, these disruptions may trigger panicked "margin call" requests, obliging counterparties to put up more cash or collateral to compensate for falling prices. As a consequence, borrowers may have to sell some of their assets at fire-sale prices, pushing prices further down, and creating further rounds of margin calls and forced sales.

One proposal for addressing this kind of systemic risk is to make the firms that create the systemic exposure pay a fair price for having created it and for imposing costs on other market participants.[13] However, this would mean measuring, pricing, and then taxing the creation of systemic risk—a potentially complex undertaking.

The many interconnections and dependencies among financial firms, in both the regulated and unregulated sectors, exacerbate systemic risk under crisis conditions. The failures and near-failures of Bear Stearns, Lehman Brothers, and AIG during the financial crisis of 2007–2009 all contributed to systemic risk by creating massive uncertainty about which of the key interconnections would transmit default risk.

The size of an institution that is in trouble can lead to panic about the scale of the default, but this is not the only concern. Market participants may fear that large-scale liquidations will disrupt markets, break the usual market interconnections, and lead to a loss of intermediation functions that then may take months, or years, to rebuild.

The Dodd-Frank Act focuses on systemic risk. It establishes a Financial Stability Oversight Council (FSOC) whose role is to identify systemic risks wherever they arise and recommend policies to regulatory bodies. A very important feature of the Dodd-Frank Act is the decision

---

[13] See V. V. Acharya, T. F. Cooley, M. P. Richardson, and I. Walter, eds., *Regulating Wall Street: The Dodd-Frank Act and the New Architecture of Global Finance*, Wiley, 2010.

to move the market for a wide range of OTC derivatives onto centralized clearing and/or exchange trading platforms. As a consequence, the counterparty risk inherent in OTC derivative transactions will be transformed into an exposure to a central counterparty. The central clearinghouse will set margins so that risk positions will be marked-to-market. Even so, the remaining central clearinghouse risk is potentially itself a threat to the financial system and must be carefully regulated and monitored. However, this should be easier than regulating private OTC markets because clearinghouses are supervised public utilities.

Corporate Risk Management: A Primer

2

Learning Objectives

Candidates, after completing this reading, should be able to:

- Evaluate some advantages and disadvantages of hedging risk exposures.
- Explain considerations and procedures in determining a firm's risk appetite and its business objectives.
- Explain how a company can determine whether to hedge specific risk factors, including the role of the board of directors and the process of mapping risks.

- Apply appropriate methods to hedge operational and financial risks, including pricing, foreign currency, and interest rate risk.
- Assess the impact of risk management instruments.

Excerpt is Chapter 2 of The Essentials of Risk Management, *Second Edition, by Michel Crouhy, Dan Galai, and Robert Mark.*

Nonfinancial companies are exposed to many traditional business risks: earnings fluctuate due to changes in the business environment, new competitors, new production technologies, and weaknesses in supply chains. Firms react in various ways: holding inventories of raw materials (in case of unexpected interruption in supply or an increase in raw material prices), storing finished products (to accommodate unexpected increases in demand), signing long-term supply contracts at a fixed price, or even conducting horizontal and vertical mergers with competitors, distributors, and suppliers.[1] This is classic business decision making but it is also, often, a form of risk management. In this chapter, we'll look at a more specific, and relatively novel, aspect of enterprise risk management: why and how should a firm choose to hedge the financial risks that might affect its business by means of financial contracts such as derivatives?

This issue has received attention from corporate management in recent years as financial risk management has become a critical corporate activity and as regulators, such as the Securities & Exchange Commission (SEC) in the United States, have insisted on increased disclosures around risk management policies and financial exposures.[2]

In this chapter, we'll focus on the practical decisions a firm must make if it decides to engage in active risk management. These include the problem of how the board sets the risk appetite of a firm, the specific procedure for mapping out a firm's individual risk exposures, and the selection of risk management tactics. We'll also sketch out how exposures can be tackled using a variety of risk management instruments such as swaps and forwards—and take a look at how this kind of reasoning has been applied by a major pharmaceutical company (Box 2-1). We'll use manufacturing corporations as our examples, since the arguments in this chapter apply generally to enterprise risk management (ERM).

---

[1] For example, Delta Air Lines bought a ConocoPhillips refinery to gain more control over its fuel costs (*The New York Times*, May 1, 2012).

[2] In the United States, the Sarbanes-Oxley (SOX) legislation enacted by the U.S. Congress in the summer of 2002 requires internal control certifications by chief executive officers (CEOs) and chief financial officers (CFOs). This legislation was prompted by a rash of extraordinary corporate governance scandals that emerged during 2001 to 2003 as a result of the 1990s equity boom. While some firms had been using risk management instruments overenthusiastically to "cook the books," others had not involved themselves sufficiently in analyzing, managing, and disclosing the fundamental risks of their business.

But before we launch into the practicalities of hedging strategies, we must first confront a theoretical problem: according to the most fundamental understanding of the interests of shareholders, executives should not actively manage the risks of their corporation at all!

WHY *NOT* TO MANAGE RISK IN THEORY . . .

Among economists and academic researchers, the starting point to this discussion is a famous analysis by two professors, Franco Modigliani and Merton Miller (M&M), laid out in 1958, which shows that the value of a firm cannot be changed merely by means of financial transactions.[3] The M&M analysis is based on an important assumption: that the capital markets are perfect, in the sense that they are taken to be highly competitive and that participants are not subject to transaction costs, commissions, contracting and information costs, or taxes. Under this assumption, M&M reasoned that whatever the firm can accomplish in the financial markets, the individual investor in the firm can also accomplish or unwind on the same terms and conditions.

This line of reasoning also lies behind the seminal work of William Sharpe, who in 1964 developed a way of pricing assets that underlies much of modern financial theory and practice: the capital asset pricing model (CAPM).[4] In his work, Sharpe establishes that in a world with perfect capital markets, firms should not worry about the risks that are specific to them, known as their idio-syncratic risks, and should base their investment decisions only on the risks they hold in common with other companies (known as their systematic or beta risks). This is because all specific risks are diversified away in a large investment portfolio and, under the perfect capital markets assumption, this diversification is assumed to be costless. Firms should therefore not engage in any risk reduction activity that individual investors can execute on their own without any disadvantage (due to economies of scale, for example).

Those opposed to active corporate risk management often argue that hedging is a zero-sum game and cannot

---

[3] F. Modigliani and M. H. Miller, "The Cost of Capital, Corporation Finance, and the Theory of Investment," *American Economic Review* 48 (1958), pp. 261–297.

[4] W. Sharpe, "Capital Asset Prices: A Theory of Market Equilibrium under Conditions of Risk," *Journal of Finance* 19 (1964), pp. 425–442.

increase earnings or cash flows. Some years ago, for example, a senior manager at a U.K. retailer pointed out, "Reducing volatility through hedging simply moves earnings and cash flows from one year to another."[5] This line of argument is implicitly based on the perfect capital markets assumption that the prices of derivatives fully reflect their risk characteristics; therefore, using such instruments cannot increase the value of the firm in any lasting way. It implies that self-insurance is a more efficient strategy, particularly because trading in derivatives incurs transaction costs.

We've listed some theoretical arguments against using derivatives for risk management, but there are also some important practical objections. Active hedging may distract management from its core business. Risk management requires specialized skills, knowledge, and infrastructure, and also entails significant data acquisition and processing effort. Especially in small and medium-sized corporations, management often lacks the skills and time necessary to engage effectively in such activity.[6] Furthermore, a risk management strategy that is not carefully structured and monitored can drag a firm down even more quickly than the underlying risk (see Box 2-2 later in this chapter).

As a final point, even a well-developed risk management strategy has compliance costs, including disclosure, accounting, and management requirements. Firms may avoid trading in derivatives in order to reduce such costs or to protect the confidential information that might be revealed by their forward transactions (for example, the scale of sales they envisage in certain currencies). In some cases, hedging that reduces volatility in the true economic value of the firm could *increase* the firm's earnings variability as transmitted to the equity markets through the firm's accounting disclosures, due to the gap between accounting earnings and economic cash flows.

. . . AND SOME REASONS *FOR* MANAGING RISK IN PRACTICE

Such arguments against hedging seem powerful, but there are strong objections and counterarguments. The assumption that capital markets operate with perfect efficiency does not reflect market realities. Also, corporations that manage financial risks often claim that firms hedge in order to reduce the chance of default, for none of the theories we described above take account of one crucial and undeniable market imperfection: the high fixed costs associated with financial distress and bankruptcy.

A related argument is that managers act in their own self-interest, rather than in the interests of shareholders (referred to as "agency risk"). Since managers may not be able to diversify the personal wealth that they have accumulated (directly and indirectly) in their company, they have an incentive to reduce volatility. It can be further argued that managers have an interest in reducing risks, whether or not they have a large personal stake in the firm, because the results of a firm provide signals to boards and investors concerning the skills of its management. Since it is not easy for shareholders to differentiate volatility that is healthy from volatility that is caused by management incompetence, managers may prefer to manage their key personal performance indicator (the equity price of their firm) directly, rather than risk the confusion of managing their firm according to the long-term economic interests of a fully diversified shareholder.

Another argument for hedging rests on the collateral effects of taxation. First, there is the effect of progressive tax rates, under which volatile earnings induce higher taxation than stable earnings.[7] The empirical evidence for this as a general argument is not very strong. There is also the claim that hedging increases the debt capacity of companies, which in turn increases interest tax deductions.[8]

[5] J. Ralfe, "Reasons to Be Hedging—1,2,3," *Risk* 9(7), 1996, pp. 20–21.

[6] In an empirical research project using data on 7,139 firms from 50 countries, Bartram, Brown and Fehle found evidence that large, profitable companies with low market-to-book ratios tend to hedge more of their financial risks than smaller, less profitable firms with greater growth opportunities. (S. Bartram, G. Brown, and F. Fehle, "International Evidence on Financial Derivatives Usage," unpublished working paper, University of North Carolina, 2004.)

[7] See Rene Stulz, "Rethinking Risk Management," *Journal of Applied Corporate Finance* 9(3), Fall 1996, pp. 8–24. The argument relates to the convexity of the tax code with increasing marginal tax rates, limits on the use of tax-loss carry forward, and minimum tax rate. Maintaining taxable income in a range so that it is neither too high nor too low can produce tax benefits.

[8] See J. Graham and D. Rogers, "Do Firms Hedge in Response to Tax Incentives?" *Journal of Finance* 57, 2002, pp. 815–839. Available at SSRN: http://ssrn.com/abstract=279959. They perform empirical testing for 442 firms and find that the statistical benefit from increased debt capacity is 1.1 % of firm value. They also find that firms hedge to reduce the expected cost of financial distress.

Certainly, many firms use derivatives for tax avoidance rather than risk management purposes, but this represents a rather separate issue.

More important, perhaps, is that risk management activities allow management better control over the firm's natural economic performance. Each firm may legitimately communicate to investors a different "risk appetite," confirmed by the board. By employing risk management tools, management can better achieve the board's objectives.

Furthermore, the theoretical arguments do not condemn risk reduction activity that offers synergies with the operations of the firm. For example, by hedging the price of a commodity that is an input to its production process, a firm can stabilize its costs and hence also its pricing policy. This stabilization of prices may in itself offer a competitive advantage in the marketplace that could not be replicated by any outside investor.

As a side argument, it's worth pointing out that individuals and firms regularly take out traditional insurance policies to insure property and other assets at a price that is higher than the expected value of the potential damage (as assessed in actuarial terms). Yet very few researchers have questioned the rationale of purchasing insurance with the same vigor as they have questioned the purchase of newer risk management products such as swaps and options.

Perhaps the most important argument in favor of hedging, however, is its potential to reduce the cost of capital and enhance the ability to finance growth. High cash flow volatility adversely affects a firm's debt capacity and the costs of its activities—no one is happy to lend money to a firm likely to suffer a liquidity crisis. This becomes particularly expensive if the firm is forced to forego profitable investment opportunities related to its comparative advantages or private information.

Campello et. al. (2011) sampled more than 1,000 firms and found that hedging reduces the cost of external financing and eases the firms' investment process. They focused on the use of interest rate and foreign currency derivatives for the period 1996–2002. They found that hedging reduces the incidence of investment restrictions in loan agreements. They also showed that hedgers were able to invest more than nonhedgers, controlling for many other factors.[9]

An earlier empirical study in the late 1990s investigated why firms use currency derivatives.[10] Rather than analyze questionnaires, the researchers looked at the characteristics of Fortune 500 nonfinancial corporations that in 1990 seemed potentially exposed to foreign currency risk (from foreign operations or from foreign-currency-denominated debt). They found that approximately 41 percent of the firms in the sample (of 372 companies) had used currency swaps, forwards, futures, options, or combinations of these instruments. The major conclusion of the study was "that firms with greater growth opportunities and tighter financial constraints are more likely to use currency derivatives." They explain this as an attempt to reduce fluctuations in cash flows so as to be able to raise capital for growth opportunities.

However, McKinsey has pointed out that boards of nonfinancial firms are often unimpressed when looking inside their firm for insight into how the firm should manage risk. Many nonfinancial companies possess only poorly structured information on the key risks facing their company, which in turn complicates decisions on the best approach to hedging their risks.[11]

The theoretical argument about why firms might legitimately want to hedge may never produce a single answer; there are a great many imperfections in the capital markets and a great many reasons why managers might want to gain more control over their firm's results. But the theoretical argument against hedging has one important practical implication. It tells us that we should not take it for granted that risk management strategies are a "good thing," but instead should examine the logic of the argument in relation to the specific circumstances and aims of the firm (and its stakeholders). Meanwhile, we can be pretty sure that firms should not enter derivatives markets to *increase* exposure to a risk type unless they can demonstrate that understanding, managing, and arbitraging this risk is one of their principal areas of expertise.

HEDGING OPERATIONS VERSUS HEDGING FINANCIAL POSITIONS

When discussing whether a particular corporation should hedge its risks, it is important to look at how the risk

---

[9] M. Campello, C. Lin, Y. Ma, and H. Zou, "The Real and Financial Implications of Corporate Hedging," *Journal of Finance* 66(5), October 2011, pp. 1615–1647.

[10] C. Geczy, B. A. Minton, and C. Schrand, "Why Firms Use Currency Derivatives," *Journal of Finance* 82(4), 1997, pp. 1323–1354.

[11] "Top-down ERM: A Pragmatic Approach to Managing Risk from the C-Suite," McKinsey working paper on Risk 22, August 2010.

arises. Here we should make a clear distinction between hedging activities related to the operations of the firm and hedging related to the balance sheet.

If a company chooses to hedge activities related to its operations, such as hedging the cost of raw materials (e.g., gold for a jewelry manufacturer), this clearly has implications for its ability to compete in the marketplace. The hedge has both a size and a price effect—i.e., it might affect both the price and the amount of products sold. Again, when an American manufacturing company buys components from a French company, it can choose whether to fix the price in euros or in U.S. dollars. If the French company insists on fixing the price in euros, the American company can opt to avoid the foreign currency risk by hedging the exposure. This is basically an operational consideration and, as we outlined above, lies outside the scope of the CAPM model, or the perfect capital markets assumption.

In a similar way, if a company exports its products to foreign countries, then the pricing policy for each market is an operational issue. For example, suppose that an Israeli high-tech company in the infrastructure business is submitting a bid to supply equipment in Germany over a period of three years, at predetermined prices in euros. If most of the high-tech firm's costs are in dollars, then it is natural for the company to hedge the future euro revenues. Why should the company retain a risky position in the currency markets? Uncertainty requires management attention and makes planning and the optimization of operations and processes more complicated. It is generally accepted that companies should concentrate on business areas in which they have comparative advantages and avoid areas where they cannot add value. It follows that reducing risk in the production process and in selling activities is usually advisable.

The story is quite different when we turn to the problem of the balance sheet of the firm. Why should a firm try to hedge the interest rate risk on a bank loan? Why should it swap a fixed rate for a variable rate, for example? In this case, the theoretical arguments we outlined above, based on the assumption that capital markets are perfect, suggest that the firm should not hedge.

Equally, however, if we believe financial markets are in some sense perfect, we might argue that investors' interests are also unlikely to be much harmed by appropriate derivatives trading. The trading, in such a case, is a "fair game." Nobody will lose from the activity, provided it is properly controlled and the firm's policy is fully transparent and disclosed to all investors.

If one argues that financial markets are not perfect, then the firm may gain some advantage from hedging its balance sheet. It may have a tax advantage, benefit from economies of scale, or have access to better information about a market than investors.

This all suggests a twofold conclusion to our discussion:

- Firms should risk-manage their operations.
- Firms may also hedge their assets and liabilities, so long as they disclose their hedging policy.

In any case, whether or not it makes use of derivative instruments, the firm must make risk management decisions. The decision not to hedge is also, in effect, a risk management decision that may harm the firm if the risk exposure turns into a financial loss.

In most cases, the relevant question is not whether corporations should engage in risk management but, rather, how they can manage and communicate their particular risks in a rational way. In Box 2-1 we can see one example of how Merck, a major pharmaceutical company, chose to describe one part of its hedging policy to investors in a particular financial year. We can see that the firm has adopted a particular line of reasoning to justify its hedging activities, and that it has tried to link some of the specific aims of its hedging activities to information about specific programs. As this example illustrates, each firm has to consider which risks to accept and which to hedge, as well as the price that it is willing to pay to manage those risks. The firm should take into account how efficiently it will be able to explain its aims to investors and other stakeholders.

PUTTING RISK MANAGEMENT INTO PRACTICE

Determining the Objective

A corporation should not engage in risk management before deciding clearly on its objectives in terms of risk and return. Without clear goals, determined and accepted by the board of directors, management is likely to engage in inconsistent, costly activities to hedge an arbitrary set of risks. Some of these goals will be specific to the firm, but others represent important general issues.

BOX 2-1   How Merck Manages Foreign Exchange and Interest Risk Exposures[1]

The Company [Merck] operates in multiple jurisdictions and, as such, virtually all sales are denominated in currencies of the local jurisdiction. Additionally, the Company has entered and will enter into acquisition, licensing, borrowings or other financial transactions that may give rise to currency and interest rate exposure.

Since the Company cannot, with certainty, foresee and mitigate against such adverse fluctuations, fluctuations in currency exchange rates and interest rates could negatively affect the Company's results of operations, financial position and cash flows.

In order to mitigate against the adverse impact of these market fluctuations, the Company will from time to time enter into hedging agreements. While hedging agreements, such as currency options and interest rate swaps, may limit some of the exposure to exchange rate and interest rate fluctuations, such attempts to mitigate these risks may be costly and not always successful.

Foreign Currency Risk Management

The Company has established revenue hedging, balance sheet risk management, and net investment hedging programs to protect against volatility of future foreign currency cash flows and changes in fair value caused by volatility in foreign exchange rates.

The objective of the revenue hedging program is to reduce the potential for longer-term unfavorable changes in foreign exchange rates to decrease the U.S. dollar value of future cash flows derived from foreign currency denominated sales, primarily the euro and Japanese yen. To achieve this objective, the Company will hedge a portion of its forecasted foreign currency denominated third-party and intercompany distributor entity sales that are expected to occur over its planning cycle, typically no more than three years into the future. The Company will layer in hedges over time, increasing the portion of third-party and intercompany distributor entity sales hedged as it gets closer to the expected date of the forecasted foreign currency denominated sales. The portion of sales hedged is based on assessments of cost-benefit profiles that consider natural offsetting exposures, revenue and exchange rate volatilities and correlations, and the cost of hedging instruments. . . . The Company manages

its anticipated transaction exposure principally with purchased local currency put options. . . . In connection with the Company's revenue hedging program, a purchased collar option strategy may be utilized. . . . The Company may also utilize forward contracts in its revenue hedging program.

The primary objective of the balance sheet risk management program is to mitigate the exposure of foreign currency denominated net monetary assets of foreign subsidiaries where the U.S. dollar is the functional currency from the effects of volatility in foreign exchange. In these instances, Merck principally utilizes forward exchange contracts, which enable the Company to buy and sell foreign currencies in the future at fixed exchange rates and economically offset the consequences of changes in foreign exchange from the monetary assets. Merck routinely enters into contracts to offset the effects of exchange on exposures denominated in developed country currencies, primarily the euro and Japanese yen. For exposures in developing country currencies, the Company will enter into forward contracts to partially offset the effects of exchange on exposures when it is deemed economical to do so based on a cost-benefit analysis that considers the magnitude of the exposure, the volatility of the exchange rate and the cost of the hedging instrument. . . .

A sensitivity analysis to changes in the value of the U.S. dollar on foreign currency denominated derivatives, investments and monetary assets and liabilities indicated that if the U.S. dollar uniformly weakened by 10% against all currency exposures of the Company at December 31, 2012, *Income before taxes* would have declined by approximately $20 million in 2012.

Foreign exchange risk is also managed through the use of foreign currency debt. The Company's senior unsecured euro-denominated notes have been designated as, and are effective as, economic hedges of the net investment in a foreign operation.

Interest Rate Risk Management

The Company may use interest rate swap contracts on certain investing and borrowing transactions to manage its net exposure to interest rate changes and to reduce its overall cost of borrowing. The Company does not use leveraged swaps and, in general, does not leverage any of its investment activities that would put principal capital at risk.

---

[1] Extracted from Merck's Form 10-K filing with the Securities & Exchange Commission, February 28, 2013.

The first step is to determine the "risk appetite" of the firm as the board defines it. Risk appetites can be expressed in a number of ways, including quantitative and qualitative statements.[12] For example, the risk appetite might set out the types of risk that the firm is willing to tolerate and, therefore, which risks should be hedged and which risks the company should assume as part of its business strategy. The risk appetite might also indicate the maximum losses the organization is willing to incur at a given confidence limit during a given time period, where such statistical calculations can be made in a way that is practical and robust. Many firms nowadays use stress testing to help articulate their risk appetite; that is, the firm analyzes the likely level of losses in a range of plausible but severely adverse scenarios and the board says clearly which losses are tolerable and which are not. The board can then direct management to mitigate or insure against extreme losses that offend against the corporate risk appetite, and the firm can budget for this activity. Chapter 3 discusses the issue of aligning the risk appetite of the firm to its strategy. One point is clear: accepting projects with positive risk-adjusted net present value (NPV) can enhance the welfare of all stakeholders.

Boards face a key dilemma when setting the risk appetite for a firm: whose interests is the firm trying to capture in its risk appetite statement? For example, debt holders are relatively conservative in the risks they would like the firm to adopt and may worry about downside risks that threaten the firm's solvency even if these risks seem to be on the borderline of plausibility. A shareholder with a large portfolio of investments, on the other hand, may find it more acceptable for a firm to remain exposed to a large but unlikely risk, so long as the returns for assuming the risk are large enough.

The objectives that the board sets out should not take the form of slogans, such as "maximum profit at minimal risk." The board should also consider which of the corporation's many risks should be hedged, and which risks the company should assume as part of its business strategy. The objectives should be set in clear, executable directives. In addition, the criteria for examining whether the objectives are attained should be set in advance. A jewelry company may decide to fully hedge its gold inventory, or it may insure the price of gold below a certain level. By following such a policy the company can remove all or some of the risk stemming from raw material prices for a given period.

The board should declare whether the aim is to hedge accounting profits or economic profits, and short-term profits or long-term profits. With regard to the former issue, the two measures of profit do not necessarily coincide, and at times their risk exposure is vastly different. Imagine a U.S. firm that purchases a plant in the United Kingdom that will serve U.K. clients, for a sum of £1 million. The investment is financed with a £1 million loan from a British bank. From an economic point of view, the sterling loan backed by a plant in the United Kingdom is fully hedged. However, if the plant is owned and managed by the U.S. company (that is, if it fails the "long arm test" that determines whether a subsidiary should be considered as an independent unit), its value is immediately translated into U.S. dollars, while the loan is kept in pounds. Hence, the company's accounting profits are exposed to foreign exchange risk: if the pound is more expensive, in terms of the dollar, at the end of the year, the accounts will be adjusted for these financial costs and will show a reduction in profits.

Should the U.S. company hedge this kind of accounting risk? If it buys a futures contract on the pound, its accounting exposure will be hedged, but the company will be exposed to economic risk! In this case, no strategy can protect both the accounting and economic risks simultaneously. (As we hinted earlier, while most managers claim that they are concerned with economic risk only, in practice many corporations, especially publicly traded corporations, hedge their accounting risks in order to avoid fluctuations in their reported earnings.)

It is the board's prerogative, subject to local regulatory provisions, to decide whether to smooth out the ups and downs of accounting profits, even at significant economic cost. Such a decision should be conveyed to management as a guiding policy for management actions. If the board is concerned with economic risk instead, this policy should also be made clear, and a budget should be allocated for this purpose.

Another important factor that the board should make clear is the time horizon for any of the risk management objectives set for management. Should hedging be planned to the end of the quarter or the end of the accounting year? Should it be set three years into

---

[12] Quantitative measures may include financial targets, e.g., capital adequacy, target debt rating, earnings volatility, credit or other external ratings. Qualitative measures may refer to reputational impact, management effort and regulatory compliance," KPMG, *Understanding and Articulating Risk Appetite*, 2008, p. 4.

the future? Hedging a future expected transaction with a long-term option or futures contract has liquidity, accounting, and tax implications. For example, should the U.S. firm hedge a sales order from a French customer that will be delivered two years from now? Remember that the income will be allowed to enter the firm's books only upon delivery, while the futures contract will be marked-to-market at the end of each quarter (see also Box 2-2). The derivatives contract may also incur a tax liability if, at the end of the tax year, it shows a profit.

It may make sense for the board to make clear certain "risk limits"—i.e., to allow management to operate within a given zone of prices and rates, and be exposed to the risk within the zone, but to disallow risk exposure beyond those limits. In such a case, the limits should be set clearly. For example, a British company might decide to avoid dollar exposures of more than $5 million. It might also decide to tolerate fluctuations of the dollar rate within the exchange rate zone of $1.45 to $1.60 to the pound, but to hedge currency risks that fall outside these limits.

Defining an objective in terms of a simple formula that can be immediately translated into clear practical instructions is rarely feasible. The objective should be broken down into clear rules that can be implemented in line with the major policy principles (such as the time horizon, and whether the hedging aims are those of bondholders or shareholders).

Mapping the Risks

After the objectives have been set and the general nature of the risks to be managed is decided upon, it is essential to map the relevant risks and to estimate their current and future magnitudes.

For example, let us assume that the board has decided to hedge *currency risks* arising from current positions and expected transactions in the next year. Now the office of the chief financial officer of the firm will have to map the specific risks likely to arise from exchange rate fluctuations. It should make a record of all assets and liabilities with values that are sensitive to exchange rate changes, and should classify all these positions in terms of the relevant currency. In addition, information should be collected from the sales or marketing division on firm orders from foreign clients for each currency that are due over the coming year, as well as on expected orders from foreign clients that will need to be fulfilled during this period. (A decision must be made about whether to hedge

unconfirmed sales. It might be decided, for example, to base the hedge on expected revenues.) Then, all expected expenses over the coming year that are denominated in foreign currencies should be traced (with the help of the production division). Again, the firm will have to decide how it is going to distinguish between firm purchasing commitments and uncertain purchase orders. The timing of cash inflows and outflows for each foreign currency can then be matched.

The same sort of mapping can be applied to other risk factors and risky positions, starting with the business risk of the firm and moving to its market risks and credit risks. Operational risk elements should also be identified.

The firm should prepare a list (a "hit parade") of the 10 most significant risk exposures of the firm. The process leading to such a list can be very rewarding to the firm in understanding the most threatening risks it faces. Each risk on the list should be characterized in terms of its potential damage and the probability of its occurrence, say, during the next 12 months.

In the United States, the SEC has since 1998 required publicly traded companies to assess and quantify their exposure to financial instruments that are linked to changes in interest rates, exchange rates, commodity prices, and equity prices. However, the SEC does not require firms to assess their underlying or "natural" exposure to changes in the same risk factors. Management, needless to say, cannot ignore these natural positions, whether they are matched to derivative positions or not.

When mapping a firm's risks, it is important to differentiate between risks that can be insured against, risks that can be hedged, and risks that are noninsurable and non-hedgeable. This classification is important because the next step is to look for instruments that might help to minimize the risk exposure of the firm.

Instruments for Risk Management

After mapping the risks, the next step is to identify instruments that can be used to risk-manage the exposures. Some of the instruments can be devised internally. For example, a U.S. firm with many assets denominated in British pounds can borrow money in pounds, in a loan transaction with the same time-to-maturity as the assets, and thus achieve a natural hedge (at least, an economic hedge, though not necessarily an accounting hedge). Similarly, a division with a euro liability may be hedged internally against another division with euro-denominated assets. Internal or "natural" hedging opportunities like this sidestep the transaction costs and many of the operational risks associated with purchasing risk management contracts and so should be considered first.

Next, the company should compare competing ways to manage risks that have been identified as transferable or insurable in the risk-mapping process, and evaluate the likely costs and benefits. The firm might decide to fully insure or offset some risks, partially insure others, and refrain from insuring some insurable risks. With regard to traditional insurance products, many large and well-diversified companies, operating in a variety of geographical areas, nowadays opt to self-insure their property (including cars, plants, and equipment). The same logic can sometimes be applied to financial risks.

Plenty of financial instruments for hedging risks have been developed over the last few decades, as we can see in Figure 2-1. The most fundamental distinction is between instruments traded on public exchanges versus over-the-counter (OTC) instruments that represent private contracts between two parties (often a corporation and a bank). Exchange-traded instruments are based on a limited number of underlying assets and are much more standardized than OTC contracts. For example, the strike prices and maturities of exchange-traded options are defined and set in advance by the exchanges in order to "commoditize" the risk management product and promote a thriving and liquid market.

Conversely, OTC products are issued by commercial and investment banks and thus can be tailored to customers' needs. For example, an OTC option on the British pound can be customized to a size and maturity that fits the needs of the customer and to a strike price that suits the client's strategy. OTC instruments can be made to "fit" a customer's risk exposure quite closely, but they tend to lack the price transparency and liquidity advantages of exchange products. Another concern in the OTC market is the credit risk associated with the counterparty to each contract. During the financial crisis of 2007–2009, many OTC contracts collapsed or endured an extended period of uncertainty about the ability of counterparties to honor them, while all exchange-based products were honored.[13]

_____

[13] Prior to the financial crisis of 2007–2009, counterparty credit risk was not considered to be a particularly key area and the concept of Credit Value Adjustment (CVA), was largely ignored in practice.

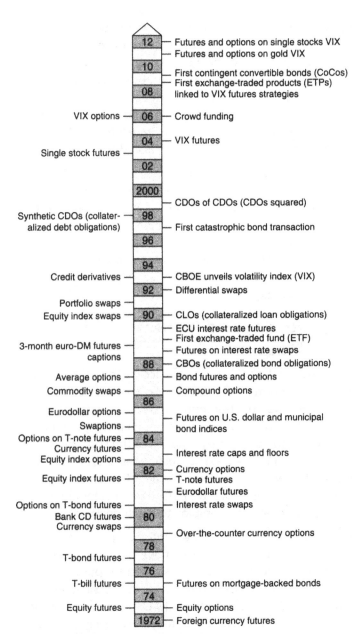

FIGURE 2-1 The evolution of financial instruments for hedging risks.

Source: The Economist. April 10, 1993, updated by the authors.

The active markets for exchange-traded instruments in the United States are mainly the Chicago Board Options Exchange (CBOE), which offers active markets in equity and index options; the Philadelphia Options Exchange, which is the leader in foreign exchange options; the International Securities Exchange (ISE), which is the leader in electronic trading of derivatives; the Chicago Board of Trade (CBOT), which runs huge markets in futures on stock indexes, bonds, and major commodities; the Chicago Mercantile Exchange (CME), with major markets in currency futures; and the International Monetary Market (IMM), with options trading on futures on foreign currencies and on bonds and interest rates. There are also active markets for options and futures in London (LIFFE), Paris, Brussels, Amsterdam (Euronext), Frankfurt, and Zurich (Eurex) and in most major countries and financial centers.

The variety of exchange-traded and, especially, OTC instruments is huge. In fact, investment bankers are willing to price almost any possible derivative based on known, traded underlying financial instruments. This leaves the corporate hedger with the considerable problem of identifying the most suitable instruments to hedge the specific risky positions of his or her firm, taking into consideration cost and liquidity.

Constructing and Implementing a Strategy

The office of the CFO must have access to all the relevant corporate information, market data, and statistical tools and models before attempting to devise a hedging strategy. The firm will need to select certain pricing and hedging models to help in the formation of the strategy. A firm can opt to purchase statistical estimates and/or models from external vendors. However, the officers in charge of risk management must have a deep understanding of the tools they are about to employ to reach decisions.

A key tactical decision is whether to hedge risks by means of "static" strategies or to plan more "dynamic" strategies. In a static strategy, a hedging instrument is purchased to match the risky position as exactly as possible and is maintained for as long as the risky position exists (or for a set horizon). This kind of strategy is relatively easy to implement and monitor. Dynamic strategies involve an ongoing series of trades that are used to calibrate the combined exposure and the derivative position. This strategy calls for much greater managerial effort in implementing and monitoring the positions, and may incur higher transaction costs.

For example, suppose that a U.S. company exporting to England is expecting to receive 5 million British pounds three months from today and wishes to hedge the downside risk—i.e., the risk that the pound will devalue against the U.S. dollar. It could simply follow the static strategy of buying a put option for the full quantity and term of the exposure. Alternatively, to hedge dynamically, the firm

might buy a longer-term put option than the three-month maturity of the exposure (longer maturity options often trade at a lower implied volatility and thus cost less per unit of risk) and adjust the quantity of the put so that it simulates the three-month put option in the static strategy. The dynamic strategy may require the hedger to adjust the put position on a daily or weekly basis and to increase or reduce the quantities of options, and possibly switch to other options with still lower relative risk premiums (maintaining the relevant hedge ratio through time). To follow a dynamic approach, the firm must possess sophisticated and reliable models with which to trade in the markets and monitor its positions—and the staff and skills to put these tools to use. But even this will not necessarily save the firm from making significant errors in communicating and implementing its risk management strategy. In Box 2-2 we take a look at a dynamic corporate risk management strategy put in place by a major U.S. energy trading company, Metallgesellschaft Refining & Marketing, Inc. (MGRM)—a strategy that went badly wrong. It's worth noting that in this case there has never been any suggestion of fraud or malpractice; problems arose purely through the nature, implementation, and communication of the corporate risk management strategy.

Another fundamental consideration in the hedging strategy is the planning horizon. The horizon can be fixed at the end of a quarter or the end of the tax year, or it might be a rolling horizon. Investment horizons should be made consistent with performance evaluations.

Other important considerations are accounting issues and potential tax effects. Accounting rules for derivatives are quite complex and are constantly being revised. Under the current rules, derivatives used for hedging must be perfectly matched to an underlying position (e.g., with regard to quantities and dates). They can then be reported together with the underlying risky positions, and no accounting profit or loss needs to be reported. If the positions are not perfectly matched, the marked-to-market profit or loss in the hedge must be recorded in the firm's accounts, even though changes in the value of the underlying exposure are not. Accounting rules affect how derivatives are presented in quarterly or year-end financial reports and how they affect the profit-and-loss statement. The MGRM case highlights the discrepancy between economic and accounting hedging. While MGRM was about fully hedged in economic terms, it was fully exposed in accounting terms, and was also not prepared to absorb liquidity risk.

In 1993 MGRM (MG Refining & Marketing), the U.S. subsidiary of Metallgesellschaft (MG), entered into contracts to supply end-user customers with 150 million barrels of oil products (gasoline and heating oil) over a period of 10 years, at fixed prices.

MGRM's fixed-price forward delivery contracts exposed it to the risk of rising energy prices. In the absence of a liquid market for long-term futures contracts, MGRM hedged this risk with both short-dated energy futures contracts on the New York Mercantile Exchange (NYMEX) and over-the-counter (OTC) swaps. The derivative positions were concentrated in short-dated futures and swaps, which had to be rolled forward monthly as they matured. Each month, the size of the derivatives position was reduced by the amount of product delivered that month, with the intention of preserving a one-to-one hedge. According to Culp and Miller (1995), "such a strategy is neither inherently unprofitable nor fatally flawed, provided top management understands the program and the long-term funding commitments necessary to make it work."[1]

This rolling hedge strategy can be profitable when markets are in a state known as "backwardation" (oil for immediate delivery commands a higher price than does oil for future delivery), but when markets are in

contango (the reverse relationship) it can result in losses. This is because when a company is rolling the hedge position in a backwardated market, the contract near expiration is sold at a higher price than the replacement contract, which has a longer delivery date, resulting in a rollover profit. The contrary applies when the market is in contango.

This meant that MGRM was exposed to curve risk (backwardation versus contango) and to basis risk, which is the risk that short-term oil prices might temporarily deviate from long-term prices. During 1993, cash prices fell from close to $20 a barrel in June to less than $15 a barrel in December, leading to $1.3 billion of margin calls that MGRM had to meet in cash. The problem was further compounded by the change in the shape of the price curve, which moved from backwardation to contango. MGRM's German parent reacted in December 1993 by liquidating the hedge, thus turning paper losses into realized losses.

Whether or not the cash drain from the negative marked-to-market of the futures positions was sustainable, the decision by the supervisory board to liquidate the hedge might not have been the optimal one. According to Culp and Miller, at least three viable alternatives should have been contemplated to avoid the price impact of unwinding the hedges in the marketplace: securing additional financing and continuing the program intact; selling the program to another firm; or unwinding the contracts with the original customers.

[1] C. Culp and M. Miller, "Blame Mismanagement, Not Speculation, for Metall's Woes," *European Wall Street Journal*, April 25, 1995.

Tax considerations can be very important because they affect the cash flows of the firm. Different derivative instruments with different maturities may incur very different tax liabilities; tax treatment is also inconsistent from country to country. This means that a multinational corporation might find it advantageous to use derivatives in one country to hedge positions that are related to its business in another country. Professional advice on tax matters is a key factor when devising hedging strategies.

A strategy is only as good as its implementation, but however skillful the implementation, some deviation from the plan can be expected. Prices in the marketplace can change and make some hedges unattractive. Since different people within the firm are often responsible for establishing risky positions and hedging positions, special care should be taken to monitor the positions. For example, if the British client in our earlier example pays the firm after

two, rather than three, months, then the three-month put must be liquidated before it matures.

Performance Evaluation

The corporate risk management system must be evaluated periodically. Crucially, the evaluation should assess the extent to which the overall goals have been achieved— not whether specific transactions made a profit or loss. Whenever a risk is hedged, the party on one side of the hedge transaction inevitably shows a profit while the counterparty inevitably shows a loss. The corporation can never know in advance which side will increase in value and which side will lose value—after all, that's why it is managing the risk in the first place. So if the goal is to eliminate risk, and risk is eliminated, then the risk manager has done the job well even if the hedged position has generated an economic or accounting loss (compared to the original, unhedged position).

Reducing earnings volatility may not be the only criterion, however. Risk managers can legitimately be evaluated in terms of how well they manage the transaction costs of hedging, including the tax payments that can arise out of employing derivatives. He or she should also act within a given budget; major deviations from the budget should be explored and explained.

When evaluating the performance of risk management, the board of directors should also decide whether or not to change the policy of the company. There is nothing wrong with a firm's changing its objectives, so long as the changes are based on thorough analysis and are consistent with the other activities and aims of the firm. Local regulatory requirements for the disclosure of risks may mean that policy changes in market risk management should be made public if the changes are material.

Corporate Governance and Risk Management

3

Learning Objectives

Candidates, after completing this reading, should be able to:

- Compare and contrast best practices in corporate governance with those of risk management.
- Assess the role and responsibilities of the board of directors in risk governance.
- Evaluate the relationship between a firm's risk appetite and its business strategy, including the role of incentives.

- Distinguish the different mechanisms for transmitting risk governance throughout an organization.
- Illustrate the interdependence of functional units within a firm as it relates to risk management.
- Assess the role and responsibilities of a firm's audit committee.

Excerpt is Chapter 4 of The Essentials of Risk Management, *Second Edition, by Michel Crouhy, Dan Galai, and Robert Mark.*

The first decade of the millennium saw two major waves of corporate failures, first in the nonfinancial sector (2001–2003) and then in the financial sector (2007–2009), both of which were attributed in part to failures of corporate governance. As a result, corporate governance[1] and its relationship to risk oversight is a continuing concern around the world, and especially in the United States and Europe.

The first wave of failures included, most notoriously, the bankruptcy of energy giant Enron in 2001, a wave of "new technology" and telecom industry accounting scandals at companies such as World Com and Global Crossing, and, to prove that the problem wasn't confined to the United States, the collapse of the Italian dairy products giant Parmalat in late 2003. In many cases, boards were provided with misleading information or there was a breakdown in the process by which information was transmitted to the board and shareholders. The breakdowns often involved financial engineering and the nondisclosure of economic risks—as well as outright fraud.

The first wave of scandals led to a wave of reforms, including legislation in the United States and reforms of corporate codes in Europe, designed to mend perceived failures in corporate governance practices and, especially, to improve financial controls and financial reporting. A striking feature of these reforms was that they sought to penalize inattention and incompetence as much as deliberate malfeasance. In the United States, the main mechanisms of reform were the Sarbanes-Oxley Act (SOX) of 2002 and associated changes in stock exchange rules, as described in Boxes 3-1 and 3-2.

However, the reforms proved insufficient[2] to avert the subprime crisis in the United States and the subsequent global financial crisis. Following a series of failures and

---

[1] "Corporate governance involves a set of relationships between a company's management, its board, its shareholders and other stakeholders. Corporate governance also provides the structure through which the objectives of the company are set, and the means of attaining those objectives and monitoring performance are determined." Preamble, OECD Principles of Corporate Governance, 2004, p. 11.

[2] Perhaps because the first wave of reforms focused on internal controls and financial reporting, rather than risk management in its wider sense including the risk of pursuing fundamentally flawed business models. Following the 2007–2009 crisis, a new emphasis on stress testing programs and "recovery and resolution" style regulatory approaches should help to guard against the danger of a firm's pursuing a flawed business model.

BOX 3-1   Sarbanes-Oxley (Sox)

In response to the series of accounting and management scandals that surfaced soon after the millennium, the U.S. Congress passed the Sarbanes-Oxley Act of 2002 (SOX). The act has created a more rigorous legal environment for the board, the management committee, internal and external auditors, and the CRO (chief risk officer).

SOX places primary responsibility on the chief executive officer and the chief financial officer of a publicly traded corporation for ensuring the accuracy of company reports filed with the Securities and Exchange Commission. SOX requires these senior corporate officers to report on the completeness and accuracy of the information contained in the reports, as well as on the effectiveness of the underlying controls.

Specifically, SOX calls for the CEO and CFO to certify quarterly and annually that the report filed with the Securities and Exchange Commission does not contain any untrue statements or omit any material facts. Senior officers must certify that the financial statements fairly present (in all material respects) the results of the corporation's operations and cash flows. They also must take responsibility for designing, establishing, and maintaining disclosure controls and procedures.

The CEO and CFO must also disclose to the audit committee and to the company's external auditors any deficiencies and material weaknesses in internal controls, as well as any fraud (material or not) involving anyone with a significant role in internal control. The act requires that senior management annually assess the effectiveness of the corporation's internal control structure and procedures for financial reporting.

The act also seeks to make sure that the board of the company includes some members who are experts in understanding financial reports. Companies are compelled to disclose the number and names of persons serving on the critical audit committee whom the board has determined to be "financial experts." A financial expert is someone with an understanding of generally accepted accounting principles and financial statements, and should also have experience with internal accounting controls and an understanding of the function of the audit committee.

near-failures of large financial institutions between 2007 and 2009, boards professed ignorance of the risks that had been assumed in the pursuit of profit—and sometimes senior management offered the same excuse. In particular, the risk management function at many firms failed to attract the attention of senior management, or the boards,

BOX 3-2	U.S. Exchanges Tighten Up the Rules

In January 2003 the U.S. Securities and Exchange Commission issued a rule—as directed by the Sarbanes-Oxley Act—that requires U.S. national securities exchanges and national securities associations (i.e., the NYSE, Amex, and Nasdaq) to make sure that their securities listing standards conform to the existing and evolving SEC rules.

These standards cover a number of areas that are critical to corporate governance and risk management, such as

- Composition of the board of directors—e.g., the board must have a majority of independent directors
- Establishment of a corporate governance committee with duties such as the development of broad corporate governance principles and oversight of the evaluation of the board and management
- Duties of the compensation committee—e.g., it should make sure that CEO compensation is aligned with corporate objectives
- Activities of the audit committee—e.g., to review external auditors' reports describing the quality of internal control procedures, and to adopt and disclose corporate governance guidelines and codes of business conduct

to the risk accumulated in structured financial products. One reason may have been a process of marginalization of the role of risk management in financial institutions during the boom years in the run-up to the crisis.

A note of frustration characterized the debate about corporate governance following the 2007–2009 crisis. Would it do any good to reform corporate governance once again with detailed legislation and new rules, when the enormous effort expended on the Sarbanes-Oxley reforms had proved inadequate to prevent a second wave of disaster?[3] Others have argued that a principles-based approach might work better, given that the regulators of the banking industry have already set out some of the key principles of improved risk governance in Pillar II of Basel II. Table 3-1 sets out some of the key areas of debate

---

[3] Some of the key legislative reforms can be seen as ways to force bank boards to do what they should have been doing all along—e.g., in the United States, the Dodd-Frank Act forces larger banks to run worst-case macroeconomic scenarios and to take the results into account in their capital planning and dividend payouts.

on financial institution corporate governance following the crisis; we return to many of these themes throughout this chapter.

Together with the Basel III reforms, these concerns and their remedies in various jurisdictions are shaping the broader corporate governance and risk management environment. More generally, the dramatic collapse in public confidence in the corporate and financial world caused by the two waves of scandals continues to put pressure on boards and their committees to carry out corporate governance risk oversight responsibilities in a more effective manner.

In this chapter we'll use the example of an archetypal bank to try to answer three critical questions:

- How does best-practice corporate governance relate to best-practice risk management?
- How do boards and senior executives organize the delegation of risk management authority through key committees and risk executives?
- How can agreed risk limits be transmitted down the line to business managers in a way that can be monitored and that makes sense in terms of day-to-day business decisions?

Our aim is to give an idea of how risk management should be articulated from the top of an organization to the bottom. We focus on banks, since this topic is particularly critical in banking, but the concepts usually apply equally to other financial institutions as well as to nonbank corporations.

SETTING THE SCENE: CORPORATE GOVERNANCE AND RISK MANAGEMENT

From a corporate governance perspective, a primary responsibility of the board is to look after the interests of shareholders. For example, does it make sense for the corporation to assume a particular risk, given the projected returns of the business activity and the potential threat to the corporation if the risk is realized? The board also needs to be sensitive to the concerns of other stakeholders such as debt holders. Debt holders are most interested in the extreme downside of risk—how likely is it that a risk will damage a corporation so badly that it will become insolvent?

TABLE 3-1 Key Post-Crisis Corporate Governance Concerns: The Banking Industry

Stakeholder priority	Inquiries into the 2007–2009 financial crisis found that there was little focus in some firms on controlling tail risks and considering truly worst-case outcomes. This has led to debate about the uniquely complicated set of stakeholders in banking institutions and how this should affect corporate governance structures. In addition to equity, banks have very large amounts of deposits, debt, and implicit guarantees from governments. Depositors, debt holders, and taxpayers have a much stronger interest in minimizing the risk of bank failure than do most shareholders, who often seem to press for short-term results. The usual solution to corporate governance issues (empowering shareholders) may therefore not be the complete solution in banking.[1]
Board composition	The crisis reignited a long-term debate about how to ensure that bank boards contain the right balance of independence, engagement, and financial industry expertise. However, analyses of failed banks do not show any clear correlation between a predominance of "expert insiders" or "independents" and either failure or success. The first large failure of the crisis, the U.K.'s Northern Rock in 2007, had a number of banking experts on its board.
Board risk oversight	One key post-crisis trend has been a realization that boards need to become much more actively involved in risk oversight. This means educating boards on risk and making sure they maintain a direct link to the risk management infrastructure (e.g., giving CROs direct reporting responsibilities to the board, and more generally re-empowering risk managers).
Risk appetite	Regulators have pushed banks to set out a formal board-approved risk appetite that defines the firm's willingness to take risk and to tolerate threats to solvency. This can then be translated into an enterprise-wide set of risk limits. Engaging the board in the limit-setting process helps to make sure that the board thinks clearly about the firm's risk-taking and what this means for day-to-day risk decisions. However, defining risk appetites and translating them successfully into limit frameworks remains a work in progress.
Compensation	One of the key levers of the board in determining bank behavior on risk is its control over compensation schemes. Some banks have begun to institute reforms such as making bonuses a smaller part of the compensation package, introducing bonus clawbacks and deferred payments to capture longer-term risks, and similar measures. Boards have a particular duty to examine how pay structures might exacerbate risk-taking and whether risk adjustment mechanisms capture all the key long-term risks.

[1] See discussion in Hamid Mehran et. al., "Corporate Governance and Banks: What Have We Learned from the Financial Crisis?" Federal Reserve Bank of New York, Staff Report no. 502, June 2011.

In particular, the board needs to be on the alert for any conflict that may arise between the interests of management in boosting returns while assuming risks, and the interests of the company's longer-term stakeholders. (This kind of conflict of interest is often referred to in the academic literature as an "agency risk.")

Conflicts of interest can easily happen if, for example, executives are rewarded with options that they can cash in if the share price of the company rises above a certain level. Such an arrangement gives management an incentive to push the share price up, but not necessarily in a sustainable way. For example, management might encourage business lines to earn short-term rewards in exchange for assuming long-term risks. By the time the chickens come home to roost, managers, including CEOs, may well have picked up their bonuses or even changed jobs.

The tension between the interests of the CEO and the interests of longer-term stakeholders helps to explain why boards of directors need to maintain their independence from executive teams, and why there is a global push to separate the role of the CEO and the chairman of the board. The bankruptcy of MF Global, a brokerage firm, in October of 2011—one of the 10 largest U.S. bankruptcies ever—offers an example of poor governance. Many commentators have pointed out the danger of the board of a company falling under the spell of a charismatic CEO.[4]

[4] Jon Corzine, the CEO of MF Global, took huge bets on European sovereign debt, eventually leading to an increase in required capital, increased margin calls as positions soured, a ratings downgrade, and a loss of confidence in the firm. MF Global was left without the cash to support its operations and was faced with a classic run on the bank. Bankruptcy followed.

This all explains why it is becoming difficult to draw a line between corporate governance and risk management, and we can see some clear effects of this at an organizational level. For example, over the last few years, many corporations have created the role of chief risk officer (CRO). A key duty of the CRO is often to act as a senior member of the management committee and to attend board meetings regularly. The board and the management committee increasingly look to the CRO to integrate corporate governance responsibilities with the risk function's existing market, credit, operational, and business risk responsibilities. Following the financial crisis of 2007–2009, many CROs were given a direct reporting line to the board or its risk committees in addition to reporting to the executive team and CEO.[5]

TRUE RISK GOVERNANCE

The primary responsibility of the board is to ensure that it develops a clear understanding of the bank's business strategy and the fundamental risks and rewards that this implies. The board also needs to make sure that risks are made transparent to managers and to stakeholders through adequate internal and external disclosure.

Although the board is not there to manage the business, it is responsible for overseeing management and holding it accountable. It must also contribute to the development of the overall strategic plan for the firm, taking into consideration how any changes might affect business opportunities and the strategy of the firm. This necessarily includes the extent and types of risks that are acceptable for the firm—i.e., the board must characterize an appropriate "risk appetite" for the firm, as we discussed in Chapter 2.[6]

The firm's risk appetite should clearly be connected to its overall business strategy and capital plan. Some business activities may simply be wrong for a given firm, given the risks they entail and the size of the activity in relation to the firm's balance sheet. Business planning, which tends to be driven by earnings goals in a competitive environment, needs to involve risk management from the beginning of the planning process, in order to test how targets fit with the firm's risk appetite and to assess potential downsides. Equally important is clear communication throughout the firm of the firm's risk appetite and risk position.

To fulfill its risk governance responsibilities, the board must ensure that the bank has put in place an effective risk management program that is consistent with these fundamental strategic and risk appetite choices. And it must make sure that there are effective procedures in place for identifying, assessing, and managing all types of risk—e.g., business risk, operational risk, market risk, liquidity risk, and credit risk. For every business disaster where a firm has knowingly taken on too much risk, there is another where the firm has failed to identify a risk, such as an underlying liquidity risk, or ignored the risk because it was thought so unlikely that it did not deserve active risk management.

The board may be challenged by the complexity of the risk management process, but the principles at a strategic level are quite simple. There are only four basic choices in risk management:

- Avoid risk by choosing not to undertake some activities.
- Transfer risk to third parties through insurance, hedging, and outsourcing.
- Mitigate risk, such as operational risk, through preventive and detective control measures.
- Accept risk, recognizing that undertaking certain risky activities should generate shareholder value.

In particular, the board should ensure that business and risk management strategies are directed at economic rather than accounting performance, contrary to what happened at Enron and some of the other firms involved in highly publicized corporate governance scandals around the turn of the millennium.

This includes making sure that all the appropriate policies, methodologies, and infrastructure are in place across the enterprise.[7] The infrastructure includes both operating

---

[5] The Basel Committee says that a bank CRO should "report and have direct access to the board and its risk committee without impediment. . . . Interaction between the CRO and the board should occur regularly. . . . Non-executive board members should have the right to meet regularly—in the absence of senior management—with the CRO." Basel Committee, *Principles for Enhancing Corporate Governance,* October 2010.

[6] See also risk appetite discussion in Senior Supervisors Group, *Risk Management Lessons from the Global Banking Crisis of 2008,* October 2009, pp. 23–24; and in KPMG, *Understanding and Articulating Risk Appetite,* 2008.

[7] The OECD's paper on *Corporate Governance and the Financial Crisis: Conclusions and Emerging Good Practices to Enhance Implementation of the Principles,* February 2010, p. 4, says that "an important conclusion is that the board's responsibility for defining strategy and risk appetite needs to be extended to establishing and overseeing enterprise-wide risk management systems."

elements (e.g., sophisticated software, hardware, data, and operational processes) and personnel.

This might sound like an onerous task, but there are various levers that the board can pull. For example, one way to gauge how seriously a company takes its risk management process is to look at the human capital that is employed:

- What kind of a career path does the risk management function offer?
- Whom do risk managers report to?
- What salaries are paid to risk managers in comparison to "reward-oriented" personnel such as traders?
- Is there a strong ethical culture in evidence?

An effective board will also establish strong ethical standards and work to ensure that it understands the degree to which management follows them. Some banks have set up ethics committees within their business divisions to try to make sure that "soft" risks such as unethical business practices don't slip through the mesh of their "hard" risk-reporting framework.

Another important lever available to the board is the firm's performance metrics and compensation strategy. The board has a critical responsibility to make sure that the way staff are rewarded and compensated is based on risk-adjusted performance and is aligned with shareholders' interests. The increase in misreporting after the millennial stock market boom paralleled the rise of equity-based compensation for CEOs, which arguably provided a perverse incentive to executives to manipulate financial results to boost the share price in the short term.

A related responsibility is to ensure that any major transactions the bank enters into are consistent with the risk authorized and the associated strategies of the bank.

The board should ensure that the information it obtains about risk management is accurate and reliable. Directors should demonstrate healthy skepticism and require information from a cross section of knowledgeable and reliable sources, such as the CEO, senior management, and internal and external auditors. Directors should be prepared to ask tough questions, and they should make themselves able to understand the answers.

The duty of the board is not, however, to undertake risk management on a day-to-day basis, but to make sure that all the mechanisms used to delegate and drive risk management decisions are functioning properly. As we discussed above, the 2007–2009 financial crisis highlighted the need to strengthen the role of the board, and therefore:[8]

- Board members need to be educated on risk issues and be given the means to explore and determine the risk appetite of the organization. They should be able to assess the risk of loss that the firm is willing to accept over a specified time horizon, taking into account its business mix and strategy, earnings goals, and competitive position. This involves understanding the firm's current risk profile and its business culture vis-à-vis the firm's risk appetite, and monitoring the firm's ongoing performance against its risk appetite.

- Board members of the risk committee need some technical sophistication with regard to the key risk disciplines as well as solid business experience so that they can build clear perspectives on risk issues.

- The risk committee of the board should remain separate from the audit committee, as different skills are required for each fiduciary responsibility.

COMMITTEES AND RISK LIMITS: OVERVIEW

We've set out some of the goals of best-practice risk governance. Now we'll take a look at some of the mechanisms that financial institutions and other nonfinancial risk-taking corporations use to translate these goals into reality.

In the following we'll focus on corporate governance in the banking industry. However, many of the same principles and structures could be applied in other industries.

At most banks, the board charges its main committees—e.g., the audit and risk management committees—with ratifying the key policies and associated procedures of the bank's risk management activities. These committees also make sure that the implementation of these key policies is effective.

---

[8] In October 2010, the Basel Committee issued principles for enhancing corporate governance that addressed such issues as the role of the board of directors, the qualification of board members, and the importance of an independent risk management function. (Basel Committee, *Principles for Enhancing Corporate Governance,* October 2010.) In the United States, the Dodd-Frank Act requires a dedicated risk committee of the board of directors for publicly traded bank holding companies with total assets of $10 billion or more, as well as for systemically important publicly traded nonbank financial companies.

The committees help to translate the overall risk appetite of the bank, approved by the board, into a set of limits that flow down through the bank's executive officers and business divisions. All banks, for example, should have in place a credit risk management committee to keep an eye on credit risk reporting, as well as a system of credit risk limits.

The exact name for each committee tends to vary quite a lot across the industry, as do the specific duties of each committee. For our purposes, we'll imagine an archetypal bank with a senior risk committee to oversee risk management practices and detailed reporting. Junior risk committees that look after specific types of risk, such as the credit risk committee, often report to this senior risk committee.

Let's now look at two specific mechanisms for risk governance, before examining how risk committees use risk metrics and limit frameworks to delegate risk authority down through the bank.

A Key Traditional Mechanism: The Special Role of the Audit Committee of the Board

The role of the audit committee of the board is critical to the board's oversight of the bank. The audit committee is responsible not only for the accuracy of the bank's financial and regulatory reporting, but also for ensuring that the bank complies with minimum or best-practice standards in other key activities, such as regulatory, legal, compliance, and risk management activities. Audit committee members are now required to be financially literate so that they can carry out their duties.

We can think of auditing as providing independent verification for the board on whether the bank is actually doing what it says it is doing. Although some of the audit committee's functions can sound quite close to risk management, it is this key verification function that separates the audit committee's work from the work of other risk committees.

The audit committee's duties involve not just checking for infringements, but also overseeing the quality of the processes that underpin financial reporting, regulatory compliance, internal controls, and risk management.

In a later section, we look specifically at how the audit function, which often has a direct reporting relationship with the audit committee, acts as an independent check on the bank's risk management process.

To function properly, an audit committee needs members with the right mix of knowledge, judgment, independence, integrity, inquisitiveness, and commitment. In most banks, a nonexecutive director leads the audit committee, and most members are nonexecutives. The audit committee also needs to establish an appropriate interaction with management—independent but productive, and with all the necessary lines of communication kept open.

The audit committee needs to ask itself several key questions with respect to each of its principal duties. For example, with respect to financial statements, the audit committee needs to be satisfied not only that the financial statements are correct, but also that the company adequately addresses the risk that the financial statements may be materially misstated (intentionally or unintentionally).

The audit committee also needs to be clear about the reporting and risk management elements of governance that it oversees on behalf of the board. These might include financial reporting, operational effectiveness, and efficiency, as well as compliance with laws and regulations. Again, the recent financial crisis revealed the weaknesses of the audit committees in many banks and financial institutions—e.g., they did not uncover the excess risk assumed by traders or the risk of building up large portfolios of structured credit products.

A Key New Mechanism: The Evolving Role of a Risk Advisory Director

Not all board members will have the skills to determine the financial condition of a complex risk-taking corporation such as a bank (or an insurance company, or an energy company).

This is especially likely if the selection of nonexecutives on the board is designed to include nonexecutives who come from outside the firm's industry and are truly independent of the corporation. This is a problem because many of the recent corporate governance scandals have shown that it is easy for executives to bamboozle nonexecutives who lack the skills to ask probing questions, or to understand the answers to these questions in a rigorous manner.

There are various ways to square this circle, including training programs for board members and establishing some kind of independent support for interpreting

BOX 3-3 What Might a Risk Advisory Director Do?

In the main text, we describe a new mechanism of corporate governance, the risk advisory director. Such a director should review, analyze, and become familiar with

- Risk management policies, methodologies, and infrastructure
- Daily and weekly risk management reports
- The overall business portfolio and how it drives risk
- Business strategies and changes that shape risk
- Internal controls to mitigate key market, credit, operational, and business risks
- Financial statements, critical accounting principles, significant accounting judgments, material accounting estimates, and off-balance-sheet financings
- Financial information and disclosures that are provided in support of securities filings
- Internal audit and external audit reports and associated management letters
- Interplay between the company and its affiliates, including intercompany pricing issues, related-party transactions, and interrelationship of the external auditors selected for each of the enterprises
- Relevant regulatory, accounting profession, industry, rating agency, and stock exchange-based requirements and best practices
- Practices of external competitors and industry trends in risk management
- Industry corporate governance and risk-related forums

- Participate in audit committee meetings to support members.
- Participate periodically in key risk committee meetings to provide independent commentary on executive risk reporting.
- Meet regularly with key members of management.
- Observe the conduct of business.
- Share insights on best-practice corporate governance and risk management with respect to best-in-class policies, methodologies, and infrastructure.
- Provide a high-level educational perspective on the risk profiles of key business areas and on the risks associated with the business model.

A key goal of the advisory director would be an ongoing examination of the interface between corporate governance and risk management in terms of risk policies, methodologies, and infrastructure.

The Special Role of the Risk Management Committee of the Board

At a bank, the risk management committee of the board is responsible for independently reviewing the identification, measurement, monitoring, and controlling of credit, market, and liquidity risks, including the adequacy of policy guidelines and systems. If the committee identifies any issues concerning operational risk, it typically refers these to the audit committee for review.

The board of directors also typically delegates to the risk management committee the responsibility for approving individual credits (e.g., loans) above a certain amount, as well as for reviewing individual credits within limits delegated to the chairman and chief executive officer by the board, but above certain reporting thresholds. These aspects are usually set out in a formal document—e.g., the "investment and lending delegation of authority resolution"—approved by the board.

The risk management committee reports back to the board on a variety of items, such as all loans and/or credits over a specified dollar limit that are special, or being made to related parties (e.g., bank officers). The risk management committee also monitors credit and securities portfolios, including major trends in credit, market, and liquidity risk levels, portfolio composition, and industry breakdowns.

information about risk and risk processes (i.e., independent of the senior executive team).

One approach is for the board to gain the support of a specialist risk advisory director—that is, a member of the board (not necessarily a voting member) who specializes in risk matters. An advisory director works to improve the overall efficiency and effectiveness of the senior risk committees and the audit committee, as well as the independence and quality of risk oversight by the main board. The concerns of such a director are listed in Box 3-3, which in effect is also a checklist of some of the key duties of the board with regard to risk management.

In terms of specific activities, the advisory director might:

The risk management committee also typically provides opportunities for separate, direct, and private communication with the chief inspector (head of internal audit), the external auditors, and the management committee.

The Special Role of the Compensation Committee of the Board

One of the main lessons of the 2007–2009 financial crisis was that compensation schemes in financial institutions encouraged disproportionate risk-taking with insufficient regard to long-term risks. Over the previous two decades, bankers and traders had increasingly been rewarded with bonuses tied to short-term profits or to business volume, incentivizing them to front-load fees and income and back-load the risks. Also, the compensation schemes were structured like a call option in that compensation increased with the upside, but there were no real penalties in the case of losses. With the help of excessive leverage, this sometimes led bank personnel to bet the entire bank on astonishingly reckless investment strategies.

In many countries, securities authorities now require public companies to set up a special board compensation committee to determine the compensation of top executives. This was driven by concerns over corporate governance, particularly the ability of CEOs to convince board members to compensate the CEO and other officers at the expense of shareholders, who had virtually no say in such decisions.

It is now widely recognized that incentive compensation should be aligned with the long-term interests of shareholders and other stakeholders, and with risk-adjusted return on capital. To the extent that this is not the case, it is important for banks to address any potential distortions. Incorporating risk management considerations into performance goals and compensation decisions has become a leading practice, and compensation planning is viewed as a key tool in enterprise-wide risk management.

However, it will always be tempting for firms to offer attractive compensation packages to revenue-generating talent. International cooperation may be necessary to prevent financial firms from arbitraging the market for human capital through their choice of jurisdiction. In September 2009, the G20 endorsed the notion that excessive compensation in the financial sector encouraged excessive risk-taking and contributed to the financial crisis. Among the G20 recommendations was the removal of guaranteed bonuses, with executives being exposed to downside risk through compensation deferral and clawbacks in the event that a strategy incurs losses in the longer term.[9] Moreover, EU regulators have adopted a rule, taking effect in 2014, which caps bankers' bonuses at one times their salary, or twice their salary if shareholders explicitly agree by a two-thirds majority. Also, in 2013 the European Parliament voted to cap bonuses in the asset management industry. Bonuses should not exceed base salaries for managers of mutual funds regulated by the European Union.

Stock-based compensation helps to align the interests of executives with those of shareholders, but it is not a panacea. Before Lehman's bankruptcy, about a third of the firm was owned by the employees, and many employees lost a large chunk of their life savings. Stock ownership can also encourage risk-taking, as shareholders' gains are not limited on the upside, while their losses are capped on the downside.

One solution could be to make employees creditors of the company by including restricted notes or bonds as part of their compensation package. Such a solution has been adopted by UBS, which will pay part of the bonuses of its most highly compensated employees with "bonus bonds"—i.e., bonds that will be forfeited if the bank's regulatory capital ratio falls below 7.5%.

Furthermore, UBS's use of contingent debt is structured to complement this compensation strategy. The contingent debt converts into equity if the capital ratio falls below 5%, a trigger set deliberately lower than the trigger for forfeiture of deferred compensation. The reason is that bond investors are expected to pay more for contingent debt if they expect management to recapitalize the distressed firm before it crosses the threshold for conversion of debt to equity.

---

[9] The Financial Stability Board's implementation standards list specific propositions and time periods for deferral, such as 40% to 60% lockup of compensation for three years. The Board also recommended that firms prohibit employees from hedging to undermine the intended risk incentive alignment. The Board also suggests that at least 50% of pay be based on shares, along with a share retention policy, as opposed to the use of guaranteed bonuses.

Compensation policies such as these should improve social welfare more generally by reducing both the likelihood and expected costs of future bailouts.[10, 11]

ROLES AND RESPONSIBILITIES IN PRACTICE

We've described the basic structures and mechanisms for risk governance at the board level. But how do these structures and mechanisms work together to make sure that the day-to-day activities of the bank conform to the board-agreed general risk appetite and the limits set by the board and management committees?

The senior risk committee of the bank recommends to the risk committee of the board an amount at risk that it is prudent for the risk committee of the board to approve. In particular, the senior risk committee of the bank determines the amount of financial risk (i.e., market risk and credit risk) and nonfinancial risk (i.e., operational risk and business risk) to be assumed by the bank as a whole, in line with the bank's business strategies. At the top of the tree, the risk committee of the board approves the bank's risk appetite each year, based on a well-defined and broad set of risk measures (such as the amount of overall interest rate risk). The risk committee of the board delegates authority to the senior risk committee of the bank, chaired by the CEO of the firm, whose membership includes, among others, the chief risk officer (CRO), the head of compliance, the heads of the business units, the CFO, and the treasurer.

---

[10] Compensation schemes similar to this have been advocated by *The Squam Lake Report* (French et. al., 2010), which recommends: "Systemically important financial institutions should be required to hold back a substantial share—perhaps 20%—of the compensation of employees who can have a meaningful impact on the survival of the firm. This holdback should be forfeited if the firm's capital ratio falls below a specified threshold. The deferral period—perhaps 5 years—should be long enough to allow much of the uncertainty about managers' activities to be resolved before the bonds mature. Except for forfeiture, the payoff on the bonds should not depend on the firm's performance, nor should managers be permitted to hedge the risk of forfeiture. The threshold for forfeiture should be crossed well before a firm violates its regulatory capital requirements and well before its contingent convertible securities convert to equity."

[11] In 2008, Credit Suisse paid a portion of senior management's bonuses in bonds linked to a pool of toxic assets, helping the firm to dispose of risky assets and free up capital.

The senior risk committee of the bank is also responsible for establishing, documenting, and enforcing all policies that involve risk, and for delegating specific business-level risk limits to the CRO of the bank. The CRO is typically a member of the management committee and is responsible, among other things, for designing the bank's risk management strategy. Specifically, the CRO is responsible for the risk policies, risk methodologies, and risk infrastructure as well as for corporate risk governance.

The senior risk committee of the bank delegates to the CRO the authority to make day-to-day decisions on its behalf, including the authority to approve risks in excess of the limits provided to the bank's various businesses as long as these limits do not breach the overall risk limits approved by the board.

At many banks, the CRO plays a pivotal role in informing the board, as well as the senior risk committee of the bank, about the appetite for risk across the bank. The CRO also communicates the views of the board and senior management down through the organization. Each business unit, for example, may be given a mandate to assume risk on behalf of the bank up to a specific risk limit. The senior risk committee of the bank must satisfy itself that the bank's infrastructure can support the bank's risk management objectives. The senior risk committee of the bank also reviews in detail and approves (say, annually) each business unit mandate in terms of their risk limits, and delegates the monitoring of these limits to the CRO.

In large banks, the process for developing and renewing this authority is explicit. For example, business unit risk authority typically expires one year after the senior risk committee of the bank approves it. The CRO may approve an extension of an authority beyond one year to accommodate the senior risk committee's schedule.

A balance needs to be struck between ensuring that a business can meet its business goals and maintaining its overall risk standards (including ensuring that limits can be properly monitored). Key infrastructure and corporate governance groups are normally consulted when preparing a business unit's mandate.

The CRO is responsible for independently monitoring the limits throughout the year. The CRO may order business units to reduce their positions or close them out because of concerns about risk such as market, credit, or operational risks.

The CRO also delegates some responsibilities to the heads of the various business units. For example, at an investment bank, the head of global trading is likely to be made responsible for the risk management and performance of all trading activities, and he or she in turn delegates the management of limits to the business managers. The business managers are responsible for the risk management and performance of the business, and they in turn delegate limits to the bank's traders.

This delegation process is summarized in Figure 3-1 with reference to market risk authorities.

At the level of each major business, there may also be a business risk committee. The business risk committee is typically made up of both business and risk personnel. The focus of the business risk committee is to make sure that business decisions are in line with the corporation's desired risk/reward trade-offs and that risks are managed appropriately at the business line level (see Box 3-4).

The business risk committee might be responsible for managing business-level design issues that set out exactly how a particular risk will be managed, reflecting the agreed-upon relationship between the business and the bank's risk management function. The business risk committee also approves policies that define the appropriate measurement and management of risk, and provides a detailed review of risk limits and risk authorities within the business unit.

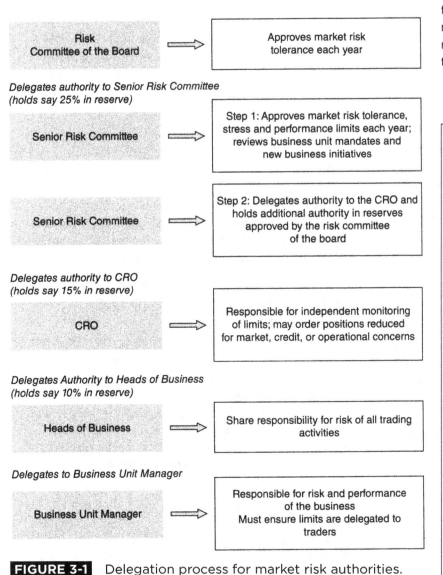

FIGURE 3-1 Delegation process for market risk authorities.

BOX 3-4 Format for Obtaining Approval of a Business Unit Mandate

The format for obtaining approval of a business unit mandate can be quite standardized, as follows:

- First, the business unit seeking approval provides an overview and points out the key decisions that need to be taken.
- Second, the business unit brings everyone up to date about the business—e.g., key achievements, risk profile, and a description of any new products (or activities) that may affect the risk profile.
- Third, the business unit outlines future initiatives.
- Fourth, the business unit proposes financial (i.e., market and credit) risk limits in line with the business strategy and the limit standards that we discuss in the main text.
- Fifth, the business unit describes all the nonfinancial risks that it is exposed to. This might include the impact of any finance, legal, compliance, business conduct, and tax issues.

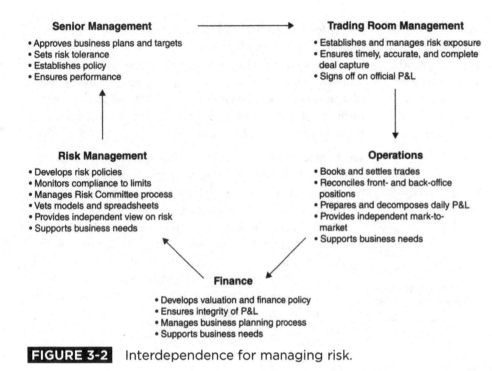

Senior Management
- Approves business plans and targets
- Sets risk tolerance
- Establishes policy
- Ensures performance

Trading Room Management
- Establishes and manages risk exposure
- Ensures timely, accurate, and complete deal capture
- Signs off on official P&L

Risk Management
- Develops risk policies
- Monitors compliance to limits
- Manages Risk Committee process
- Vets models and spreadsheets
- Provides independent view on risk
- Supports business needs

Operations
- Books and settles trades
- Reconciles front- and back-office positions
- Prepares and decomposes daily P&L
- Provides independent mark-to-market
- Supports business needs

Finance
- Develops valuation and finance policy
- Ensures integrity of P&L
- Manages business planning process
- Supports business needs

FIGURE 3-2 Interdependence for managing risk.

Below the board committee level, executives and business managers are necessarily dependent upon each other when they try to manage and report on risk in a bank (Figure 3-2). Business managers also ensure timely, accurate, and complete deal capture and sign-off on the official profit and loss (P&L) statement.

The bank's operations function is particularly critical to risk oversight. In the case of an investment bank, for example, it is this function that independently books trades, settles trades, and reconciles front- and back-office positions—which should provide the core record of all the bank's dealings. Operations staff also prepare the P&L report and independent valuations (e.g., mark to market of the bank's positions) and support the operational needs of the various businesses.

Meanwhile, the bank's finance function develops valuation and finance policy and ensures the integrity of the P&L, including reviews of any independent valuation processes. Finance also manages the business planning process and supports the financial needs of the various businesses.

The financial crisis highlighted the need to re-empower risk officers in financial institutions, particularly at a senior level. The key lessons are:

- CROs should not just be after-the-fact risk managers but also risk strategists; that is, they should play a significant role in determining the risks that the bank

assumes as well as helping to manage those risks. To ensure there is a strategic focus on risk management at a high level, the CRO in a bank or other financial institution should report to the chief executive officer (CEO) and have a seat on the risk management committee of the board.

- The CRO should engage directly, on a regular basis, with the risk committee of the board. The CRO should also report regularly to the full board to review risk issues and exposures. A strong independent voice will mean that the CRO will have a mandate to bring to the attention of both line and senior management, or the board, any situation that could materially violate risk appetite guidelines.

- The CRO should be independent of line business management and have a strong enough voice to make a meaningful impact on decisions.

- The CRO must evaluate all new financial products to verify that the expected return is consistent with the risks undertaken, and that the risks are consistent with the business strategy of the institution.

LIMITS AND LIMIT STANDARDS POLICIES

To achieve best-practice corporate governance, a corporation must be able to tie its board-approved risk appetite and risk tolerances to particular business strategies. This means, in turn, that an appropriate set of limits and authorities must be developed for each portfolio of business and for each type of risk (within each portfolio of business), as well as for the entire portfolio.

Market risk limits serve to control the risk that arises from changes in the absolute price (or rate) of an asset. Credit risk limits serve to control and limit the number of defaults as well as limit a downward migration in the quality of the credit portfolio (e.g., the loan book). The bank will also want to set tight policies regarding exposure to both asset/liability management risk and market liquidity risk, especially in the case of illiquid products.

The exact nature of each limit varies quite widely, depending on the bank's activities, size, and sophistication. It is best practice for institutions to set down on paper the process by which they establish risk limits, review risk exposures, approve limit exceptions, and develop the analytic methodologies used to calculate the bank's risk exposures.

At many banks, best-practice risk governance will call for the development and implementation of sophisticated risk metrics, such as value-at-risk (VaR) measures for market risk and credit risk or potential exposure limits by risk grade for credit risk.

Risk-sensitive measures such as VaR are useful for expressing risk in normal market conditions and for most kinds of portfolios, but less good in extreme circumstances or for specialized portfolios (e.g., certain kinds of option portfolios). So limits should also be related to scenario and stress testing measures to make sure the bank can survive worst-case scenarios—e.g., extreme volatility in the markets.

Most institutions employ two types of limits—let's call them limit type A and limit type B. Type A (often referred to as tier 1) limits might include a single overall limit for each asset class (e.g., a single limit for interest rate products), as well as a single overall stress test limit and a cumulative loss from peak limit. Type B (often referred to as tier 2) limits are more general and cover authorized business and concentration limits (e.g., by credit class, industry, maturity, region, and so on).

The setting of the risk limit level in terms of a particular metric should be consistent with certain underlying standards for risk limits (proposed by the risk management function and approved by the senior risk committee).

It's not realistic on practical grounds to set limits so that they are likely to be fully utilized in the normal course of events—that would be bound to lead to limit transgressions. Instead, limit setting needs to take into account an assessment of the business unit's historical usage of limits. For example, type A limits for market risk might be set at a level such that the business, in the normal course of its activities and in normal markets, has exposures of about 40% to 60% of its limit. Peak usage of limits, in normal markets, should generate exposures of perhaps 85% of the limit.

A consistent limit structure helps a bank to consolidate its approach to risk across many businesses and activities.

Additionally, if the limits are expressed in a common language of risk, such as economic capital, then type B limits can be made fungible across business lines. Nevertheless, such transfers would require the joint approval of the head of a business and the CRO.

If banks had followed the above principles and procedures, many of the troubles revealed during the financial crisis of 2007–2009 could have been prevented.

STANDARDS FOR MONITORING RISK

Once a bank has set out its risk limits in a way that is meaningful to its business lines, how should it monitor those limits to make sure they are followed? Let's take the example of market risk, which is perhaps the most time-sensitive of limits.

First, all market risk positions should be valued daily. Units that are independent of traders should prepare daily profit and loss statements and provide them to (nontrading) senior management. All the assumptions used in the models to price transactions and to value positions should be independently verified.

There should be timely and meaningful reports to measure the compliance of the trading team with risk policy and risk limits. There should be a timely escalation procedure for any limit exceptions or transgressions—i.e., it should be clear what a manager must do if his or her subordinates breach the limits.

The variance between the actual volatility of the value of a portfolio and that predicted by means of the bank's risk methodology should be evaluated. Stress simulations should be executed to determine the impact of major market or credit risk changes on the P&L.

The bank must distinguish between data used for monitoring type A limits (where data must be independent of risk-takers) and data used to supply other kinds of management information. For other types of analysis, where timeliness is the key requirement, risk managers may be forced to use front-office systems as the most appropriate sources. For example, real-time risk measurement, such as that used to monitor intraday trading exposures, may simply have to be derived from front-office systems.

But data used in limit monitoring must be:

- Independent of the front office
- Reconciled with the official books of the bank in order to ensure their integrity

- Derived from consolidated data feeds
- In a data format that allows risk to be properly measured—e.g., it might employ the market risk VaR or credit risk VaR methodology

Business units should be under strict orders to advise the risk management function that they might exceed a limit well before the limit excess happens. For example, there might be an alert when an exposure is at, say, 85% of the type A or type B limit. The CRO, jointly with the head of the business line, might then petition the senior risk committee of the bank for a temporary increase in limits. The business risk committee should also approve the need for an increase in limits prior to the request being passed to the senior risk committee of the bank.

If risk management is advised of a planned excess, then it should be more likely that the excess will be approved—this gives the business unit a necessary incentive to provide early warnings.

What happens if the limit is breached? The risk management function, as illustrated in Figure 3-3, should immediately put any excess on a daily "limit type A or limit type B exception report," with an appropriate explanation and a plan of action to cope with the excess. The head of risk management may authorize the use of a reserve.

Limit type A excesses must be cleared or corrected immediately. Limit type B excesses should be cleared or approved within a relatively short time frame—say, a week. The risk managers should then report all limit excesses across the bank in an exception report, which may be discussed at a daily risk meeting and which should distinguish between limit type A and type B excesses. No manager should have the power to exclude excesses from the daily excess report.

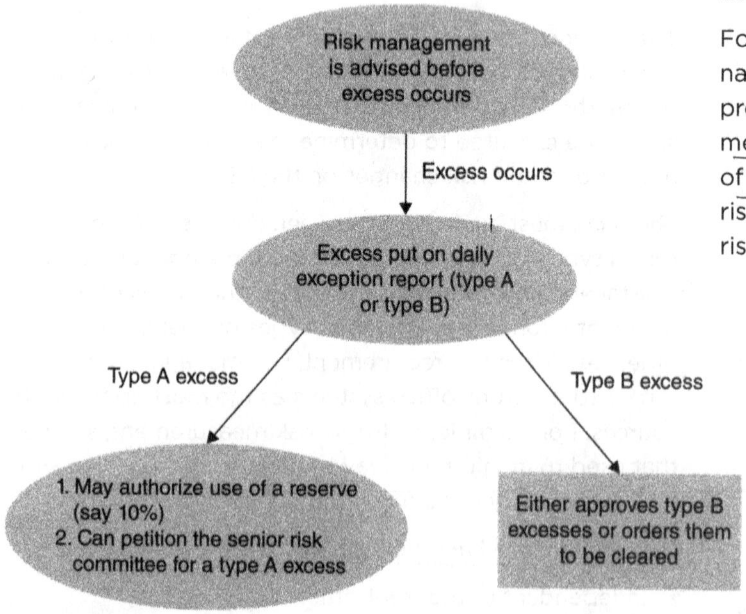

It should be noted that when limits become effective, they impose a hidden cost: the bank cannot assume additional risk and thus may have to give up profitable opportunities. As a limit is approached, the opportunity cost of the limit should be evaluated so that the bank can decide in good order whether or not the limit should be relaxed.

WHAT IS THE ROLE OF THE AUDIT FUNCTION?

We've set out, in general terms, a risk management process that should be able to support best-practice risk governance. But how does the board know that the executives and business managers are living up to the board's stated intentions (and to minimum legal and regulatory requirements)?

The answer lies in the bank's audit function and the periodic investigations it carries out across the bank. A key role of the audit function is to provide an independent assessment of the design and implementation of the bank's risk management.

For example, regulatory guidelines typically call for internal audit groups to review the overall risk management process. This means addressing the adequacy of documentation, the effectiveness of the process, the integrity of the risk management system, the organization of the risk control unit, the integration of risk measures into daily risk management, and so on.

Let's again take the example of market risk. Regulatory guidelines typically call for auditors to address the approval process for vetting derivatives pricing models and valuation systems used by front- and back-office personnel, the validation of any significant change in the risk measurement process, and the scope of risks captured by the risk measurement model.

Regulators also require that internal auditors examine the integrity of the management information system and the independence, accuracy, and completeness of position data.

FIGURE 3-3 Limit excess escalation procedure.

Above and beyond any local regulatory requirements, a key audit objective should be to evaluate the design and conceptual soundness of the risk measures (including the methodologies associated with stress testing). Internal auditors should verify the accuracy of models through an examination of the back-testing process.

Audit should also evaluate the soundness of elements of the risk management information system (the "risk MIS"), such as the processes used for coding and implementation of internal models. This should include examining controls over market position data capture, as well as controls over the parameter estimation processes (e.g., volatility and correlation assumptions).

Audit responsibilities often include providing assurance as to the design and conceptual soundness of the financial rates database that is used to generate parameters entered into the market VaR and credit VaR analytic engines. Audit also reviews the adequacy and effectiveness of the procedures for monitoring risk, the progress of plans to upgrade risk management systems, the adequacy and effectiveness of application controls within the risk MIS, and the reliability of the vetting processes.

Audit should also examine the documentation relating to compliance with the qualitative/quantitative criteria outlined in any regulatory guidelines. Audit should comment on the reliability of any value-at-risk reporting framework.

Box 3-5 sets out in general terms what a statement of audit's findings on the risk management function might look like. It also helps to make clear the dangers that might arise from any confusion between the role of risk management and that of audit. Box 3-6, in contrast, looks at an approach to scoring the risk management function that might be adopted by third parties (such as rating agencies, which need to compare the risk management structures of many different organizations).

Internal auditors have devised international standards to provide objective assurance about control, governance, and risk management. The Institute of Internal Auditors (IIA) provides guidance that has been organized into an International Professional Practices Framework (IPPF), offering both mandatory and strongly recommended guidance. The IPPF has performance standards that encompass a variety of activities.[12]

---

[12] See the Professional Guidance section of the IIA's website. These IIA standards include Managing the Internal Audit Activity, Nature of Work, Engagement Planning, Performing the

---

BOX 3-5 **Example: Statement of Audit Findings**

If all is well from a risk management perspective, then audit should state that adequate processes exist for providing reliable risk control and ensuring compliance with regulatory criteria.

For example, in short form, the audit group's conclusion regarding risk control in a bank trading business might be:

- The risk control unit is independent of the business units.
- The internal risk models are utilized by business management.
- The bank's risk measurement model captures all material risks.

Furthermore, if all is well, then the audit group should state that adequate and effective processes exist for

- Risk-pricing models and valuation systems used by front-and back-office personnel
- Documenting the risk management systems and processes
- Validating any significant change in the risk measurement process
- Ensuring the integrity of the risk management information system
- Capturing position data (and ensuring that any positions that are not captured do not materially affect risk reporting)
- Verifying the consistency, timeliness, and reliability of data sources used to run internal models, and that the data sources are independent
- Ensuring the accuracy and appropriateness of volatility and correlation assumptions
- Ensuring the accuracy of the valuation and risk transformation calculations
- Verifying the model's accuracy through frequent back-testing

---

Engagement, Communicating Results, Monitoring Progress, and Resolution of Senior Management's Acceptance of Risk. The Governance and Risk Management Standards are a subset of the Nature of Work standard. The Risk Management standards cover topics such as evaluating an organization's risk exposure, evaluating fraud risks, reviewing risk during consulting, and risk knowledge gained during consultancy.

Is It Possible to Score the Quality of an Institution's Risk Management?

In much of this chapter, we talk about establishing the right structures for best-practice risk governance. But is there any way to score risk management practice across an institution so that both the institution itself and external observers can gain some objective idea of the institution's risk management culture and standards?

One of the authors has worked with a credit rating agency to construct such a score.

Under this approach, the risks underlying each aspect of the enterprise risk management function within institutions are assessed using a questionnaire tailored along three key dimensions:

- Policies—e.g., is the tolerance for risk consistent with the business strategy? Is risk properly communicated internally and externally?
- Methodologies—e.g., are the risk methodologies tied into performance measurement? Are risk stress testing methodologies performed? Are the mathematical models properly vetted? Does senior management understand the risks in the models?
- Infrastructure—e.g., are the appropriate people and operational processes (such as data, software, systems, and quality of personnel) in place to control and report on the risks?

The basic PMI (policies, methodologies, infrastructure) framework can be used for most industries; within each of the three key dimensions, more detailed questions can be developed that tackle aspects relevant to a particular industry.

For example, for trading financial institutions, we might require a description of the process around limits delegation for market risk and credit risk (as it pertains to the trading book).

Gathering this information involves supplying questionnaires and also scheduling the time of senior management at the trading institution for review sessions. The completed assessments would be presented to an internal committee at the rating agency, where the primary credit analyst will take them into consideration in the rating agency's overall review of the institution.

A negative assessment could affect the credit rating of the institution—a clear indicator of how important the nexus between risk management, corporate governance, and risk disclosure has become.

There has been some discussion in the banking industry about whether the audit function should control the operational risk management function at the bank—after all, audit has a natural interest in the quality of internal controls.

Unfortunately, allowing the audit function to develop a bank's operational risk management function is an error. Audit's independence from the risk management function is a prerequisite for the value of any assurances it gives to the board. Unless this independence is preserved, there is a danger that audit will end up trying to give an independent opinion about the quality of risk management activities that audit itself has designed or helped administer. This would imply a classic conflict of interest right at the heart of bank risk governance.

CONCLUSION: STEPS TO SUCCESS

In complex risk-taking organizations, it's not possible to separate best-practice risk management from best-practice corporate governance.

Boards can't monitor and control the financial condition of a risk-taking institution without excellent risk management and risk metrics. Meanwhile, the risk management function depends on sponsors at the senior executive and board level to gain the investment it requires—and the influence it needs to balance out powerful business leaders.

It's worth stressing an important lesson of business history: Many fatal risks in a corporation are associated with business strategies that at first look like runaway successes. It's only later on that the overlooked or discounted risks come home to roost.

Recent history provides us with ample evidence. Subprime loans, and the structured products backed by such loans, looked very lucrative due to the high promised yield. But investors and institutions failed to correctly assess the risks, including the possible effect of a drop in the price of houses across the whole United States together with an economic recession.

At a best-practice institution, everything flows from a clear and agreed-upon risk management policy at the top. For example, senior management and the board must approve a clear notion of the institution's risk appetite and set out how this is to be linked to an enforceable system of limits and risk metrics.

Without this kind of platform, it's very difficult for risk managers further down the management chain to make key decisions on how they approach and measure risk. For example, without a clearly communicated concept of an institution's risk appetite, how would risk managers define a "worst-case risk" in any extreme risk scenario analysis? How would they decide whether the institution could live with the small chance of a worst-case outcome or, alternatively, avoid any risk to solvency by severely limiting business volumes or even closing down a business line (in the face of attractive profits)?

The risk committees of the institution also need to be involved, to some degree, in setting the basic risk measurement methodologies employed by the institution. Most banks know that they have to be able to define their risk in terms of market risk and credit risk, but banks have also now extended their risk measurement framework to include more sophisticated approaches to liquidity risk and operational risk, as well as a whole new class of enterprise stress tests. It's important that risk committees understand the strengths and weaknesses of any new metrics if they are to make sense of risk reports.

There are also unavoidable strategic, political, and investment reasons why the board and top executive management must be closely involved in determining an institution's risk management strategy. Without their involvement, how can the managers of the institution agree on a credible organizational infrastructure that avoids both gaps and duplications in risk oversight? The key to designing an efficient organization is to ensure that the roles and responsibilities of each risk mechanism and unit are carefully spelled out and remain complementary to one another. Meanwhile, data for risk analysis, including enterprise-wide macroeconomic stress testing, has to be drawn from many business lines and bank functions. An enterprise-wide perspective is increasingly essential.

We should not think of board and top management time spent on risk management as time spent purely on the defensive "risk control" aspects of the business. A best-practice risk system can be applied to gain offensive advantages. A board with a sound understanding of the risk profile of its key existing or anticipated business lines can support aggressive strategic decisions with much more confidence. Sophisticated risk measures such as VaR, stress testing, and economic capital offer a way of setting risk limits, but they are also vital in helping the institution decide which business lines are profitable (once risk is taken into account).

Ideally, businesses would use the risk infrastructure as a tactical management tool in deal analysis and pricing, and also take account of its results in incentive compensation schemes, to help make sure that risk management and business decisions are aligned.

A joint approach to corporate governance and risk management has become a critical component of a globally integrated best-practice institution—from board level to business line.

What Is ERM?

4

■ Learning Objectives

Candidates, after completing this reading, should be able to:

- Describe enterprise risk management (ERM) and compare and contrast differing definitions of ERM.
- Compare the benefits and costs of ERM and describe the motivations for a firm to adopt an ERM initiative.

- Describe the role and responsibilities of a chief risk officer (CRO) and assess how the CRO should interact with other senior management.
- Distinguish between components of an ERM program.

Excerpt is Chapter 4 of Enterprise Risk Management: From Incentives to Controls, *Second Edition, by James Lam.*

Earlier, we reviewed the concepts and processes applicable to almost all of the risks that a company will face. We also argued that all risks can be thought of as a bell curve. Certainly, it is a prerequisite that a company develop an effective process for each of its significant risks. But it is not enough to build a separate process for each risk in isolation.

Risks are by their very nature dynamic, fluid, and highly interdependent. As such, they cannot be broken into separate components and managed independently. Enterprises operating in today's volatile environment require a much more integrated approach to managing their portfolio of risks.

This has not always been recognized. Traditionally, companies managed risk in organizational silos. Market, credit, and operational risks were treated separately and often dealt with by different individuals or functions within an institution. For example, credit experts evaluated the risk of default, mortgage specialists analyzed prepayment risk, traders were responsible for market risks, and actuaries handled liability, mortality, and other insurance-related risks. Corporate functions such as finance and audit handled other operational risks, and senior line managers addressed business risks.

However, it has become increasingly apparent that such a fragmented approach simply doesn't work, because risks are highly interdependent and cannot be segmented and managed by entirely independent units. The risks associated with most businesses are not one-to-one matches for the primary risks (market, credit, operational, and insurance) implied by most traditional organizational structures. Attempting to manage them as if they are is likely to prove inefficient and potentially dangerous. Risks can fall through the cracks, risk inter-dependencies and portfolio effects may not be captured, and organizational gaps and redundancies can result in suboptimal performance. For example, imagine that a company is about to launch a new product or business in a foreign country. Such an initiative would require:

- The business unit to establish the right pricing and market-entry strategies;

- The treasury function to provide funding and protection against interest rate and foreign-exchange (FX) risks;

- The Information Technology (IT) and operations function to support the business; and

- The legal and insurance functions to address regulatory and liability issues.

It is not difficult to see how an integrated approach could more effectively manage these risks. An enterprise risk management (ERM) function would be responsible for establishing firm-wide policies and standards, coordinate risk management activities across business units and functions, and provide overall risk monitoring for senior management and the board.

Nor is risk monitoring any more efficient under the silo approach. The problem is that individual risk functions measure and report their specific risks using different methodologies and formats. For example, the treasury function might report on interest rate and FX risk exposures, and use value-at-risk as its core risk measurement methodology. On the other hand, the credit function would report delinquencies and outstanding credit exposures, and measure such exposures in terms of outstanding balances, while the audit function would report outstanding audit items and assign some sort of audit score, and so on.

Senior management and the board get pieces of the puzzle, but not the whole picture. In many companies, the risk functions produce literally hundreds of pages of risk reports, month after month. Yet, oftentimes, they still don't manage to provide management and the board with useful risk information. A good acid test is to ask if the senior management knows the answers to the following basic questions:

- What are the company's top 10 risks?

- Are any of our business objectives at risk?

- Do we have key risk indicators that track our critical risk exposures against risk tolerance levels?

- What were the company's actual losses and incidents, and did we identify these risks in previous risk assessment reports?

- Are we in compliance with laws, regulations, and corporate risk policies?

If a company is uncertain about the answers to any of these questions, then it is likely to benefit from a more integrated approach to handling all aspects of risk— enterprise risk management (ERM).[1]

---

[1] Other popular terms used to describe enterprise risk management include firm-wide risk management, integrated risk management, and holistic risk management.

ERM DEFINITIONS

Since the practice of ERM is still relatively new, there have yet to be any widely accepted industry standards with regard to the definition of ERM. As such, a multitude of different definitions is available, all of which highlight and prioritize different aspects of ERM. Consider, for example, a definition provided by the Committee of Sponsoring Organizations of the Treadway Commission (COSO) in 2004:

> "ERM is a process, effected by an entity's board of directors, management, and other personnel, applied in strategy setting and across the enterprise, designed to identify potential events that may affect the entity, and manage risk to be within its appetite, to provide reasonable assurance regarding the achievement of entity objectives."

Another definition was established by the International Organization of Standardization (ISO 31000):

> Risk is the "effect of uncertainty on objectives" and risk management refers to "coordinated activities to direct and control an organization with regard to risk."

While the COSO and ISO definitions provide useful concepts (e.g., linkage to objectives), I think it is important that ERM is defined as a value added function. Therefore, I would suggest the following definition:

> Risk is a variable that can cause deviation from an expected outcome. ERM is a comprehensive and integrated framework for managing key risks in order to achieve business objectives, minimize unexpected earnings volatility, and maximize firm value.

The lack of a standard ERM definition can cause confusion for a company looking to set up an ERM framework. No ERM definition is perfect or applicable to every organization. My general advice is for each organization to adopt an ERM definition and framework that best fit their business scope and complexity.

THE BENEFITS OF ERM

ERM is all about integration, in three ways.

First, enterprise risk management requires an integrated risk organization. This most often means a centralized risk management unit reporting to the CEO and the Board in support of their corporate- and board-level risk oversight responsibilities. A growing number of companies now have a Chief Risk Officer (CRO) who is responsible for overseeing all aspects of risk within the organization—we'll consider this development later.

Second, enterprise risk management requires the integration of risk transfer strategies. Under the silo approach, risk transfer strategies were executed at a transactional or individual risk level. For example, financial derivatives were used to hedge market risk and insurance to transfer out operational risk. However, this approach doesn't incorporate diversification within or across the risk types in a portfolio, and thus tends to result in over-hedging and excessive insurance cover. An ERM approach, by contrast, takes a portfolio view of all types of risk within a company and rationalizes the use of derivatives, insurance, and alternative risk transfer products to hedge only the residual risk deemed undesirable by management.

Third, enterprise risk management requires the integration of risk management into the business processes of a company. Rather than the defensive or control-oriented approaches used to manage downside risk and earnings volatility, enterprise risk management optimizes business performance by supporting and influencing pricing, resource allocation, and other business decisions. It is during this stage that risk management becomes an offensive weapon for management.

All this integration is not easy. For most companies, the implementation of ERM implies a multi-year initiative that requires ongoing senior management sponsorship and sustained investments in human and technological resources. Ironically, the amount of time and resources dedicated to risk management is not necessarily very different for leading and lagging organizations.

The most crucial difference is this: leading organizations make rational investments in risk management and are proactive, optimizing their risk profiles. Lagging organizations, on the other hand, make disconnected investments and are reactive, fighting one crisis after another. The investments of the leading companies in risk management are more than offset by improved efficiency and reduced losses.

Let's discuss the three major benefits to ERM: increased organizational effectiveness, better risk reporting, and improved business performance.

Centralized & integrated unit

Organizational Effectiveness

Most companies already have risk management and corporate-oversight functions, such as finance/insurance, audit and compliance. In addition, there may be specialist risk units: for example, investment banks usually have market risk management units, while energy companies have commodity risk managers.

The appointment of a chief risk officer and the establishment of an enterprise risk function provide the top-down coordination necessary to make these various functions work cohesively and efficiently. An integrated team can better address not only the individual risks facing the company, but also the interdependencies between these risks.

Risk Reporting *(enterprise level & not in silos)*

As previously noted, one of the key requirements of risk management is that it should produce timely and relevant risk reporting for the senior management and board of directors. As we also noted, however, this is frequently not the case. In a silo framework, either no one takes responsibility for overall risk reporting, and/or every risk-related unit supplies inconsistent and sometimes contradictory reports.

An enterprise risk function can prioritize the level and content of risk reporting that should go to senior management and the board: an enterprise-wide perspective on aggregate losses, policy exceptions, risk incidents, key exposures, and early-warning indicators. This might take the form of a risk dashboard that includes timely and concise information on the company's key risks. Of course, this goes beyond the senior management level; the objective of ERM reporting is by its nature to increase risk transparency throughout an organization.

Business Performance *(portfolio view of risks)*

Companies that adopt an ERM approach have experienced significant improvements in business performance. Figure 4-1 provides examples of reported benefits of ERM from a cross-section of companies. ERM supports key management decisions such as capital allocation, product development and pricing, and mergers and acquisitions. This leads to improvements such as reduced losses, lower earnings volatility, increased earnings, and improved shareholder value.

These improvements result from taking a portfolio view of all risks; managing the linkages between risk, capital, and profitability; and rationalizing the company's risk transfer strategies. The result is not just outright risk reduction: companies that understand the true risk/return economics of a business can take more of the profitable risks that make sense for the company and less of the ones that don't.

Despite all these benefits, many companies would balk at the prospect of a full-blown ERM initiative were it not for the existence of heavy internal and external pressures. In the business world, managers are often galvanized into action

Benefit	Company	Actual Results
Market value improvement	Top money center bank	Outperformed S&P 500 banks by 58% in stock price performance
Early warning of risks	Large commercial bank	Assessment of top risks identified over 80% of future losses; global risk limits cut by one-third prior to Russian crisis
Loss reduction	Top asset-management company	30% reduction in the loss ratio enterprise-wide; up to 80% reduction in losses at specific business units
Regulatory capital relief	Large international commercial and investment bank	$1 Billion reduction of regulatory capital requirements, or about 8–10%
Risk transfer rationalization	Large property and casualty insurance company	$40 million in cost savings, or 13% of annual reinsurance premium
Insurance premium reduction	Large manufacturing company	20–25% reduction in annual insurance premium

FIGURE 4-1 ERM benefits.

after a near miss—either a disaster averted within their own organization or an actual crisis at a similar organization.

In response, the board and senior management are likely to question the effectiveness of the control environment and the adequacy of risk reporting within their company. To put it another way, they will begin to question how well they really know the organization's major risk exposures.

Such incidents are also often followed by critical assessments from auditors and regulators—both groups which are constitutionally concerned with the effectiveness of risk management. Consequently, regulators focus on all aspects of risk during examinations, setting risk-based capital and compliance requirements, and reinforcing key roles for the board and senior management in the risk management process.

This introspection often leads to the emergence of a risk champion among the senior executives who will sponsor a major program to establish an enterprise risk management approach. As noted above, this risk champion is increasingly becoming a formalized senior management position—the chief risk officer, or CRO.

Aside from this, direct pressure also comes from influential stakeholders such as shareholders, employees, ratings agencies, and analysts. Not only do such stakeholders expect more earnings predictability, management have fewer excuses today for not providing it. Over the past few years, volatility-based models such as value-at-risk (VaR) and risk-adjusted return on capital (RAROC) have been applied to measure all types of market risk within an organization; their use is now spreading to credit risk, and even to operational risk. The increasing availability and liquidity of alternative risk transfer products—such as credit derivatives and catastrophe bonds—also means that companies are no longer stuck with many of the unpalatable risks they previously had no choice but to hold. Overall, the availability of such tools makes it more difficult and less acceptable for companies to carry on with more primitive and inefficient alternatives. Managing risk is management's job.

THE CHIEF RISK OFFICER

The role of a chief risk officer has received a lot of attention within the risk management community, as well as from the finance and general management audiences. Articles on chief risk officers and ERM appear frequently in trade publications such as *Risk Magazine* and *Risk and Insurance,* but have also been covered in general

publications such as *CFO* magazine, the *Wall Street Journal,* and even *USA Today.*

. . .

Today, the role of the CRO has been widely adopted in risk-intensive businesses such as financial institutions, energy firms, and non-financial corporations with significant investment activities and/or foreign operations. Today, I would estimate that as many as up to 80% of the biggest U.S. financial institutions have CROs.

The recent financial and economic meltdowns have increased the demand for comprehensive ERM frameworks. As an indication of this increased demand, executive management training programs in ERM are increasingly offered by leading business schools. For example, in November 2010, Harvard Business School implemented a five-day program designed to train CEOs, COOs, and CROs in managing risk as corporate leaders: there have been two other sessions to date, one in February 2012, and one just recently, in February 2013.[2]

Typical reports to the CRO are the heads of credit risk, market risk, operational risk, insurance, and portfolio management. Other functions that the CRO is commonly responsible for include risk policy, capital management, risk analytics and reporting, and risk management within individual business units. In general, the office of the CRO is directly responsible for:

- Providing the overall leadership, vision, and direction for enterprise risk management;
- Establishing an integrated risk management framework for all aspects of risks across the organization;
- Developing risk management policies, including the quantification of the firm's risk appetite through specific risk limits;
- Implementing a set of risk indicators and reports, including losses and incidents, key risk exposures, and early warning indicators;
- Allocating economic capital to business activities based on risk, and optimizing the company's risk portfolio through business activities and risk transfer strategies;
- Communicating the company's risk profile to key stakeholders such as the board of directors, regulators, stock analysts, rating agencies, and business partners; and

---

[2] Winokur, L.A. "The Rise of the Risk Leader: A Reappraisal," *Risk Professional,* April 2012, 20.

- Developing the analytical, systems, and data management capabilities to support the risk management program

Still, given that enterprise risk management is still a relatively new field, many of the kinks have yet to be smoothed out of the Chief Risk Officer role. For example, there are still substantial amounts of ambiguity with regard to where the CRO stands in the hierarchy between the board of directors and other C-level positions, such as CEOs, CFOs, and COOs.

In many instances, the CRO reports to the CFO or CEO—but this can make firms vulnerable to internal friction when serious clashes of interest occur between corporate leaders. For example, when Paul Moore, former head of regulatory risk at HBOS, claimed that he had been "fired . . . for warning about reckless lending," the resulting investigations led to the resignation of HBOS' chief executive, Sir James Crosby, as the deputy chairman of the Financial Services Authority.[3]

One organizational solution is to establish a dotted-line reporting relationship between the chief risk officer and the board or board risk committee. Under extreme circumstances (e.g., CEO/CFO fraud, major reputational or regulatory issues, excessive risk taking beyond risk appetite tolerances), that dotted line may convert to a solid line so that the chief risk officer can go directly to the board without fear for his or her job security or compensation. Ultimately, to be effective, risk management must have an independent voice. A direct communication channel to the board is one way to ensure that this voice is heard.[4]

For these dotted-line reporting structures between the CRO and the board (and between the business line risk officers and the CRO), it is critical that an organization clearly establish and document the ground rules. Basic ground rules include risk escalation and communication protocols, and the role of the board or CRO in hiring/firing, annual goal setting, and compensation decisions of risk and compliance professions who report to them.

Another board risk oversight option is to alter existing audit committees to incorporate risk management. In a survey of the S&P 500, "58% of respondents said that their audit committees were responsible for risk management."[5] However, this presents problems of its own; oftentimes, audit committees are already working at maximum capacity just handling audit matters, and are unable to properly oversee ERM as well. Henry Ristuccia, of Deloitte, affirms that unless the "audit committee [can improve] its grasp of risk management . . . a separate risk committee needs to be formed."[6]

The lack of an ERM standard is also a significant barrier to the positive development of the CRO role. Mona Leung, CFO of Alliant Credit Union, says that "we have too many varying definitions" of enterprise risk management, with the result that ERM means something different to every company, and is implemented in different ways. Of course, firms from different industries should (and must) tailor their approaches to risk management in order to meet the requirements of their specific business models and regulatory frameworks, but nonetheless, it is important to have a general ERM standard.

Despite the remaining ambivalences in the structure of the CRO role, I believe that it has elevated the risk management profession in some important ways. First and foremost, the appointment of executive managers whose primary focus is risk management has improved the visibility and organizational effectiveness of that function at many companies. The successes of these appointments have only increased the recognition and acceptance for the CRO position.

Second, the CRO position provides an attractive career path for risk professionals who want to take a broader view of risk and business management. In the past, risk professionals could only aspire to become the head of a narrowly focused risk function such as credit or audit. Nearly 70 percent of the 175 participants in one online seminar that I gave on September 13, 2000, said they aspired to become CROs.

Today, CROs have begun to move even further up the corporate ladder by becoming serious contenders for the positions of CEO and CFO. For example, Matthew Feldman, formerly CRO of the Federal Home Loan Bank of Chicago, was appointed its CEO and President in May of 2008. Likewise, Deutsche Bank CRO Hugo Banziger was a candidate for UBS CEO. Kevin Buehler, of McKinsey &

---

[3] Davy, Peter. "Cinderella Moment," *Wall Street Journal,* October 5, 2010.

[4] Lam, James. "Structuring for Accountability," *Risk Progressional,* June 2009, 44.

[5] Banham, Russ. "Disaster Averted," *CFO Magazine,* April 1, 2011, 2.

[6] Ibid.

Co.'s, affirms that the gradual movement of CROs from control functions to more strategic roles is the primary contributing factor to their success, and that with the coming years, this progress is only likely to accelerate.[7]

. . .

Some argue that a company shouldn't have a CRO because that job is already fulfilled by the CEO or the CFO. Supporting this argument is the fact that the CEO is always going to be ultimately responsible for the risk (and return) performance of the company, and that many risk departments are part of the CFO's organization. So why create another C-level position of CRO and detract from the CEO's or CFO's responsibilities?

The answer is the same reason that companies create roles for other C-level positions, such as chief information officers or chief marketing officers. These roles are defined because they represent a core competency that is critical to the success for the company—the CEO needs the experience and technical skills that these seasoned professionals bring. Perhaps not every company should have a full-time CRO, but the role should be an explicit one and not simply one implied for the CEO or CFO.

For companies operating in the financial or energy markets, or other industries where risk management represents a core competency, the CRO position should be considered a serious possibility. A CRO would also benefit companies in which the full breadth of risk management experience does not exist within the senior management team, or if the build-up of required risk management infrastructure requires the full-time attention of an experienced risk professional.

What should a company look for in a CRO? An ideal CRO would have superb skills in five areas. The first would be the leadership skills to hire and retain talented risk professionals and establish the overall vision for ERM. The second would be the evangelical skills to convert skeptics into believers, particularly when it comes to overcoming natural resistance from the business units. Third would be the stewardship to safeguard the company's financial and reputational assets. Fourth would be to have the technical skills in strategic, business, credit, market, and operational risks. And, last but not least, fifth would be to have consulting skills in educating the board and senior management, as well as helping business

units implement risk management at the enterprise level. While it is unlikely that any single individual would possess all of these skills, it is important that these competencies exist either in the CRO or elsewhere within his or her organization.

COMPONENTS OF ERM

A successful ERM program can be broken down into seven key components (see Figure 4-2). Each of these components must be developed and linked to work as an integrated whole. The seven components include:

1. Corporate governance to ensure that the board of directors and management have established the appropriate organizational processes and corporate controls to measure and manage risk across the company.

2. Line management to integrate risk management into the revenue-generating activities of the company (including business development, product and relationship management, pricing, and so on).

3. Portfolio management to aggregate risk exposures, incorporate diversification effects, and monitor risk concentrations against established risk limits.

4. Risk transfer to mitigate risk exposures that are deemed too high, or are more cost-effective to transfer out to a third party than to hold in the company's risk portfolio.

5. Risk analytics to provide the risk measurement, analysis, and reporting tools to quantify the company's risk exposures as well as track external drivers.

1. Corporate Governance
Establish top-down risk management

2. Line Management Business strategy alignment	3. Portfolio Management Think and act like a "fund manager"	4. Risk Transfer Transfer out concentrated or inefficient risks

5. Risk Analytics Develop advanced analytical tools	6. Data and Technology Resources Integrate data and system capabilities

7. Stakeholders Management
Improve risk transparency for key stakeholders

FIGURE 4-2   Seven components of ERM.

[7] Winokur, L. A. "The Rise of the Risk Leader: A Reappraisal," *Risk Professional*, April 2012, 17.

6. Data and technology resources to support the analytics and reporting processes.

7. Stakeholder management to communicate and report the company's risk information to its key stakeholders.

Let's consider these in turn.

Corporate Governance

Corporate governance ensures that the board of directors and management have established the appropriate organizational processes and corporate controls to measure and manage risk across the company. The mandate for effective corporate governance has been brought to the forefront by regulatory and industry initiatives around the world. These initiates include the Treadway Report from the United States, the Turnbull Report from the UK, and the Dey Report from Canada. All of these made recommendations for establishing corporate controls and emphasized the responsibilities of the board of directors and senior management. Additionally, the Sarbanes-Oxley Act provides both specific requirements and severe penalties for non-compliance.

From an ERM perspective, the responsibilities of the board of directors and senior management include:

- Defining the organization's risk appetite in terms of risk policies, loss tolerance, risk-to-capital leverage, and target debt rating.

- Ensuring that the organization has the risk management skills and risk absorption capability to support its business strategy.

- Establishing the organizational structure of the ERM framework and defining the roles and responsibilities for risk management, including the role of chief risk officer.

- Implementing an integrated risk measurement and management framework for strategic, business, operational, financial, and compliance risks.

- Establishing risk assessment and audit processes, as well as benchmarking company practices against industry best practices.

- Shaping the organization's risk culture by setting the tone from the top not only through words but also through actions, and reinforcing that commitment through incentives.

- Providing appropriate opportunities for organizational learning, including lessons learned from previous problems, as well as ongoing training and development.

Line Management

Perhaps the most important phase in the assessment and pricing of risk is at its inception. Line management must align business strategy with corporate risk policy when pursuing new business and growth opportunities. The risks of business transactions should be fully assessed and incorporated into pricing and profitability targets in the execution of business strategy.

Specifically, expected losses and the cost of risk capital should be included in the pricing of a product or the required return of an investment project. In business development, risk acceptance criteria should be established to ensure that risk management issues are considered in new product and market opportunities. Transaction and business review processes should be developed to ensure the appropriate due diligence. Efficient and transparent review processes will allow line managers to develop a better understanding of those risks that they can accept independently and those that require corporate approval or management.

Portfolio Management

The overall risk portfolio of an organization should not just happen—that is, it should not just be the cumulative effect of business transactions conducted entirely independently. Rather, management should act like a fund manager and set portfolio targets and risk limits to ensure appropriate diversification and optimal portfolio returns.

The concept of active portfolio management can be applied to all the risks within an organization. Diversification effects from natural hedges can only be fully captured if an organization's risks are viewed as a whole, in a portfolio. More importantly, the portfolio management function provides a direct link between risk management and shareholder value maximization.

For example, a key barrier for many insurance companies in implementing ERM is that each of the financial risks within the overall business portfolio is managed independently. The actuarial function is responsible for estimating liability risks arising for the company's insurance policies; the investment group invests the company's cash flows in fixed-income and equity investments. The interest rate risk function hedges mismatches between assets and liabilities. However, an insurance company which has implemented ERM would manage all of its liability, investment, interest rate, and other risks as an integrated whole in order to optimize overall risk/return. The integration of financial risks is one step in the ERM process, while strategic, business, and operational risks must also be considered in the overall ERM framework.

Risk Transfer *(hedge strategies)*

Portfolio management objectives are supported by risk transfer strategies that lower the cost of transferring out undesirable risks, and also increase the organization's capacity to originate desirable but concentrated risks. To reduce undesirable risks, management should evaluate derivatives, insurance, and hybrid products on a consistent basis and select the most cost-effective alternative. For example, corporations such as Honeywell and Mead have used alternative risk transfer (ART) products that combine traditional insurance protection with financial risk protection. By bundling various risks, risk managers have achieved estimated savings of 20 to 30% in the cost of risk transfer.

A company can dramatically reduce its hedging and insurance costs—even without third-party protection—by incorporating the natural hedges that exist in any risk portfolio. In the course of doing business, companies naturally develop risk concentrations in their areas of specialization. The good news is that they should be very capable of analyzing, structuring, and pricing those risks. The bad news is that any risk concentration can be dangerous. By transferring undesirable risks to the secondary market—through credit derivatives or securitization, for example—an organization can increase its risk origination capacity and revenue without accumulating highly concentrated risk positions.

Finally, management can purchase desirable risks that they cannot directly originate on a timely basis, or swap undesirable risk exposures for desirable risk exposures through a derivative contract.

Risk Analytics

The development of advanced risk analytics has supported efforts to quantify and manage credit, market, and operational risks on a more consistent basis. The same techniques that allow for the quantification of risk exposures and risk-adjusted profitability can be used to evaluate risk transfer products such as derivatives, insurance, and hybrid products. For example, management can increase shareholder value through risk transfer provided that the cost of risk transfer is lower than the cost of risk retention for a given risk exposure (e.g., 12% all-in cost of risk transfer versus 15% cost of risk capital).

Alternatively, if management wants to reduce its risk exposure, risk analytics can be used to determine the most cost-effective way to accomplish that objective. In addition to risk mitigation, advanced risk analytics can also be used to significantly improve net present value (NPV)- or economic value added (EVA)-based decision tools. The use of scenario analyses and dynamic simulations, for example, can support strategic planning by analyzing the probabilities and outcomes of different business strategies as well as the potential impact on shareholder value.

Data and Technology Resources

One of the greatest challenges for enterprise risk management is the aggregation of underlying business and market data. Business data includes transactional and risk positions captured in different front- and back-office systems; market data includes prices, volatilities, and correlations. In addition to data aggregation, standards and processes must be established to improve the quality of data that is fed into the risk systems.

As far as risk technology goes, there is no single vendor software package that provides a total solution for enterprise risk management. Organizations still have to either build, buy, and customize or outsource the required functionality. Despite the data and system challenges, companies should not wait for a perfect system solution to become available before establishing an enterprise risk management program. Rather, they should make the best use of what is available and at the same time apply rapid prototyping techniques to drive the systems-development process. Additionally, companies should consider tapping into the power of the Internet/Intranet in the design of an enterprise risk technology platform.

Stakeholder Management

Risk management is not just an internal management process. It should also be used to improve risk transparency in a firm's relationship with key stakeholders. The board of directors, for example, needs periodic reports and updates on the major risks faced by the organization in order to review and approve risk management policies for controlling those risks. Regulators need to be assured that sound business practices are in place, and that business operations are in compliance with regulatory requirements. Equity analysts and rating agencies need risk information to develop their investment and credit opinions.

An important objective for management in communicating and reporting to these key stakeholders is an assurance that appropriate risk management strategies are in effect. Otherwise, the company (and its stock price) will not get full credit, since interested parties will see the risks but may not see the controls. The increasing emphasis of analyst presentations and annual reports on a company's risk management capabilities is evidence of the importance now placed on stakeholder communication. . . .

Risk-Taking and Risk Management by Banks

5

Learning Objectives

Candidates, after completing this reading, should be able to:

- Assess methods which banks can use to determine their optimal level of risk exposure, and explain how the optimal level of risk can differ across banks.
- Describe implications for a bank if it takes too little or too much risk compared to its optimal level.
- Explain ways in which risk management can add or destroy value for a bank.

- Describe structural challenges and limitations to effective risk management, including the use of VaR in setting limits.
- Assess the potential impact of a bank's governance, incentive structure, and risk culture on its risk profile and its performance.

Excerpt is Risk-Taking and Risk Management by Banks, *by René Stulz, Journal of Applied Corporate Finance.*

Most people who do not work in business view risk as a bad thing, the possibility of unwanted outcomes. But risk-taking is of course an essential part of business activity; without a willingness to take risk there is generally very little expected reward. And banks—the subject of this article—have opportunities to take risks that have a positive expected payoff or reward when the opportunities are viewed on a stand-alone basis. We will refer to such risks throughout this paper as "good" risks.

One might be tempted to conclude that the main job of effective risk management at banks is to limit exposure to risk, and hence to the possibility of bad outcomes. However, such a view of risk management ignores the reality that banks cannot succeed without taking risks—but risks that, as already noted, are expected to have a profitable outcome. As a consequence, taking actions that reduce risk can prove costly for shareholders when the lower risk is achieved mainly by avoiding valuable investments and activities with higher risk.

Thus, when viewed from the perspective of shareholders, the goal of corporate risk management is not to reduce or minimize risk. But if effective risk management does not mean low risk, then what does it mean? How is it implemented? What are its limitations? And what can be done to make it more effective? In the pages that follow, I provide a framework that can be used by practitioners to understand the role, the organization, and the limitations of risk management in helping banks to increase shareholder value.

HOW DOES RISK MANAGEMENT ADD VALUE?

In what Merton Miller once called "the economist's frictionless dream world of perfect markets," the value of companies would not be affected by corporate efforts to manage financial risks, such as the effects on profitability and value of changes in interest rates or commodity prices. That is to say, given a certain level and stability of operating earnings, whether a company chooses to hedge such financial price exposures should be largely a matter of indifference to investors.

But in the real world of taxes and transactions costs, the most compelling argument for managing financial risks is that bad outcomes can lead to financial distress, and financial distress can be very costly (especially for banks,

as we shall see).[1] When companies get into financial trouble, they often lose their ability to carry out their strategies effectively and find it more difficult and expensive to conduct their businesses. As a result, the value of a company's equity today is reduced by the present value of the *expected* future costs of financial distress. And to the extent a company's risk management function succeeds in reducing these expected distress costs (by more than the costs incurred by the function), it increases the value of the firm.

Banks are different from most industrial companies in the sense that they typically create value for shareholders through their liabilities as well as their assets. In particular, they attract deposits that, thanks to their liquidity and the federal guarantees behind them, provide most banks with a low-cost source of funding. At least for "retail" banks, the value of the franchise depends in large part on the bank's success in gathering deposits. And a bank's ability to issue deposits—that is, claims that are valued in large part because of their liquidity as well as any supporting federal guarantees—depends importantly on the perceived risk of the bank. For this reason alone, risk management is a critical part of the business model of banks in a way that it is not for non-financial firms.[2]

But as we have already seen, the goal of risk management for banks is not to eliminate or minimize risk, but rather to determine the *optimal* level of risk—the level that maximizes bank value subject to the constraints imposed by regulators, laws, and regulations. A well-governed bank will have processes in place to identify this optimal amount of risk, and to make sure that its risk does not differ too much from this amount.

In theory, the rule that guides a bank's investment and risk-taking decisions should be the same as the one that guides all public companies. That is, like all companies, a bank should take any project that is expected to earn more than its cost of capital, while taking into account the costs associated with the impact of the project on the bank's total risk. The problem, however, is that anticipating the effects of new projects on a bank's risk is complicated by the reality that, at least in banks of any size, risk-taking decisions are made throughout the organization that when taken together are capable of increasing

---

[1] Smith and Stulz (1985).

[2] See DeAngelo and Stulz (2015).

the bank's probability of financial distress. As a result, decisions to take on new projects and associated risks cannot be evaluated in isolation; they must be assessed in terms of their impact on the overall risk of the bank.

In principle, if there is an optimal level of risk for a bank, the costs associated with taking on a new project or activity that increases the bank's total risk should be traded off against the potential gain from taking the risk. But that said, there are some projects it would never make sense for a bank to take on—activities that are clearly negative-NPV projects that can be expected to destroy value as stand-alone risks. And let's call such projects "bad risks" to distinguish them from the other, potentially value-adding activities. Such projects have *negative expected* outcomes.

One example is a trading desk's writing of *underpriced*, deep-out-of-the-money puts based on traders' expectation that if the puts are not exercised and the desk ends up booking the premiums as income, the traders will receive higher bonuses. For the traders themselves (though not the banks they work for), this seems like a can't-lose proposition: after all, if the puts do end up being exercised, the traders would have been unlikely to receive a bonus anyway because asset values would had to have fallen by a lot. But for the bank's shareholders, such a trading strategy is clearly a negative NPV project as a stand-alone project since the bank is selling an asset for less than it is worth.

But now let's consider the case of writing puts that traders believe to be overvalued. In that case, the trading strategy would be a positive-NPV project on a stand-alone basis, and so a "good risk." But whether taking such a risk adds value for the bank as a whole depends on its effect on the overall risk position of the bank. In both cases, the one involving a bad risk and the other a good risk, there is an increase in the bank's total risk. While it is clear that taking the bad risk makes no sense for the bank, whether it makes sense to take the good risk cannot be decided on a stand-alone basis. In evaluating the case for taking on the good risks, a bank's risk managers must try to ensure that the expected gains outweigh the costs associated with the expected increase in the bank's overall risk.

And this brings us to another major challenge for risk management in banks: When risk-taking is decentralized—as it is bound to be for most organizations—for most

risk-taking actions the tradeoff between a project's contribution to the bank's risk and its expected return cannot be made in real time. What is needed instead is a short-cut—one that enables traders and their supervisors to focus on individual risks separately while at the same time giving the bank's management the means to manage the bank's overall risk. The main challenge in developing and operating such a two-level risk evaluation system is to prevent the oversight function from rejecting projects that are valuable for the institution despite their risk.

Thus, there are two fundamentally different ways that risk management can destroy value for a bank. First, it can fail to ensure that the bank has the right amount of risk—a failure that can come about in a number of different ways: it can fail to uncover bad risks that should be eliminated; it can mismeasure good risks and end up misclassifying them as bad; or it can fail in its task of measuring the bank's total risk. The second main way that a risk management system can destroy value is by failing to exercise the right amount of flexibility when the circumstances call for it—for example, blocking increases in risk that, if allowed, would actually increase the bank's value. For instance, in the fall of 2008, it was not unusual for risk managers to impose blanket restrictions on trading because of the high level of uncertainty. More recently, energy traders at major banks have been sidelined because of concerns about capital requirements. However, such restrictions have meant that traders could not exploit mispricings that were unusually large and would have created value for their banks. As I discuss later, when risk management becomes too inflexible, risk managers come to be viewed within the institution as "policemen," obstacles to be circumvented rather than partners in creating value. Striking the right balance between helping the firm take risks efficiently and ensuring that employees don't take risks that destroy value is a critical challenge for risk management in any bank.

In the rest of this paper, I start by discussing the determinants of the optimal level of risk for companies in general and then in the case of banks. Next I examine the role of governance and risk management in helping a bank achieve its optimal level of risk. Then I turn to an analysis of the organization of the risk management function. And last, after discussing the proper uses and limitations of risk management tools like value at risk (VaR) that are commonly used in banks, I show how such limitations create an important role for well-designed incentives and an effective corporate culture.

STEP ONE: DETERMINING A BANK'S RISK APPETITE

In a market economy, there are compelling reasons for corporations to be run to maximize shareholder wealth. These reasons apply to banks as well. But no corporation maximizes shareholder wealth in a vacuum. In particular, corporations are constrained in their actions by laws and regulations. Laws and regulations play a special role in the case of banks because the failures or weaknesses of banks can have damaging effects on the financial system and the economy.

But when thinking about the effects of regulation, it's important to recognize that market forces also play a role in causing banks to limit their risks. Indeed, if a bank is managed to maximize shareholder wealth, it will choose a level of risk that is consistent with that objective. As some of the world's largest banks were reminded during the crisis, banks that operate with too much risk cannot conduct their business even if regulators allow them to do so because they find it hard to fund themselves.

While deposit insurance guarantees depositors against losses, it does not guarantee their continuous access to their deposits. Further, many short-term liabilities of banks are not insured. To the extent that safe and liquid deposits are a source of value for banks, the market's perception that a bank has too much risk can reduce its value by limiting its ability to attract such deposits. Although some borrowers have no reason to care if the bank they borrow from is too risky, others will care. Borrowers that rely on their relationship with the bank could see that relationship jeopardized or lost if the bank becomes distressed—such borrowers may therefore seek to borrow elsewhere rather than deal with a risky bank.[3] If the bank is in the derivatives business, counterparties will be reluctant to deal with it if it is too risky. A bank that is perceived as fragile might also find it difficult or expensive to hire potential employees reluctant to make bank-specific investments in human capital.

Other reasons can be cited for how excessive risk can reduce a bank's value in the eyes of its shareholders. Nevertheless, as already noted, a bank that takes no risk whatsoever probably won't be worth much either. As a general rule, banks have to take some risks to create wealth for their shareholders.

There are many ways to define risk. For risk to affect the value of a bank to its shareholders, it must affect either the bank's expected future cash flows or the rate at which these cash flows are discounted.

And let's start with the effects of risk on a bank's operating cash flow. Just the possibility that an unexpected downturn in a bank's cash flow could lead to its financial distress sometime in the future should reduce the value of the bank today. In other words, the market will adjust its estimate of the bank's going concern value for the probability that the bank will experience financial distress and, as a result, will no longer be able to carry out its strategy and maintain operations as before.

Viewed from the perspective of shareholder value, then, the main risk of a bank that has to be managed is the risk of financial distress. But how do we evaluate and measure such risk?

Let's begin by assuming that the bank's risk of financial distress is reflected with reasonable accuracy by its credit rating (if it has one). For reasons we've already discussed, the optimal rating of a bank is unlikely to be the highest rating, which is AAA. For almost all public corporations, industrial companies as well as banks, achieving a AAA rating would require the sacrifice of too many valuable risky projects. No U.S. bank holding company today has an AAA rating, and only a handful outside the U.S. do.

But let's suppose that the value of a specific bank is expected to be the highest when operating with an A rating. The first point to keep in mind here is that an A rating, although several notches below AAA, is still consistent with a very low probability of default. From 1981 to 2011, the annual average default rate for A-rated credits was 0.08%, according to Standard & Poor's.[4] And this means that by targeting a certain credit rating, a bank's management is also targeting a specific probability of default and, along with it, the bank's desired level of risk. For that institution, a rating higher than A will necessarily limit its activities, possibly forcing it to give up some existing operations as well as planned projects. At the same time, a rating lower than A could make it difficult or impossible

---

[3] See for instance, Poloncheck, Slovin, and Sushka (1993) for evidence that corporate rate borrowers are affected adversely when their relationship bank becomes distressed.

[4] http://www.standardandpoors.com/ratings/articles/en/us/?articleType=HTML&assetID=1245331026864.

for the bank to continue some value-creating activities. For example, banks with significant derivatives operations generally maintain at least an A rating to address their customers' concerns about counterparty risk. Moreover, as a general rule, banks with larger deposit franchises and relationship lending operations tend to have higher credit ratings than institutions that rely mainly on fee-based, transactional activities.

And so banks with very different strategies, or liability and asset structures, could well end up having very different credit ratings, and different attitudes toward risk. To help make this point, Figure 5-1 shows the relation between credit ratings and bank value for two different kinds of banks—and let's call them "Bank Safe" and "Bank Risky." In both cases, the relation between ratings and bank value is "concave," which means that there is a single value-maximizing credit rating or risk posture. In the case of Bank Safe, the value of the bank falls sharply if it turns out to be riskier—whether because of a shift in management strategy or a change in external circumstances—than its target rating. Banks with large amounts of non-insured deposits tend to look like Bank Safe.

Bank Risky has a very different relation between its value and its rating. Its target rating is BBB, and its value increases substantially as it increases its risk towards its target—and falls sharply when it exceeds it. For both banks, having too much risk is extremely costly in terms of their value. But, for Bank Safe having too little risk appears to have little cost while for Bank Risky it has a large cost.

The main lesson here, then, is the importance of expected financial distress costs when determining the value-maximizing risk profile for banks. And as our simple example suggests, the size and importance of financial distress costs—and hence a bank's optimal credit rating—will depend on a bank's business model and investment opportunities.[5] As we have already seen, most banks that expect to add value mainly through "traditional" activities such as deposit-gathering and relationship lending will choose to maintain a low-risk profile. And the same is true of financial institutions with credit-sensitive operations like derivatives dealing and third-party guarantee businesses. By contrast, banks and other financial institutions with less reliance on deposit-gathering activities are likely to see more value in targeting a less restrictive

_____

[5] With the approach presented so far, bank value is highest if it achieves a specific target rating that depends on characteristics of the bank such as its strategy and business model. Not all banks, of course, have ratings. But since a rating corresponds to a probability of default, banks without rating could still use them to figure out the probability of default that is optimal for them. Obviously, banks might choose to tailor their risk in a more complex way. They might want to specify how they are affected by specific shocks. For instance, a bank might choose to set a level of risk such that it can survive a major recession with a downgrade of only one notch. One obvious difficulty with the use of such additional criteria to evaluate and monitor a bank's risk is that the criteria—and the constraints imposed by them—could be inconsistent and their impact on bank value might be hard to assess. At the same time, however, multiple criteria and constraints could help ensure that the bank is better prepared to weather shocks that do materialize.

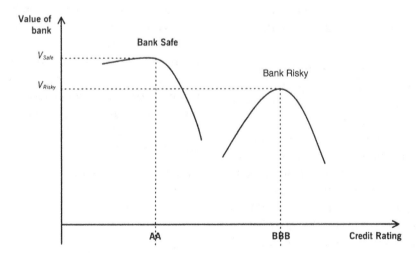

FIGURE 5-1 Bank value as a function of bank risk measure by the bank's credit rating.

credit posture. For instance, Capital One Financial, which focuses on credit cards, has a BBB rating from S&P, which would cause problems for a bank that relies heavily on deposit-gathering and relationships.

In this sense, a bank's credit rating and risk posture reflect what is often referred to as its "appetite" for risk. A bank's risk appetite is top management's assessment, usually with some input from the bank's chief risk officer, of the expected effect on the bank's risk and value of taking on more risky investments and activities. And because this assessment can change with changes in the bank's opportunities, a bank's risk appetite should not be determined once and for all, but continuously monitored and reevaluated. What's more, a bank's risk appetite should not be defined in such a precise way that a small shift in opportunities will affect it.

Taking Social Costs into Account

As already stated, the critical difference between banks and less regulated industrial companies is the potential for bank failures to have system-wide effects. If a producer of widgets fails, as long as there are other producers of widgets, the impact on society will generally be very limited. The same is not true if a large bank or a group of smaller banks fail.

But despite the social importance of limiting the systemic risk created by banks, there is no reason to expect that banks with less systemic risk will be worth more to their shareholders (in fact, as we will soon see, what research we have suggests that investors generally assign higher values to financial institutions that assume more risk). And this means that the activities of banks that aim to maximize value for their shareholders could end up generating an amount of systemic risk that is excessive from the perspective of society.

Because of the role of banks in the economy and the consequences of bank failures, regulators impose restrictions on banks' ability to take risks on the asset side and require banks to satisfy minimal capital requirements. And this of course means that banks choose their level of risk subject to external constraints. But the critical point is that such constraints do not change our earlier conclusions: namely, that there is an optimal level of risk for a bank—one that affects the interests and concerns of both bank regulators and bank investors—and that that level of risk differs across banks in ways that reflect their business models.

Moreover, because the optimal level of risk differs across banks, the costs to shareholders of constraints imposed by regulators are not equal across banks. For instance, my own recent study with Nicole Boyson and Ruediger Fahlenbrach shows that banks with high deposit franchise value have incentives to, and do indeed, choose lower risk strategies; and as a result, such banks tend to operate with amounts of capital well in excess of their requirements.[6] For instance, in our sample of banks, the behavior of Wells Fargo over the last ten years fits the model of a bank with high franchise value that chooses a conservative risk posture with Tier 1 capital well in excess of existing requirements. But for other banks with riskier strategies, capital requirements are likely to be binding.

GOVERNANCE AND RISK TAKING

As we have seen, then, bank shareholders still expect bank managers to aim to maximize shareholder wealth, and hence a well-governed bank should have mechanisms in place that encourage bank managers to make value-maximizing trade-offs between risk and reward, all while operating within the constraints imposed by regulation. In this section, I address some key considerations when designing a firm's governance of its risk management function.

As we saw earlier, for each bank there is a positive level of risk that can be expected to maximize its value for shareholders. Good governance should begin by ensuring that the firm chooses that level of risk. This means ensuring that the firm has processes in place that enable it to measure its risk, understand how its value is related to risk, and maintain the right level of risk.

One obvious concern, for shareholders and regulators alike, is that management could do a poor job of managing the firm's risk, or have incentives to take risks that are not in the interest of the shareholders. To address this concern, the board has to ensure that the firm has a risk management organization in place that is capable of measuring and overseeing the management of risk so that the actual level of risk taken is consistent with the firm's stated risk appetite.

Understanding whether a company is taking the right risks is a rather complex and technical task. Even if the board has the expertise to assess and oversee management's

---

[6] Boyson, Fahlenbrach, and Stulz (2014).

efforts in measuring and managing risks, it may be difficult for the board to develop such an understanding. While boards require their companies' accounting methods and procedures to be evaluated and signed off on by third-party auditors, they do not typically require assessments of a firm's risk accounting procedures (though auditors may comment on various aspects of it). Such risk audits could be valuable tools in helping boards reach the proper level of comfort that management is managing a bank's risk properly.

One important implication of this view of effective risk governance is that, as discussed earlier, it does not mean eliminating risk-taking, or necessarily even reducing it. In fact, a bank management team left to its own devices may well choose to take less risk than what is best for the shareholders. But as we have also noted, because the optimal amount of risk from the perspective of the shareholders need not be the optimal amount for society, better governance does not necessarily lead to safer banks. More effective governance can be expected to lead to banks that are not only more valuable, but in many cases also more risky.

What empirical research we have does not support the proposition that better governance in banks leads to less risk. The recent global financial crisis provides a natural experiment for testing this proposition. If it were correct, we might expect better governed banks to have been less affected by the crisis since they would have been less exposed to risks that manifested themselves during the crisis—provided, of course, that management correctly measured those risks.

Recent studies have found little support for that prediction. For instance, my own research found that banks with more "shareholder friendly" boards performed worse during the crisis than other banks, not better.[7] Another study has reported that banks deemed to have better governance operated with less capital and experienced higher levels of insolvency risk, especially in fiscally stronger countries, than banks with weaker governance systems.[8] And despite the post-crisis push for more financial expertise on boards, yet another study reported finding no

evidence of greater ability to weather the crisis by banks whose boards had more financial expertise.[9] Finally, studies—including one I co-authored[10]—showed that banks where management had large equity stakes also performed worse during the crisis.

All this evidence, then, implies that better governance did not enable banks to perform better during the crisis. Of course, the implication is not that better governance is bad for shareholders. What it should make clear, however, is that better governance does not necessarily mean less risk. Better governance meant taking risks that were expected to be rewarding for shareholders, given that bank managers and their shareholders generally viewed the possibility of a crisis as an exceedingly low-probability event.

THE ORGANIZATION OF RISK MANAGEMENT

Consider a bank where employees throughout the organization can take risks. And suppose also that the top management could know exactly what the bank's risk is at each point in time and could instantly hedge all risks at zero cost.

In this case, risk management would be straightforward. Having determined its risk appetite, the bank could control its risk through hedging by top management. As long as risk-takers in the bank took only projects that were expected to create value (regardless of their risk), top management would have no reason to monitor the bank's risk in the sense of assessing and, where necessary, limiting risk decisions made by its employees. All the bank would have to do is measure the risk taken within the bank and control it through hedging.

Real-world banks cannot control risk this way for at least three important reasons:

1. **Limitations of risk measurement technology:** While real-time risk measures exist for a number of activities within banks, such measures do not exist for banks as a whole. Further, risk measurement is not just imperfect, but can be highly imprecise. Finally, risk measurement can be affected by behavioral

---

[7] See Beltratti and Stulz (2012) and Erkens et al. (2012).

[8] See Anginer, Demirguc-Kunt, Huizinga, and Ma (2013, 2014), which provide a more general exploration of the relation between governance, performance, and capitalization using an international dataset.

[9] See Minton, Taillard, and Williamson (2014).

[10] See Fahlenbrach and Stulz (2011).

biases; for example, excessive optimism and "group-think" can lead important issues to be ignored or underappreciated.[11]

2. **Limitations of hedging:** Even if a bank had a precise measure of its overall risk, it does not follow that it could safely manage its overall risk through hedging by top management. Some risks cannot be hedged, and hedges may not work out as planned.

3. **Limitations of control resulting from incentives:** Risk-takers are often rewarded in ways that give them incentives to take risks that are more valuable to themselves than to their organizations. This problem is made worse by the limitations of risk measurement tools.

These three limitations mean that risk must be monitored and managed throughout the organization. Risk managers play a critical role in measuring, monitoring, and managing risk. Yet, despite their name, risk managers do not really manage risk themselves. They mostly measure and monitor it, and then *help those who manage risk*.

For example, consider the interactions between the head of a trading desk at a bank and the risk managers. The head of the trading desk will be constantly changing the risk taken by the desk when responding to opportunities as well as to the constraints placed on the desk by risk management and senior management. And this means that the head of the trading desk will effectively be managing the risk of the desk, subject to the limits imposed on his risk-taking. Risk management will monitor the risk of the desk to ensure that it stays within its limits. But the limits are effectively set by decisions made at the top of the organization. And in this sense, the top risk manager of a bank (or any large company) is the CEO, not the CRO.

The risk-taking framework presented earlier can be used to help an organization understand the kind of risk management function that is most likely to contribute to shareholder value. If a bank's value is relatively insensitive to its overall level of risk, there is little room for risk management to add much value by ensuring that the bank's aggregate risk is at its optimal level. By contrast, in those cases where too much risk-taking results in a sharp drop in a bank's value, a risk management function that is designed to limit excessive risk-taking while still allowing the bank to pursue promising opportunities has the

potential to create a lot of value. In such a case, effective risk management could show up in the form of a higher P/E multiple—one that reflects investors' confidence in the bank's ability to maintain its current earnings and cash flows under most conditions.

This risk-taking framework can also be used when assessing how independent the risk management function should be. One widely held view, as already noted, is that risk management is the equivalent of the audit function, whose value depends in large part on the auditor's independence from the firm being audited. In practice, however, there are two important reasons why the risk management function cannot operate completely independently of the businesses.

First, unlike auditors, whose job is to verify profits that have already been earned, effective risk managers must continuously monitor risk-taking and be proactive in ensuring that risk limits are enforced. They often help employees contemplating an action to assess the associated risk, especially when the action could lead to the breach of some limit. Risk managers, to be sure, can end up preventing employees from taking actions that could increase firm value. But in a well-organized risk management function, they can and should be used to help employees increase firm value by devising strategies that are less risky but not less profitable.

The second potential problem with a completely independent risk management function is that, if risk managers come to be viewed as a kind of risk "police," they will face obstacles in gathering information and understanding strategies, and are likely to be kept out of the information flow that is critical to assessing risk. As a consequence, risk managers may not learn of model weaknesses or new risks until it is too late.

The right degree of independence for risk managers cannot be achieved by formal rules alone. The reporting lines of risk managers may be completely separate from the businesses whose risks they are monitoring; but if they have the ambition and opportunity to move into that business line, formal independence may not lead to the desired independence.[12] And to the extent that the performance of risk managers is partly evaluated, whether formally or informally, by the business lines they monitor, the resulting interdependence can have very different

---

[11] Greenbaum (2014).

[12] See Landier, Sraer, and Thesmar (2009).

implications depending on the culture of the institution. In institutions with weak commitments by business lines to manage risk effectively, this incomplete independence can provide a way for the business lines to retaliate against "uncooperative" risk managers and can lead to a situation where the businesses take risks they should not. But in institutions with a strong commitment to manage risk, such interdependence can help in creating incentives for a constructive collaboration between risk managers and business units—one that aims to achieve the company's goals while staying within existing risk limits.

USING VaR TO TARGET RISK

The financial risk management functions of many banks rely heavily on the use of a measure called value-at-risk, or VaR. For banks whose overall risk position can be captured using VaR, the risk management framework presented earlier can be implemented in a fairly straightforward way. But, as I discuss later, this approach has some important limitations.

To make use of VaR within this risk framework, a bank's management would begin by translating its risk appetite into a targeted probability of experiencing losses that are expected to result in financial distress or in default. And let's say the bank's top management has determined that it wants to limit its probability of default or failure within a single year to 0.06%, which, as we saw earlier, is consistent with a AA credit rating. This means that the bank is expected to fail less than once in a thousand years.

Suppose that the bank has $100 billion of assets and $10 billion of equity. If all the risks the bank faces are measured by the bank-wide VaR,[13] the bank should have only a 0.06% probability of experiencing a loss that exceeds its cushion of $10 billion. But if the bank's risk manager determines that the bank has a bank-wide VaR of $15 billion, it has taken too much risk. In that case, the bank's management should either reduce the risk of its assets or raise additional equity.

VaR can also be estimated for any risk-taking unit within a bank.[14] For instance, a VaR can be estimated for the book of a trader as well as for the unit the trader belongs to. Starting from the smallest units for which VaR is estimated, VaRs can be aggregated in such a way that the bank-wide VaR is a function of the VaRs of these units as well as the correlations among the risks of these units. Further, using the VaRs of the smallest units and the correlations, it is possible to assess how each unit contributes to the risk of the bank. For instance, a bank could estimate how much of the risk of the bank as measured by VaR is accounted for by a specific trader. And the fact that the bank-wide VaR results from the aggregation of the VaRs of the units of the bank means that risk management can target the bank's VaR by setting limits on the VaRs of all the units. If all units are within their limits, the VaR of the bank should not exceed the level consistent with its risk appetite.

THE LIMITS OF RISK MEASUREMENT

But having made the case for firm-wide risk measurement, there are obvious difficulties in using VaR to measure risk at the firm level. First, aggregating VaR measures to obtain a firm-wide risk VaR measure is fraught with problems. Second, VaR does not capture all risks. Third, VaR has substantial model risk.

Using the same risk framework presented earlier, let's again assume that a bank formulates its risk appetite in terms of a targeted probability of default—a condition that is assumed to occur if and when the bank incurs a loss large enough to wipe out its equity buffer. Hence, to properly target a probability of default, the firm has to measure correctly the risk of a loss that exceeds the size of the equity buffer. This means that *all* risks that could lead to losses have to be modeled. If the firm targets a probability of default of 0.06% but fails to capture some major risks, its VaR and probability of default will be significantly understated.

A typical approach for a bank is to divide risks into three categories: market, credit, and operational risks. Basel II introduced that three-part division, and it requires banks to hold capital against each of these types of risk. For most banks, however, a firm-wide VaR that is obtained by aggregating market, credit, and operational risks will not reflect all risks. For example, such an approach often fails to capture some core business risks that are not modeled as part of operational risk. For many banks, non-interest income is a large component of revenue. This income

[13] A loss that is exceeded only with a probability p over one year is the value-at-risk over one year at the probability level p. It follows that the risk framework leads directly to the use of value-at-risk (VaR) as a firm-wide risk measure. For illustration of an application of the concept to an insurance company, see Nocco and Stulz (2006).

[14] See, for instance, Litterman (1996).

is not only variable, but tends to be low when the bank experiences losses on loans. Such income has to be modeled when assessing the amount of equity necessary to support the targeted probability of default. Also potentially important, interest rate risks—both those in the banking book and arising from liabilities—are typically not reflected in firm-wide VaRs.

If a bank divides risks between market, credit, and operational risks, it has to aggregate these risks to obtain a firm-wide measure of risk.[15] This aggregation requires estimates of the correlations between these types of risks. And it turns out that aggregate risk is very sensitive to these estimates. To see this, suppose that a bank has VaRs of $1 for each of its three main risks. If the correlations are 1.0 among the risks, the bank-wide VaR is $3. But if the correlations are 0, the bank-wide VaR falls to $1.73. Unfortunately, the data needed to estimate such correlations are hard to come by. Yet, these correlation estimates make an enormous difference in the amount of equity that is required to target a given default probability. Mistakes in correlation estimates could lead a bank to have too little capital and to have an actual probability of default much larger than its targeted one.

No discussion of risk management can be complete without addressing the issue of risks that are not known—the famous "black swans" of Nassim Taleb or the "unknown unknowns" of Donald Rumsfeld. Such low-probability risks generally become relevant and consequential only when assessing annual VaRs at extremely low probability levels, such as the 0.06% level. Precisely because the losses corresponding to such a VaR are likely to be caused by such rare events, one's understanding and analysis of such events may well become important. As already noted, the use of historical data and established statistical techniques cannot alone be sufficient to estimate a VaR at the 0.06% level because the data generally encompass a period that is too short to develop an accurate representation of extreme losses that have an annual probability of less than 0.06% of occurring.

As we saw earlier, a VaR of 0.06% is one that should be exceeded less than one year in a thousand. In other words, the bank that targets a 0.06% probability of default should be able to survive just about any crisis. This suggests another approach to investigating whether

---

[15] Rosenberg and Schoenbaum (2006).

the VaR is correctly estimated. Since the bank should survive almost all crises, a simple way to assess whether the bank's targeting of the probability of default is done correctly is to simulate what the performance of the bank would be if historical crises were to repeat themselves.

This approach amounts to performing the "stress tests" that many of the world's largest banks have been subjected to in recent years. If such tests show that the bank would be unable to survive past crises, it is likely that its VaR is biased. More generally, however, stress tests can help understand the risks that a bank is exposed to and whether it has enough equity to withstand the realization of such risks.

INCENTIVES, CULTURE, AND RISK MANAGEMENT

Risk measurement is never perfect. Even if it were, there would still be the problem that firm value does not depend on risk alone. As we have seen, risk management with a rigid structure and inflexible limits designed to ensure that a bank's risk never exceeds some pre-specified level may well succeed in controlling risk; but in so doing, it may also prevent the institution from creating wealth for its shareholders. In a bank, risk management is part of the production technology. When risk management works well, the institution creates more value in part because of its ability to issue more liquid claims and its resulting greater capacity to take those business risks it has a comparative advantage in managing.

As already noted, there is an unfortunate tendency among some board members and regulators to think of the risk management function as a compliance function like auditing. There is, to be sure, an important compliance element to risk management. If a limit is set for a specific risk, the risk function must monitor to ensure that the limit is respected—and it must understand limit exceedances and be involved in decisions on how to respond to them. Whereas auditors are never in a position to conclude that departures from GAAP can create shareholder wealth, risk managers must understand the bank's businesses and personnel well enough to know when limit exceedances should be allowed and when a business line should be forced to respect a limit. Risk managers also have to determine or help determine when limits have to be changed and when it is appropriate for the institution to adjust its risk appetite.

Another way of saying this is that banks, like all businesses, continually face tradeoffs between risk and expected return. To complicate matters, risk and expected return are measured imperfectly. If the costs to an institution associated with having more risk than optimal are extremely high, that institution may benefit from having a risk management organization that operates as a police department whose main job is to enforce the rules. In this case, it would also make sense for the organization to account for limitations in risk measurement by imposing a substantial risk buffer—that is, set a limit for the risk measure that is lower than the objective to account for the fact that the risk measure might understate risk. But firms often face a different situation—namely, one where they can lose a lot from not being able to take advantage of opportunities that might be precluded by an inflexible risk organization. Further, difficulties in assessing risk mean that a risk management organization might make incorrect risk assessments without having a dialogue with business units. But having such a dialogue is likely to be very difficult if the risk management function is viewed as a compliance unit rather than an essential part of the firm that seeks to implement policies that increase firm value.

If many people in an organization are focused on making sure that the institution takes risks that increase firm value, risk management becomes a resource in making this possible. Lines of business within banks cannot know by themselves the extent to which the risks they take increase value because the amount of risk the bank can take at a given point in time depends on other risks taken by other lines of business. Hence, risk management has to bring the perspective of the firm to bear on at least major risk-taking decisions to help ensure that the firm itself is taking the right amount of risk.

In taking the perspective of the firm as a whole, risk managers face potential conflicts with managers whose main concern is the profitability of their own units. Hence, for risk management to work well, executives within the firm must have reasons to care about the firm as a whole. This requires incentives that reward them if they create value for the firm while holding them accountable for taking risks that destroy value.

Setting the correct incentives for risk-taking is a complex undertaking. Many banks have developed bank-wide mechanisms based on the concept of "risk capital" (sometimes also called "economic capital") that are used to evaluate the costs of taking specific risks. For a bank, risk capital is the amount of capital required to support the firm-wide level of risk that is consistent with the bank's risk appetite. Using the concept of risk capital, when a unit of the bank takes an additional risk, the bank can maintain its aggregate level of risk by acquiring more equity capital. But this capital has a cost that must be accounted for and allocated to the unit taking the risk. Taking into account this equity capital cost may mean that it is no longer worthwhile to take the risk.

Incentives should be set right, but they should also have limits. It is impossible to set up an incentive plan that is so precisely calibrated that it leads executives to take the right actions in every situation. Employment contracts are by their very nature incomplete, and executives must deal with situations that nobody contemplated. A further issue is that not all risks can be quantified or defined. As a bank focuses on specific risks that it quantifies and can account for in employee reviews and incentive plans, there is an incentive for employees to take risks that are not quantified and monitored.

Because of the limits of risk management and incentives, the ability of a firm to manage risk properly depends on its corporate culture as well.[16] Within a corporation, culture is the set of shared beliefs and norms that tells people how to act when there are no formal rules. As such, corporate culture is in large part the result of experience and learning. According to one definition, "Culture is what a group learns over a period of time as that group solves its problems of survival in an external environment and its problems of internal integration."[17] And mainly for this reason, culture is hard to change. It also has to be transmitted to new hires—and it may leave with key employees.

There is little empirical work on the relation between culture and corporate outcomes, in large part because of the difficulty of measuring the dimensions of culture. Two recent studies have used data from independent surveys of corporate employees about the attractiveness of the corporate workplace. One of the studies reports finding that companies where managers are viewed by their employees as trustworthy and ethical are more profitable and have higher valuations.[18] But the other study finds that improvements in shareholder governance change some

---

[16] For a recent review, see Bouwman (2013).

[17] Schein (1990).

[18] Guiso, Sapienza, and Zingales (2013).

aspects of a firm's culture for the worse, in the sense that its attentiveness to customers and employee integrity are both said to suffer as emphasis on near-term results increases.[19] According to that study, shareholders gain initially from the better governance, but these gains are partly offset over time because of the change in the culture of the firm.

The literature on culture does not focus on risk-taking or on other questions that are distinctive to the financial industry. But in a recent study, two colleagues and I show that certain characteristics of banks that could be viewed as indicative of their culture are helpful in understanding how banks responded to and were affected by crisis. More specifically, we find that the extent of underperformance by individual large banks during the 1998 crisis proved to be a remarkably accurate predictor of the degree of those same banks' underperformance during the recent crisis. In fact, a bank's relative stock performance during the 1998 crisis had as much explanatory power for the performance of the bank in the recent crisis as its leverage or capital ratio.[20] This finding suggests that there are bank characteristics that persist through time that help explain banks' level of risk. And a bank's culture could be a big part of this—in other words, certain aspects of the banks' practices and behavior quite apart from their fundamentals appear to have caused them to remain susceptible to crisis, even after experiencing shocks that might have caused them to become more crisis-resistant.

When thinking about this finding, it's important to keep in mind that companies in the financial industry differ considerably from non-financial firms in the extent to which employees are empowered to make decisions that affect risk. For example, a loan officer who can decide whether a loan is granted makes a decision to take a risk. She may have information about that risk that nobody else has in the organization. And no one may ever know whether the decision was right from the perspective of the firm for a number of reasons. First, it may not be possible for the loan officer to communicate credibly the information she has. Second, the loan officer may have incentives to make loans that she knows should not be made. Third, loan outcomes by themselves are of limited use in evaluating a loan officer's performance because expected defaults are not zero, and even "good" loans can turn out badly.

One solution for the bank is to minimize the discretion of the loan officer by relying mainly on statistical models for the decision. But such a solution can be costly by reducing the organization's flexibility, its option to use valuable "soft" information possessed by its loan officers or others. Instead of relying exclusively on statistical models, a bank's culture could be used to provide a more flexible way of constraining loan officer discretion that leads to better outcomes for the bank. A bank with an underwriting culture that is highly focused on the interests of the bank will make it harder for its loan officers to deviate from the social norms within the bank.

CONCLUSION

The success of banks and the health of the financial system depend critically on how they take risks. A bank's ability to measure and manage risks creates value for shareholders. But there is no simple recipe that enables a bank to measure and manage risks more effectively. For risk-taking to maximize shareholder wealth, a bank has to have the right risk management, but also the right governance, the right incentives, and the right culture. An organization of risk management that is optimal for one bank may be value-reducing for another. Ultimately, the success of risk management in performing its functions depends not just on the quality of its models and its data, but also on judgment, incentives, and culture. Nevertheless, while better risk management should lead to better risk-taking, there is no reason for a bank with good risk management to have low risk.

René Stulz holds the Everett D. Reese Chair of Banking and Monetary Economics at Ohio State University's Fisher College of Business, and is affiliated with NBER, ECGI, and the Wharton Financial Institutions Center.

References

Aebi, Vincent, Gabriele Sabato, and Markus Schmid, 2012, Risk management, corporate governance, and bank performance in the financial crisis, *Journal of Banking and Finance* 36, 3213–3226.

Anginer, Deniz, Asli Demirguc-Kunt, Harry Huizinga, and Kebin Ma, 2013, How does corporate governance affect bank capitalization strategies?, Policy Research Working Paper, The World Bank.

---

[19] Popadak (2013).

[20] Fahlenbrach, Prilmeier, and Stulz (2012).

Anginer, Deniz, Asli Demirguc-Kunt, Harry Huizinga, and Kebin Ma, 2014, Corporate governance and bank insolvency risk: International evidence, CentEr Working Paper, Tilburg University.

Beltratti, Andrea, and René M. Stulz, 2012, The credit crisis around the globe: Why did some banks perform better?, *Journal of Financial Economics* 105, 1-17.

Berg, Tobias, 2014, Playing the devil's advocate: The causal effect of risk management on loan quality, working paper, Bonn University.

Bouwman, Christa H.S., 2013, The role of corporate culture in mergers and acquisitions, in Mergers and Acquisitions, Etienne Perrault, ed., NOVA Science Publishers.

Cartwright, Susan, and Cary L. Cooper, 1993, The role of culture compatibility in successful organizational marriage, *Academy of Management Executive* 7, 57-70.

Cheng, Ing-Haw, Harrison Hong, and Jose Scheinkman, 2010, Yesterday's heroes: Compensation and creative risk-taking, NBER Working Paper.

DeAngelo, Harry, and René M. Stulz, 2014, Liquid-claim production, risk management, and capital structure: Why high leverage is optimal for banks, *Journal of Financial Economics*, forthcoming.

De Haan, Jakob, and Razvan Vlahu, 2013, Corporate governance of banks: A survey, DNB working paper.

Erkens, David, Mingyi Hung, and Pedro Matos, 2012, Corporate governance in the 2007-2008 financial crisis: Evidence from financial institutions worldwide, *Journal of Corporate Finance* 18, 389-411.

Fahlenbrach, Rüdiger, and René M. Stulz, 2011, Bank CEO incentives and the credit crisis, *Journal of Financial Economics* 99, 11-26.

Fahlenbrach, Rüdiger, Robert Prilmeier, and René M. Stulz, 2012, This time is the same: Using bank performance in 1998 to explain bank performance during the recent financial crisis, *Journal of Finance* 67, 2139-2185.

Greenbaum, Stuart I., 2014, Tail risk perspectives, unpublished paper.

Guiso, Luigi, Paola Sapienza, and Luigi Zingales, 2013, The value of corporate culture, *Journal of Financial Economics*, forthcoming.

Hall, Matthew, Anette Mikes, and Yuval Millo, 2013, How do risk managers become influential? A field study in two financial institutions, Harvard Business School Working Paper.

Kaplan, Robert S., and Annette Mikes, 2012, Managing risks: A new framework, *Harvard Business Review*.

Laeven, Luc, and Ross Levine, 2009, Bank governance, regulation and risk taking, *Journal of Financial Economics* 93, 259-275.

Lingel, Anna, and Elizabeth Sheedy, 2012, The influence of risk governance on risk outcomes—international evidence, unpublished working paper, Macquarie University.

Litterman, Robert, 1996, Hot Spots™ and hedges, *Journal of Portfolio Management*, Special Issue, 52-75.

Mikes, Anette, Matthew Hall, and Yuval Millo, 2013, How experts gain influence, *Harvard Business Review* 91. 70-74.

Minton, Bernadette, Jerome Taillard, and Rohan Williamson, 2013, Financial expertise of the board, risk taking and performance: Evidence from bank holding companies, *Journal of Financial and Quantitative Analysis*, forthcoming.

Nocco, Brian, and René M. Stulz, 2006, Enterprise risk management: Theory and practice, *Journal of Applied Corporate Finance* 18, 8-20.

O'Reilly, Charles A., Jennifer Chatman, and David F. Caldwell, 1991, People and organizational culture: A profile comparison approach to assessing person-organization fit, *Academy of Management Journal* 34, 487-516.

Polonchek, John A., Myron B. Slovin, and Marie E. Sushka, 1993, The value of bank durability: Borrowers as bank stakeholders, *Journal of Finance* 48, 247-266.

Popadak, Jillian, 2013, A corporate culture channel: How increased shareholder governance reduces value, unpublished working paper, The Wharton School.

Schein, Edgar H., 1990, Organizational culture, *American Psychologist* 45, 109-119.

Sorensen, Jesper B., 2002, The strength of corporate culture and the reliability of firm performance, *Administrative Science Quarterly* 47, 70-91.

Stulz, René M., 2003, Risk management and derivatives, South-Western Publishing.

Stulz, René M., 2008, Risk management failures: What are they and when do they happen?, *Journal of Applied Corporate Finance* 20, 39-48.

Thakor, Anjan, 2013, Bank capital and financial stability: Economic tradeoff or Faustian bargain, *Annual Review of Financial Economics*, forthcoming.

Financial Disasters

Learning Objectives

Candidates, after completing this reading, should be able to:

- Analyze the key factors that led to and derive the lessons learned from the following risk management case studies:
  - Chase Manhattan and their involvement with Drysdale Securities
  - Kidder Peabody
  - Barings
- Allied Irish Bank
- Union Bank of Switzerland (UBS)
- Société Générale
- Long Term Capital Management (LTCM)
- Metallgesellschaft
- Bankers Trust
- JPMorgan, Citigroup, and Enron

Excerpt is Chapter 4 of Financial Risk Management: A Practitioner's Guide to Managing Market and Credit Risk (+Website), *Second Edition, by Steven Allen.*

One of the fundamental goals of financial risk management is to avoid the types of disasters that can threaten the viability of a firm. So we should expect that a study of such events that have occurred in the past will prove instructive. A complete catalog of all such incidents is beyond the scope of this chapter, but I have tried to include the most enlightening examples that relate to the operation of financial markets, as this is the chapter's primary focus.

A broad categorization of financial disasters involves a three-part division:

1. Cases in which the firm or its investors and lenders were seriously misled about the size and nature of the positions it had.

2. Cases in which the firm and its investors and lenders had reasonable knowledge of its positions, but had losses resulting from unexpectedly large market moves.

3. Cases in which losses did not result from positions held by the firm, but instead resulted from fiduciary or reputational exposure to positions held by the firm's customers.

DISASTERS DUE TO MISLEADING REPORTING

A striking feature of all the financial disasters we will study involving cases in which a firm or its investors and lenders have been misled about the size and nature of its positions is that they all involve a significant degree of deliberation on the part of some individuals to create or exploit incorrect information. This is not to say situations do not exist in which firms are misled without any deliberation on the part of any individual. Everyone who has been in the financial industry for some time knows of many instances when everyone at the firm was misled about the nature of positions because a ticket was entered into a system incorrectly. Most typically, this will represent a purchase entered as a sale, or vice versa. However, although the size of such errors and the time it takes to detect them can sometimes lead to substantial losses, I am not aware of any such incident that has resulted in losses that were large enough to threaten the viability of a firm.

An error in legal interpretation can also seriously mislead a firm about its positions without any deliberate exploitation of the situation. However, such cases, although they can result in large losses, tend to be spread across many firms rather than concentrated at a single firm, perhaps because lawyers tend to check potentially controversial legal opinions with one another. The best-known case of this type was when derivatives contracted by British municipalities were voided.

If we accept that all cases of financial disaster due to firms being misled about their positions involve some degree of complicity on the part of some individuals, we cannot regard them completely as cases of incorrectly reported positions. Some of the individuals involved know the correct positions, at least approximately, whereas others are thoroughly misinformed. Understanding such cases therefore requires examining two different questions:

1. Why does the first group persist in taking large positions they know can lead to large losses for the firm despite their knowledge of the positions?

2. How do they succeed in keeping this knowledge from the second group, who we can presume would put a stop to the position taking if they were fully informed?

I will suggest that the answer to the first question tends to be fairly uniform across disasters, while the answer to the second question varies.

The willingness to take large risky positions is driven by moral hazard. Moral hazard represents an asymmetry in reward structure and an asymmetry in information; in other words, the group with the best information on the nature of the risk of a position has a greater participation in potential upside than potential downside. This often leads insiders to desire large risky positions that offer them commensurately large potential gains. The idea is that traders own an option on their profits; therefore, they will gain from increasing volatility. The normal counterweights against this are the attempts by representatives of senior management, stockholders, creditors, and government regulators, who all own a larger share of the potential downside than the traders, to place controls on the amount of risk taken. However, when those who could exercise this control substantially lack knowledge of the positions, the temptation exists for traders to exploit the control weakness to run inflated positions. This action often leads to another motivation spurring the growth of risky positions—the Ponzi scheme.

Some traders who take risky positions that are unauthorized but disguised by a control weakness will make profits on these positions. These positions are then possibly closed down without anyone being the wiser. However, some unauthorized positions will lead to losses, and traders will be strongly tempted to take on even larger, riskier positions in an attempt to cover up unauthorized losses. This is where the Ponzi scheme comes in. I think it helps to explain how losses from unauthorized positions can grow to be so overwhelmingly large. Stigum (1989) quotes an "astute trader" with regard to the losses in the Chase/Drysdale financial disaster: "I find it puzzling that Drysdale could lose so much so fast. If you charged me to lose one-fourth of a billion, I think it would be hard to do; I would probably end up making money some of the time because I would buy something going down and it would go up. They must have been extraordinarily good at losing money." I would suggest that the reason traders whose positions are unauthorized can be so "extraordinarily good at losing money" is that normal constraints that force them to justify positions to outsiders are lacking and small unauthorized losses already put them at risk of their jobs and reputations. With no significant downside left, truly reckless positions are undertaken in an attempt to make enough money to cover the previous losses. This is closely related to double-or-nothing betting strategies, which can start with very small stakes and quickly mushroom to extraordinary levels in an effort to get back to even.

This snowballing pattern can be seen in many financial disasters. Nick Leeson's losses on behalf of Barings were just $21 million in 1993, $185 million in 1994, and $619 million in just the first two months of 1995 (Chew 1996, Table 10.2). John Rusnak's unauthorized trading at Allied Irish Bank (AIB) accumulated losses of $90 million in its first five years through 1999, $210 million in 2000, and $374 million in 2001 (Ludwig 2002, Section H). Joseph Jett's phantom trades at Kidder Peabody started off small and ended with booked trades in excess of the quantity of all bonds the U.S. Treasury had issued.

The key to preventing financial disasters based on misrepresented positions is therefore the ability to spot unauthorized position taking in a timely enough fashion to prevent this explosive growth in position size. The lessons we can learn from these cases primarily center on why it took so long for knowledge of the misreported positions to spread from an insider group to the firm's management. We will examine each case by providing a brief summary of how the unauthorized position arose, how it failed to come to management's attention, and what lessons can be learned. In each instance, I provide references for those seeking more detailed knowledge of the case.

Chase Manhattan Bank/Drysdale Securities

Incident

In three months of 1976, Drysdale Government Securities, a newly founded subsidiary of an established firm, succeeded in obtaining unsecured borrowing of about $300 million by exploiting a flaw in the market practices for computing the value of U.S. government bond collateral. This unsecured borrowing exceeded any amount Drysdale would have been approved for, given that the firm had only $20 million in capital. Drysdale used the borrowed money to take outright positions in bond markets. When the traders lost money on the positions they put on, they lacked cash with which to pay back their borrowings. Drysdale went bankrupt, losing virtually all of the $300 million in unsecured borrowings. Chase Manhattan absorbed almost all of these losses because it had brokered most of Drysdale's securities borrowings. Although Chase employees believed they were only acting as agents on these transactions and were not taking any direct risk on behalf of Chase, the legal documentation of the securities borrowings did not support their claim.

Result

Chase's financial viability was not threatened by losses of this size, but the losses were large enough to severely damage its reputation and stock valuation for several years.

How the Unauthorized Positions Arose

Misrepresentation in obtaining loans is unfortunately not that uncommon in bank lending. A classic example would be Anthony De Angelis, the "Salad Oil King," who, in 1963, obtained $175 million in loans supposedly secured by large salad oil holdings, which turned out to be vast drums filled with water with a thin layer of salad oil floating on top. Lending officers who came to check on their collateral were bamboozled into only looking at a sample from the top of each tank.

The following are some reasons for featuring the Drysdale shenanigans in this section rather than discussing any number of other cases of misrepresentation:

- Drysdale utilized a weakness in trading markets to obtain its funds.
- Drysdale lost the borrowed money in the financial markets.
- It is highly unusual for a single firm to bear this large a proportion of this large a borrowing sting.

There is not much question as to how Drysdale managed to obtain the unsecured funds. The firm took systematic advantage of a computational shortcut in determining the value of borrowed securities. To save time and effort, borrowed securities were routinely valued as collateral without accounting for accrued coupon interest. By seeking to borrow large amounts of securities with high coupons and a short time left until the next coupon date, Drysdale could take maximum advantage of the difference in the amount of cash the borrowed security could be sold for (which included accrued interest) and the amount of cash collateral that needed to be posted against the borrowed security (which did not include accrued interest).

How the Unauthorized Positions Failed to Be Detected

Chase Manhattan allowed such a sizable position to be built up largely because it believed that the firm's capital was not at risk. The relatively inexperienced managers running the securities borrowing and lending operation were convinced they were simply acting as intermediaries between Drysdale and a large group of bond lenders. Through their inexperience, they failed both to realize that the wording in the borrowing agreements would most likely be found by a court to indicate that Chase was taking full responsibility for payments due against the securities borrowings and to realize the need for experienced legal counsel to review the contracts.

How the Unauthorized Positions Were Eventually Detected

There was some limit to the size of bond positions Drysdale could borrow, even given the assumption that the borrowings were fully collateralized. At some point, the size of the losses exceeded the amount of unauthorized borrowings Drysdale could raise and the firm had to declare bankruptcy.

Lessons Learned

The securities industry as a whole learned that it needed to make its methods for computing collateral value on bond borrowings more precise. Chase, and other firms that may have had similar control deficiencies, learned the need for a process that forced areas contemplating new product offerings to receive prior approval from representatives of the principal risk control functions within the firm.

Further Reading

Chapter 14 of Stigum (1989) gives a detailed description of the Chase/Drysdale incident, some prior misadventures in bond borrowing collateralization, and the subsequent market reforms.

Kidder Peabody

Incident

Between 1992 and 1994, Joseph Jett, head of the government bond trading desk at Kidder Peabody, entered into a series of trades that were incorrectly reported in the firm's accounting system, artificially inflating reported profits. When this was ultimately corrected in April 1994, $350 million in previously reported gains had to be reversed.

Result

Although Jett's trades had not resulted in any actual loss of cash for Kidder, the announcement of such a massive misreporting of earnings triggered a substantial loss of confidence in the competence of the firm's management by customers and General Electric, which owned Kidder. In October 1994, General Electric sold Kidder to Paine Webber, which dismantled the firm.

How the Unauthorized Positions Arose

A flaw in accounting for forward transactions in the computer system for government bond trading failed to take into account the present valuing of the forward. This enabled a trader purchasing a cash bond and delivering it at a forward price to book an instant profit. Over the period between booking and delivery, the profit would inevitably dissipate, since the cash position had a financing cost that was unmatched by any financing gain on the forward position.

Had the computer system been used as it was originally intended (for a handful of forward trades with only a few days to forward delivery), the size of error would have been small. However, the system permitted entry not only of contracted forward trades, but also of intended forward delivery of bonds to the U.S. Treasury, which did not actually need to be acted on, but could be rolled forward into further intentions to deliver in the future. Both the size of the forward positions and the length of the forward delivery period were constantly increased to magnify the accounting error. This permitted a classic Ponzi scheme of ever-mounting hypothetical profits covering the fact that previously promised profits never materialized.

Although it has never been completely clear how thoroughly Jett understood the full mechanics of the illusion, he had certainly worked out the link between his entry of forward trades and the recording of profit, and increasingly exploited the opportunity.

How the Unauthorized Positions Failed to Be Detected

Suspicions regarding the source of Jett's extraordinary profit performance were widespread throughout the episode. It was broadly perceived that no plausible account was being offered of a successful trading strategy that would explain the size of reported earnings. On several occasions, accusations were made that spelled out exactly the mechanism behind the inflated reporting. Jett seemed to have had a talent for developing explanations that succeeded in totally confusing everyone (including, perhaps, himself) as to what was going on. However, he was clearly aided and abetted by a management satisfied enough not to take too close a look at what seemed like a magical source of profits.

How the Unauthorized Positions Were Eventually Detected

Large increases in the size of his reported positions and earnings eventually triggered a more thorough investigation of Jett's operation.

Lessons to Be Learned

Two lessons can be drawn from this: Always investigate a stream of large unexpected profits thoroughly and make sure you completely understand the source. Periodically review models and systems to see if changes in the way they are being used require changes in simplifying assumptions.

Further Reading

Jett has written a detailed account of the whole affair (see Jett 1999). However, his talent for obscurity remains and it is not possible to tell from his account just what he believes generated either his large profits or the subsequent losses. For an account of the mechanics of the deception, one must rely on the investigation conducted by Gary Lynch on behalf of Kidder. Summaries of this investigation can be found in Hansell (1997), Mayer (1995), and Weiss (1994).

Barings Bank

Incident

The incident involved the loss of roughly $1.25 billion due to the unauthorized trading activities during 1993 to 1995 of a single, relatively junior trader named Nick Leeson.

Result

The size of the losses relative to Barings Bank's capital along with potential additional losses on outstanding trades forced Barings into bankruptcy in February 1995.

How the Unauthorized Positions Arose

Leeson, who was supposed to be running a low-risk, limited return arbitrage business for Barings in Singapore, was actually taking increasingly large speculative positions in Japanese stocks and interest rate futures and options. He disguised his speculative position taking by reporting that he was taking the positions on behalf of fictitious customers. By booking the losses to these nonexistent customer accounts, he was able to manufacture fairly substantial reported profits for his own accounts, enabling him to earn a $720,000 bonus in 1994.

How the Unauthorized Positions Failed to Be Detected

A certain amount of credit must be given to Leeson's industriousness in perpetrating a deliberate fraud. He worked hard at creating false accounts and was able to exploit his knowledge of weaknesses in the firm's controls. However, anyone reading an account of the incident will have to give primary credit to the stupendous incompetence on the part of Barings' management, which ignored every known control rule and failed to act on myriad obvious indications of something being wrong. What is particularly amazing is that all those trades were carried out in exchange-traded markets that require immediate cash settlement of all positions, thereby severely limiting the ability to hide positions (although Leeson did even manage to get some false reporting past the futures exchange to reduce the amount of cash required).

The most blatant of management failures was an attempt to save money by allowing Leeson to function as head of trading and the back office at an isolated branch. Even when auditors' reports warned about the danger of allowing Leeson to settle his own trades, thereby depriving the firm of an independent check on his activities, Barings' management persisted in their folly. Equally damning was management's failure to inquire how a low-risk trading strategy was supposedly generating such a large profit. Even when covering these supposed customer losses on the exchanges required Barings to send massive amounts of cash to the Singapore branch, no inquires were launched as to the cause. A large part of this failure can be attributed to the very poor structuring of management information so that different risk control areas could be looking at reports that did not tie together. The funding area would see a report indicating that cash was required to cover losses of a customer, not the firm, thereby avoiding alarm bells about the trading losses. A logical consequence is that credit exposure to customers must be large since the supposed covering of customer losses would entail a loan from Barings to the customer. However, information provided to the credit risk area was not integrated with information provided to funding and showed no such credit extension.

How the Unauthorized Positions Were Eventually Detected

The size of losses Leeson was trying to cover up eventually got too overwhelming and he took flight, leaving behind an admission of irregularities.

Lessons to Be Learned

One might be tempted to say that the primary lesson is that there are limits to how incompetent you can be and still hope to manage a major financial firm. However, to try to take away something positive, the major lessons would be the absolute necessity of an independent trading back office, the need to make thorough inquiries about unexpected sources of profit (or loss), and the need to make thorough inquiries about any large unanticipated movement of cash.

Further Reading

A concise and excellent summary of the Barings case constitutes Chapter 10 of Chew (1996). Chapter 11 of Mayer (1997) contains less insight on the causes, but is strong on the financial and political maneuvers required to avoid serious damage to the financial system from the Barings failure. Leeson has written a full-length book that appears

to be reasonably honest as to how he evaded detection (Leeson 1996). Fay (1996) and Rawnsley (1995) are also full-length accounts.

Allied Irish Bank (AIB)

Incident

John Rusnak, a currency option trader in charge of a very small trading book in AIB's Allfirst First Maryland Bancorp subsidiary, entered into massive unauthorized trades during the period 1997 through 2002, ultimately resulting in $691 million in losses.

Result

This resulted in a major blow to AIB's reputation and stock price.

How the Unauthorized Positions Arose

Rusnak was supposed to be running a small arbitrage between foreign exchange (FX) options and FX spot and forward markets. He was actually running large outright positions and disguising them from management.

How the Unauthorized Positions Failed to Be Detected

To quote the investigating report, "Mr. Rusnak was unusually clever and devious." He invented imaginary trades that offset his real trades, making his trading positions appear small. He persuaded back-office personnel not to check these bogus trades. He obtained cash to cover his losses by selling deep-in-the-money options, which provided cash up front in exchange for a high probability of needing to pay out even more cash at a later date, and covered up his position by offsetting these real trades with further imaginary trades. He entered false positions into the firm's system for calculating value-at-risk (VaR) to mislead managers about the size of his positions.

In many ways, Rusnak's pattern of behavior was a close copy of Nick Leeson's at Barings, using similar imaginary transactions to cover up real ones. Rusnak operated without Leeson's advantage of running his own back office, but had the offsetting advantage that he was operating in an over-the-counter market in which there was not an immediate need to put up cash against losses. He also was extremely modest in the amount of false profit he claimed so he did not set off the warning flags of large unexplained profits from small operations that Leeson and

Jett at Kidder Peabody had triggered in their desire to collect large bonuses.

Like Barings, AIB's management and risk control units demonstrated a fairly startling level of incompetence in failing to figure out that something was amiss. AIB at least has the excuse that Rusnak's business continued to look small and insignificant, so it never drew much management attention. However, the scope and length of time over which Rusnak's deception continued provided ample opportunity for even the most minimal level of controls to catch up with him.

The most egregious was the back office's failure to confirm all trades. Rusnak succeeded in convincing back-office personnel that not all of these trades needed to be confirmed. He relied partly on an argument that trades whose initial payments offset one another didn't really need to be checked since they did not give rise to net immediate cash flow, ignoring the fact that the purported trades had different terms and hence significant impact on future cash flows. He relied partly on booking imaginary trades with counterparties in the Asian time zone, making confirmation for U.S.-based back-office staff a potentially unpleasant task involving middle-of-the-night phone calls, perhaps making it easier to persuade them that this work was not really necessary. He also relied on arguments that costs should be cut by weakening or eliminating key controls.

Once this outside control was missing, the way was opened for the ongoing manipulation of trading records. Auditors could have caught this, but the spot audits performed used far too small a sample. Suspicious movements in cash balances, daily trading profit and loss (P&L), sizes of gross positions, and levels of daily turnover were all ignored by Rusnak's managers through a combination of inexperience in FX options and overreliance on trust in Rusnak's supposedly excellent character as a substitute for vigilant supervision. His management was too willing to withhold information from control functions and too compliant with Rusnak's bullying of operations personnel as part of a general culture of hostility toward control staff. This is precisely the sort of front-office pressure that reduces support staff independence.

How the Unauthorized Positions Were Eventually Detected

In December 2001, a back-office supervisor noticed trade tickets that did not have confirmations attached. When informed that the back-office personnel did not believe all trades required confirmations, he insisted that confirmation be sought for existing unconfirmed trades. Although it took some time for the instructions to be carried out, when they finally were carried out in early February 2002, despite some efforts by Rusnak to forge written confirmations and bully the back office into not seeking verbal confirmations, his fraud was brought to light within a few days.

Lessons to Be Learned

This incident does not provide many new lessons beyond the lessons that should already have been learned from Barings. This case does emphasize the need to avoid engaging in small ventures in which the firm lacks any depth of expertise—there is simply too much reliance on the knowledge and probity of a single individual.

On the positive side, the investigative report on this fraud has provided risk control units throughout the financial industry with a set of delicious quotes that are sure to be trotted out anytime they feel threatened by cost-cutting measures or front-office bullying and lack of cooperation. The following are a few choice samples from Ludwig (2002):

- When one risk control analyst questioned why a risk measurement system was taking market inputs from a front-office-controlled system rather than from an independent source, she was told that AIB "would not pay for a $10,000 data feed from Reuters to the back office."

- When questioned about confirmations, "Mr. Rusnak became angry. He said he was making money for the bank, and that if the back office continued to question everything he did, they would drive him to quit. . . . Mr. Rusnak's supervisor warned that if Mr. Rusnak left the bank, the loss of his profitable trading would force job cuts in the back office."

- "When required, Mr. Rusnak was able to use a strong personality to bully those who questioned him, particularly in Operations." His supervisors "tolerated numerous instances of severe friction between Mr. Rusnak and the back-office staff."

- Rusnak's supervisor "discouraged outside control groups from gaining access to information in his area and reflexively supported Mr. Rusnak whenever questions about his trading arose."

- "[I]n response to general efforts to reduce expense and increase revenues, the Allfirst treasurer permitted the weakening or elimination of key controls for which he was responsible. . . . Mr. Rusnak was able to manipulate this concern for additional cost cutting into his fraud."

Further Reading

I have relied heavily on the very thorough report issued by Ludwig (2002).

Union Bank of Switzerland (UBS)

Incident

This incident involves losses of between $400 million and $700 million in equity derivatives during 1997, which appear to have been exacerbated by lack of internal controls. A loss of $700 million during 1998 was due to a large position in Long-Term Capital Management (LTCM).

Result

The 1997 losses forced UBS into a merger on unfavorable terms with Swiss Bank Corporation (SBC) at the end of 1997. The 1998 losses came after that merger.

Were the Positions Unauthorized?

Less is known about the UBS disaster than the other incidents discussed in this chapter. Even the size of the losses has never been fully disclosed. Considerable controversy exists about whether the 1997 losses just reflected poor decision making or unlucky outcomes or whether an improper control structure led to positions that management would not have authorized. The 1998 losses were the result of a position that certainly had been approved by the UBS management, but evidence suggests that it failed to receive adequate scrutiny from the firm's risk controllers and that it was not adequately disclosed to the SBC management that took over the firm.

What seems uncontroversial is that the equity derivatives business was being run without the degree of management oversight that would be normally expected in a firm of the size and sophistication of UBS, but there is disagreement about how much this situation contributed to the losses. The equity derivatives department was given an unusual degree of independence within the firm with little oversight by, or sharing of information with, the corporate risk managers. The person with senior risk management authority for the department doubled as head of quantitative analytics. As head of analytics, he was both a contributor to the business decisions he was responsible for reviewing and had his compensation tied to trading results, which are both violations of the fundamental principles of independent oversight.

The equity derivative losses appear to have been primarily due to four factors:

1. A change in British tax laws, which impacted the value of some long-dated stock options.

2. A large position in Japanese bank warrants, which was inadequately hedged against a significant drop in the underlying stocks.

3. An overly aggressive valuation of long-dated options on equity baskets, utilizing correlation assumptions that were out of line with those used by competitors.

4. Losses on other long-dated basket options, which may have been due to modeling deficiencies.

The first two transactions were ones where UBS had similar positions to many of its competitors so it would be difficult to accuse the firm of excessive risk taking, although its Japanese warrant positions appear to have been unreasonably large relative to competitors. The last two problems appear to have been more unique to UBS. Many competitors made accusations that its prices for trades were off the market.

The losses related to LTCM came as the result of a position personally approved by Mathis Cabiallavetta, the UBS CEO, so they were certainly authorized in one sense. However, accusations have been made that the trades were approved without adequate review by risk control areas and were never properly represented in the firm's risk management systems. Although about 40% of the exposure represented a direct investment in LTCM that had large potential profits to weigh against the risk, about 60% of the exposure was an option written on the value of LTCM shares. However, there was no effective way in which such an option could be risk managed given the illiquidity of LTCM shares and restrictions that LTCM placed on UBS delta hedging the position.

The imbalance in risk/reward trade-off for an option that was that difficult to risk manage had caused other investment banks to reject the proposed trade. UBS appears to have entered into the option because of its desire for a direct investment in LTCM, which LTCM tied to agreement to the option. Agreeing to this type of bundled transaction can certainly be a legitimate business decision, but it is unclear whether the full risk of the option had been analyzed by UBS or whether stress tests of the two positions taken together had been performed.

Lessons Learned

This incident emphasizes the need for independent risk oversight.

Further Reading

The fullest account of the equity derivative losses is contained in a book by Schutz (2000), which contains many lurid accusations about improper dealings between the equity derivatives department and senior management of the firm. Schutz has been accused of inaccuracy in some of these charges—see Derivative Strategies (1998) for details. There is also a good summary in the January 31, 1998, issue of the *Economist*.

A good account of the LTCM transaction is Shirreff (1998). Lowenstein (2000), an account of the LTCM collapse, also covers the UBS story in some detail.

Société Générale

Incident

In January 2008, Société Générale reported trading losses of $7.1 billion that the firm attributed to unauthorized activity by a junior trader, Jérôme Kerviel.

Result

The large loss severely damaged Société Générale's reputation and required it to raise a large amount of new capital.

How the Unauthorized Positions Arose

In this section and the next, I am drawing primarily on the Société Générale Special Committee of the Board of Directors Report to Shareholders of May 22, 2008 (I'll abbreviate references to it as SpecComm) and its accompanying Mission Green Report of the Société Générale General Inspection Department (I'll abbreviate it as MG).

Kerviel took very large unauthorized positions in equities and exchange-traded futures, beginning in July 2005 and ending when his concealment of positions was uncovered in January 2008. His primary method for concealing these unauthorized positions was to enter fictitious transactions that offset the risk and P&L of his true trades. The fictitious nature of these transactions was hidden mostly by

creating transactions with forward start dates and then, relying on his knowledge of when control personnel would seek confirmation of a forward-dated trade, canceling the trade prior to the date that confirmation would be sought (Kerviel had previously worked in the middle office of the firm, which may have provided him with particular insight into the actions of control personnel). Not surprisingly, given his need to constantly replace canceled fictitious transactions with new ones, there were a large number of these trades, 947 transactions according to MG Focus 4. How was Kerviel able to enter this many fictitious trades before discovery of his fraud?

How the Unauthorized Positions Failed to Be Detected

Trade Cancellation There was no procedure in place that required control functions to confirm information entered for a trade that was then canceled and Kerviel knew this, nor was there a system in place for red-flagging an unusual level of trade cancellations. SpecComm, point 10, notes that the back and middle office gave "priority to the correct execution of trades" and showed "an absence of an adequate degree of sensitivity to fraud risks." The head of equity derivatives at a European bank is quoted as saying, "If he was able to cancel a trade and book a new one before the confirm was sent out, the clock [for obtaining confirmation] would start again. But at our bank, we actively monitor cancel-and-correct activity for each trader, which is standard practice at most institutions. It would stick out like a sore thumb if you had one trader who was perpetually cancelling and correcting trades" (Davies 2008). Hugo Banziger, chief risk officer of Deutsche Bank, is quoted as saying, "Routine IT controls can monitor unusual trades put on and cancelled—this is a particularly effective control mechanism" (Davies 2008). It certainly appears from the account in MG that no such procedures were in place at Société Générale, and even the inquiry to confirm the counterparty on a canceled trade that eventually led to Kerviel's downfall in January 2008 appears to have been a matter of chance (MG Focus 6).

Supervision Kerviel's immediate manager resigned in January 2007. For two and a half months, until the manager was replaced, Kerviel's positions were validated by his desk's senior trader. Day-to-day supervision of Kerviel by the new manager, who started in April 2007, was weak (SpecComm, point 9; MG, page 6). While Kerviel had begun his fraudulent activities prior to January 2007, the size of his unauthorized positions increased explosively at this time (MG Focus 10).

Trading Assistant The trading assistant who worked with Kerviel in entering trades, who would have the most immediate potential access to seeing how he was manipulating the trading system, may have been operating in collusion with Kerviel. This has not been confirmed (MG, page 3, notes that this is an allegation under investigation by the courts), but, in any case, the trading assistant appears to have accepted Kerviel's directions without questioning. This would have helped Kerviel's credibility with control functions, since the trading assistant reported to a control function and was the primary point of contact of other control functions regarding Kerviel's positions (MG, page 4).

Vacation Policy The normal precaution of forcing a trader to take two consecutive weeks of vacation in a year, during which time his positions would be managed by another trader, was not followed (MG, page 7). This control could easily have caused the collapse of a scheme based on constant rolling forward of fraudulent trading entries.

Gross Positions There were no limits or other monitoring of Kerviel's gross positions, only his net positions (Spec-Comm, point 10, notes the "lack of certain controls liable to identify the fraudulent mechanisms, such as the control of the positions' nominal value"). Had gross positions been monitored, this would have revealed the abnormally large size of his activities and might have raised suspicions as to what the purpose was of such large positions. Henning Giescke, chief risk officer of the UniCredit Group, is quoted as saying, "In high-volume businesses, banks have to look at gross as well as net position. This allows an institution to look at each trader's book to see whether they are taking too much risk, regardless of whether the net position is neutral" (Davies 2008). The chief risk officer of a UK bank is quoted as saying, "To effectively manage basis risk, you have to be able to see how the outright position—the notional—performs against the hedge. It is inconceivable such a sophisticated institution could have missed this. Modern systems are able to stress-test positions, and to do this you automatically need the notional amount" (Davies 2008). Kerviel's unusually high amount of brokerage commissions (MG, page 6), related to his high level of gross positions, could also have provided a warning sign.

Cash and Collateral The use of fictitious transactions to conceal positions will often create positions of unusual size in cash and required collateral—since the fictitious trades do not generate any cash or collateral movements, there is nothing to balance out the cash and collateral needs of the real trades. This provides good opportunities for fraud detection. The reason that Société Générale's control functions did not respond to these clues is that cash and collateral reports and inquiry procedures lacked sufficient granularity to detect unusual movements at the level of a single trader (MG Focus 13).

P&L Concealment of trading positions will not always lead to unusual earnings patterns. A trader who is trying to conceal losses may be satisfied simply to show a small positive P&L. But some fraudulent traders will show unusual profits, either because their unauthorized positions have resulted in large gains for which they want to be compensated or because their success in hiding losing positions encourages them to also claim some phantom gains to fund bonuses. Kerviel was reporting trading gains in excess of levels his authorized position taking could have accounted for, and this should have given his management and the control functions a warning sign to investigate closely the source of his earnings (MG Focus 12). These warning signs were apparently not pursued.

How the Unauthorized Positions Were Eventually Detected

One of Kerviel's fictitious trades was identified as fabricated by control personnel as part of routine monitoring of positions, leading to a thorough investigation. Kerviel's attempts to deflect the inquiry by forging confirmations proved fruitless. It appears that it was just a matter of chance that this particular inquiry led to identification of the fraud.

Lessons to Be Learned

What new lessons can we draw from this control failure? From one point of view, the answer is not much—Kerviel's methods for eluding scrutiny of his positions were very close to those used in previous incidents such as those of Kidder Peabody, Barings, and Allied Irish Bank. But, from another viewpoint, we can learn quite a bit, since clear patterns are emerging when we look across episodes.

The obvious lessons for control personnel are to tighten procedures that may lead to detection of fictitious trade entries. The specific lessons follow.

Trade Cancellation Institute systems for monitoring patterns of trade cancellation. Flag any trader who appears to be using an unusually high number of such cancellations. Any trader flagged should have a reasonably large sample of the cancellations checked to make sure that they represent real trades by checking details of the transaction with the counterparty.

Supervision Control personnel should be aware of situations in which traders are being supervised by temporary or new managers. Tightened control procedures should be employed.

Trading Assistant Control personnel must remember that even in situations where there is no suspicion of dishonesty, trading assistants are often under intense pressure from the traders with whom they work closely. Their job performance ratings and future career paths often depend on the trader, regardless of official reporting lines. The greater prestige, experience, and possible bullying tactics of a trader can often convince a trading assistant to see things from the trader's viewpoint. Other control personnel must be cognizant of these realities and not place too much reliance on the presumed independence of the trading assistant.

Vacation Policy Rules for mandatory time away from work should be enforced.

Gross Positions Gross positions must be monitored and highlighted in control reports. This is particularly important since unusually high ratios of gross to net positions are a warning sign of potentially inadequately measured basis risk as well as a possible flag for unauthorized activities. The Kidder Peabody and Allied Irish Bank frauds could also have been uncovered by investigating unusually high ratios of gross to net trading.

Cash and Collateral Cash and collateral requirements should be monitored down to the individual trader level. Better monitoring of cash and credit flows would have also been instrumental in uncovering the Barings and Allied Irish Bank frauds.

P&L Any patterns of P&L that are unusual relative to expectations need to be identified and investigated by both management and the control functions. Identification

of unusual patterns can be comparisons to historical experience, to budgeted targets, and to the performance of traders with similar levels of authority. Investigation of suspicious earnings patterns could also have led to earlier discovery of the Kidder Peabody and Barings frauds.

Further Reading

I have relied primarily on the Société Générale Special Committee of the Board of Directors Report to Shareholders (2008) and its accompanying Société Générale Mission Green Report (2008).

Other Cases

Other disasters involving unauthorized positions are covered more briefly, because they had less of an impact on the firm involved, because it is harder to uncover details on what occurred, or because they do not have any lessons to teach beyond those of the cases already discussed:

- Toshihida Iguchi of Daiwa Bank's New York office lost $1.1 billion trading Treasury bonds between 1984 and 1995. He hid his losses and made his operation appear to be quite profitable by forging trading slips, which enabled him to sell without authorization bonds held in customer accounts to produce funds he could claim were part of his trading profit. His fraud was aided by a situation similar to Nick Leeson's at Barings—Iguchi was head of both trading and the back-office support function. In addition to the losses, Daiwa lost its license to trade in the United States, but this was primarily due to its failure to promptly disclose the fraud once senior executives of the firm learned of it. A more detailed account of this by Rob Jameson of ERisk can be found on their website, www.erisk.com.

- The Sumitomo Corporation of Japan lost $2.6 billion in a failed attempt by Yasuo Hamanaka, a senior trader, to corner the world's copper market—that is, to drive up prices by controlling a large portion of the available supply. Sumitomo management claimed that Hamanaka had employed fraudulent means in hiding the size of his positions from them. Hamanaka claimed that he had disclosed the positions to senior management. Hamanaka was sent to jail for his actions. The available details are sketchy, but some can be found in Dwyer (1996), *Asiaweek* (1996), Kooi (1996), and McKay (1999).

- Askin Capital Management and Granite Capital, hedge funds that invested in mortgage securities, went bankrupt in 1994 with losses of $600 million. It was revealed that David Askin, the manager of the funds, was valuing positions with his own marks substituted for dealer quotes and using these position values in reports to investors in the funds and in marketing materials to attract new clients. For a brief discussion, see Mayer (1997).

- Merrill Lynch reportedly lost $350 million in trading mortgage securities in 1987, due to risk reporting that used a 13-year duration for all securities created from a pool of 30-year mortgages. Although this duration is roughly correct for an undivided pool of 30-year mortgages, the correct duration is 30 years when the interest-only (IO) part is sold and the principal-only (PO) part is kept, as Merrill was doing. See Crouhy, Galai, and Mark (2001).

- National Westminster Bank in 1997 reported a loss on interest rate caps and swaptions of about $140 million. The losses were attributed to trades dating back to 1994 and had been masked by deliberate use by traders of incorrect volatility inputs for less liquid maturities. The loss of confidence in management caused by this incident may have contributed to NatWest's sale to the Royal Bank of Scotland. I have heard from market sources that the traders were taking advantage of the middle-office saving costs by checking only a sample of volatility marks against market sources, although it is unclear how the traders were able to determine in advance which quotes would be checked. A more detailed account is Wolfe (2001).

- The large Swiss bank UBS in 2011 reported a loss of $2.3 billion due to unauthorized trading by Kweku Adoboli, a relatively junior equity trader. This incident cost the CEO of UBS his job. Adoboli's ability to enter into unauthorized trades appears to have been engineered by means very similar to those of Kerviel in the Société Générale incident. He took advantage of intimate knowledge of back-office control procedures to identify a loophole. Trades with forward settlement greater than 15 days were not being immediately confirmed with counterparties; confirmation was delayed until closer to the settlement date. If the trade was canceled prior to the date on which the confirmation would have been confirmed, no confirmation ever took

place. Adoboli appears to have been able to utilize this loophole to disguise his real positions by entering bogus offsetting forward positions and then canceling the fictitious positions prior to the date they would have been confirmed, replacing them with new fictitious forwards. For this to have gone on for any period of time, there must have also been flaws in UBS's monitoring of excessive cancellations. Due to an ongoing criminal prosecution against Adoboli at the time of my writing, not many public details are available. Wilson (2011) is a good summary of what is known about the mechanics of the unauthorized trades, and Broom (2011) summarizes the devastating impact the revelation of this faulty control environment had on UBS.

DISASTERS DUE TO LARGE MARKET MOVES

We will now look at financial disasters that were not caused by incorrect position information, but were caused by unanticipated market moves. The first question that should be asked is: How is a disaster possible if positions are known? No matter what strategy is chosen, as losses start to mount beyond acceptable bounds, why aren't the positions closed out? The answer is lack of liquidity. We will focus on this aspect of these disasters.

Long-Term Capital Management (LTCM)

The case we will consider at greatest length is that of the large hedge fund managed by Long-Term Capital Management (LTCM), which came close to bankruptcy in 1998. In many ways, it represents an ideal example for this type of case since all of its positions were marked to a market value daily, the market values were supplied by the dealers on the other end of each trade, no accusations have been made of anyone at LTCM providing misleading information about positions taken, and the near failure came in the midst of some of the largest market moves in recent memory.

To review the facts, LTCM had been formed in 1994 by about a dozen partners. Many of these partners had previously worked together at Salomon Brothers in a highly successful proprietary trading group. Over the period from 1994 until early 1998, the LTCM fund produced quite spectacular returns for its investors. From the beginning, the partners made clear that they would be highly secretive about the particulars of their investment portfolio, even by the standard of other hedge funds. (Since hedge funds are open only to wealthy investors and cannot be publicly offered the way mutual funds are, they are not subject to legal requirements to disclose their holdings.)

Within the firm, however, the management style favored sharing information openly, and essentially every investment decision was made by all the partners acting together, an approach that virtually eliminates the possibility of a rogue trader making decisions based on information concealed from other members of the firm. Although it is true that outside investors in the fund did not have access to much information beyond the month-end valuation of its assets and the track record of its performance, it is equally true that the investors knew these rules prior to their decision to invest. Since the partners who managed the fund were such strong believers in the fund that they had invested most of their net worth in it (several even borrowed to invest more than their net worth), their incentives were closely aligned with investors (in other words, there was little room for moral hazard). If anything, the concentration of partner assets in the fund should have led to more risk-averse decision making than might have been optimal for outside investors, who invested only a small portion of their wealth in the fund, with the exception of UBS.

In fact, even if investors had been given access to more information, there is little they could have done with it, since they were locked into their investments for extended time periods (generally, three years). This reflected the basic investment philosophy of LTCM, which was to locate trading opportunities that represented what the partners believed were temporary disruptions in price relationships due to short-term market pressures, which were almost certain to be reversed over longer time periods. To take advantage of such opportunities, they needed to know they had access to patient capital that would not be withdrawn if markets seemed to be temporarily going against them. This also helped to explain why LTCM was so secretive about its holdings. These were not quick in-and-out trades, but long-term holdings, and they needed to prevent other firms from learning the positions and trading against them.

The following are two examples of the types of positions the LTCM fund was taking:

1. LTCM was long U.S. interest rate swaps and short U.S. government bonds at a time when these spreads were at historically high levels. Over the life of the trade, this position will make money as long as the average spread between the London Interbank Offered Rate (LIBOR) at which swaps are reset and the repurchase agreement (RP) rates at which government bonds are funded is not higher than the spread at which the trade was entered into. Over longer time periods, the range for the average of LIBOR-RP spreads is not that wide, but in the short run, swap spreads can show large swings based on relative investor demand for the safety of governments versus the higher yield of corporate bonds (with corporate bond issuers then demanding interest rate swaps to convert fixed debt to floating debt).

2. LTCM sold equity options at historically high implied volatilities. Over the life of the trade, this position will make money if the actual volatility is lower than the implied volatility, but in the short run, investor demand for protection against stock market crashes can raise implied volatilities to very high levels. Perold (1999a) presents further analysis of why LTCM viewed these trades as excellent long-term investments and presents several other examples of positions it entered into.

One additional element was needed to obtain the potential returns LTCM was looking for. LTCM needed to be able to finance positions for longer terms in order to be able to ensure there was no pressure on them to sell positions before they reached the price relationships LTCM was waiting for. However, the banks and investment banks who financed hedge fund positions were the very competitors that they least wanted to share information on holdings with. How were they to persuade firms to take credit risk without knowing much about the trading positions of the hedge fund?

To understand why the lenders were comfortable in doing this, we need to digress a moment into how credit works in a futures exchange. A futures exchange represents the extreme of being willing to lend without knowledge of the borrower. Someone who purchases, for example, a bond for future delivery needs to deposit only a small percentage of the agreed purchase price as margin and does not need to disclose anything about one's financial condition. The futures exchange is counting on the nature of the transaction itself to provide confidence that money will not be lost in the transaction. This is because anytime the value of the bond falls, the purchaser is required to immediately provide added margin to fully cover the decline in value. If the purchaser does not do so, the position is closed out without delay. Loss is possible only if the price has declined so much since the last time the price fell and margin was added that the incremental price drop exceeds the amount of initial margin or if closing out the option results in a large price move. The probability of this occurring is kept low by setting initial margins high enough, restricting the size of position that can be taken by any one investor, and designing futures contracts to cover sufficiently standardized products to ensure enough liquidity that the closing out of a trade will not cause a big price jump.

LTCM wanted to deal in over-the-counter markets as well as on futures exchanges partly because it wanted to deal in some contracts more individually tailored than those available on futures exchanges and partly because of the position size restrictions of exchanges. However, the mechanism used to assure lenders in over-the-counter markets is similar—there is a requirement to cover declines in market value by immediately putting up cash. If a firm fails to put up the cash, then positions are closed out. LTCM almost always negotiated terms that avoided posting the initial margin. Lenders were satisfied with the lack of initial margin based on the size of the LTCM fund's equity, the track record of its excellent returns, and the firm's recognized investment management skills. Lenders retained the option of demanding initial margin if fund equity fell too much.

This dependence on short-term swings in valuation represented a potential Achilles' heel for LTCM's long-term focused investment strategy. Because the firm was seeking opportunities where market pressures were causing deviation from long-run relationships, a strong possibility always existed that these same market pressures would push the deviation even further. LTCM would then immediately need to come up with cash to fund the change in market valuation. This would not be a problem if some of the trades were moving in its favor at the same time as others were moving against it, since LTCM would receive cash on upswings in value to balance having to put up cash on downswings (again, the same structure as exchange-traded futures). However, if many of its trades were to move against it in tandem, LTCM would need to raise cash quickly, either from investors or by cutting positions.

In the actual events of August and September 1998, this is exactly what led to LTCM's rapid downfall. The initial trigger was a combination of the Russian debt default of August, which unsettled the markets, and the June 1998 decision by Salomon Brothers to liquidate proprietary positions it was holding, which were similar to many of those held by LTCM. The LTCM fund's equity began to decline precipitously from $4.1 billion as of the end of July 1998, and it was very reluctant to cut positions in a turbulent market in which any large position sale could easily move the valuations even further against it. This left the option of seeking new equity from investors. LTCM pursued this path vigorously, but the very act of doing so created two perverse effects. First, rumors of LTCM's predicament caused competitors to drive market prices even further against what they guessed were LTCM's positions, in anticipation of LTCM being forced to unload the positions at distressed prices. Second, to persuade potential investors to provide new money in the midst of volatile markets, LTCM was forced to disclose information about the actual positions it held. As competitors learned more about the actual positions, their pressure on market prices in the direction unfavorable to LTCM intensified.

As market valuations continued to move against LTCM and the lack of liquidity made it even more unlikely that reducing positions would be a viable plan, it became increasingly probable that in the absence of a truly large infusion of new equity, the LTCM fund would be bankrupt. Its creditors started to prepare to close out LTCM's positions, but quickly came to fear that they were so large and the markets were so illiquid that the creditors would suffer serious losses in the course of doing so. The lenders were also concerned that the impact of closing out these positions would depress values in the already fragile markets and thereby cause considerable damage to other positions held by the creditors and other investment firms they were financing.

Ultimately, 14 of the largest creditors, all major investment banks or commercial banks with large investment banking operations, contributed a fresh $3.65 billion in equity investment into the LTCM fund to permit the firm to keep operating and allow for a substantial time period in which to close out positions. In return, the creditors received substantial control over fund management. The existing investors had their investments valued at the then current market value of $400 million, so they had only a 10% share in the positions of the fund. Although some of the partners remained employed to help wind down investments, it was the consortium of 14 creditors who now exercised control and insisted on winding down all positions.

As a result, the markets calmed down. By 2000, the fund had been wound down with the 14 creditors having recovered all of the equity they had invested and having avoided any losses on the LTCM positions they had held at the time of the bailout. This outcome lends support to two propositions: LTCM was largely right about the long-term values underlying its positions, and the creditors were right to see the primary problem as one of liquidity, which required patience to ride out.

Please note that the bailout was not primarily a rescue of LTCM's investors or management, but a rescue of LTCM's creditors by a concerted action of these creditors. Even recently, I continue to encounter the view that the bailout involved the use of U.S. government funds, helped the LTCM investors and management avoid the consequences of their mistakes, and therefore contributed to an attitude that some firms are "too big to fail" and so can afford to take extra risks because they can count on the government absorbing some of their losses.

I do not think evidence is available to support any of these claims. Interested readers can form their own conclusions by looking at the detailed account of the negotiations on the rescue package in Lowenstein (2000). An opposing viewpoint can be found in Shirreff (2000). The only government involvement was some coordination by the Federal Reserve, acting out of legitimate concern for the potential impact on the financial markets. The LTCM creditors took a risk by investing money in the fund, but did so in their own self-interest, believing (correctly, as it turns out) that they were thereby lowering their total risk of loss. LTCM's investors and managers had little left to lose at the point of the bailout since they could not lose more than their initial investment. It is true that, without a rescue, the fund would have been liquidated, which would have almost certainly wiped out the remaining $400 million market value of the investors. However, in exchange for this rescue, they were able to retain only a 10% interest in the fund's positions, since the $3.65 billion in new investment was explicitly not being used to enable new trades, but only to wind down the existing positions.

LTCM management was certainly aware of the potential for short-term market movements to disrupt the fund's fundamental trading strategy of focusing on longer-term relationships. The firm tried to limit this risk by insisting

that its positions pass value-at-risk (VaR) tests based on whether potential losses over one month due to adverse market moves would reduce equity to unacceptable levels. Where LTCM seems to have fallen short of best practices was a failure to supplement VaR measures with a full set of stress test scenarios. It did run stress versions of VaR based on a higher than historical level of correlations, but it is doubtful that this offers the same degree of conservatism as a set of fully worked-through scenarios.

A lesson that all market participants have learned from the LTCM incident is that a stress scenario is needed to look at the impact of a competitor holding similar positions exiting the market, as when Salomon decided to cut back on proprietary trading. However, even by best practice standards of the time, LTCM should have constructed a stress test based on common economic factors that could cause impacts across its positions, such as a flight to quality by investors, which would widen all credit spreads, including swap spreads, and increase premiums on buying protection against stock market crashes, hence increasing option volatility.

Another point on which LTCM's risk management could be criticized is a failure to account for the illiquidity of its largest positions in its VaR or stress runs. LTCM knew that the position valuations it was receiving from dealers did not reflect the concentration of some of LTCM's positions, either because dealers were not taking liquidity into account in their marks or because each dealer knew only a small part of LTCM's total size in its largest positions.

Two other criticisms have been made of LTCM's management of risk with which I disagree. One is that a simple computation of leverage would have shown that LTCM's positions were too risky. However, leverage by itself is not an adequate measure of risk of default. It must be multiplied by volatility of the firm's assets. But this just gets us back to testing through VaR or stress scenarios. The second criticism is that LTCM showed unreasonable faith in the outcome of models. I see no evidence to support this claim. Major positions LTCM entered into—U.S. swap spreads to narrow, equity volatilities to decline—were ones that many proprietary position takers had entered into. For example, the bias in equity implied volatilities due to demand for downside protection by shareholders had long been widely recognized as a fairly certain profit opportunity for investors with long-enough time horizons. That some firms made more use of models to inform their trading judgments while others relied more on trader experience tells me nothing about the relative quality of their decision making.

Most of the focus of LTCM studies has been on the decision making of LTCM management and the losses of the investors. I believe this emphasis is misplaced. It is a fairly common occurrence, and to be expected, that investment funds will have severe drops in valuation. The bankruptcy of an investment fund does not ordinarily threaten the stability of the financial system the way the bankruptcy of a firm that makes markets or is a critical part of the payments system would. It just represents the losses of a small number of investors. Nor is there a major difference in consequences between bankruptcy and a large loss short of bankruptcy for an investment fund. It shouldn't matter to investors whether a fund in which they have invested $10 million goes bankrupt or a fund in which they have invested $30 million loses a third of its value. By contrast, losses short of bankruptcy hurt only the stockholders of a bank, whereas bankruptcy of a bank could hurt depositors and lead to loss of confidence in the banking system.

The reason that an LTCM failure came close to disrupting the financial markets and required a major rescue operation was its potential impact on the creditors to LTCM, so we need to take a closer look at their role in the story. In retrospect, the creditors to LTCM believed they had been too lax in their credit standards, and the incident triggered a major industry study of credit practices relating to trading counterparties (Counterparty Risk Management Policy Group 1999).

Some suggestions for improved practices, many of which are extensively addressed in this study, have been:

- A greater reluctance to allow trading without initial margin for counterparties whose principal business is investing and trading. A counterparty that has other substantial business lines—for example, auto manufacturing or retail banking—is unlikely to have all of its economic resources threatened by a large move in financial markets. However, a firm that is primarily engaged in these markets is vulnerable to illiquidity spreading from one market to another as firms close out positions in one market to meet margin calls in another market. For such firms, initial margin is needed as a cushion against market volatility.

- Factoring the potential costs of liquidating positions in an adverse market environment into estimates of

the price at which trades can be unwound. These estimates should be based on the size of positions as well as the general liquidity of the market. These potential liquidation costs should impact estimates of the amount of credit being extended and requirements for initial margin.

- A push for greater disclosure by counterparties of their trading strategies and positions. Reliance on historical records of return as an indicator of the volatility of a portfolio can be very misleading because it cannot capture the impact of changes in trading style. Increased allowance for liquidation costs of positions will be very inexact if the creditor only knows the positions that a counterparty holds with the creditor without knowing the impact of other positions held. To try to deal with counterparties' legitimate fears that disclosure of their positions will lead to taking advantage of this knowledge, creditors are implementing more stringent internal policies against the sharing of information between the firm's credit officers and the firm's traders.

- Better use of stress tests in assessing credit risk. To some extent, this involves using more extreme stresses than were previously used in measuring risk to reflect the increased market volatility that has been experienced in recent years. However, a major emphasis is also on more integration of market risk and credit risk stress testing to take into account overlap in risks. In the LTCM case, this would have required recognition by a creditor to LTCM that many of the largest positions being held by LTCM were also being held by other investment funds to which the firm had counterparty credit exposure, as well as by the firm's own proprietary traders. A full stress test would then look at the losses that would be incurred by a large market move and subsequent decrease in liquidity across all of these similar positions.

A complete account of the LTCM case covering all aspects of the history of the fund and its managers, the involvement of creditors, and the negotiations over its rescue can be found in Lowenstein (2000). The Harvard Business School case studies of Perold (1999a, 1999b) provide a detailed but concise analysis of the fund's investment strategy and the dilemma that it faced in August 1998.

Metallgesellschaft (MG)

The disaster at Metallgesellschaft (MG) reveals another aspect of liquidity management. In 1992, an American subsidiary of MG, Metallgesellschaft Refining and Marketing (MGRM), began a program of entering into long-term contracts to supply customers with gas and oil products at fixed costs and to hedge these contracts with short-term gas and oil futures. Although some controversy exists about how effective this hedging strategy was from a P&L standpoint, as we'll discuss in just a moment, the fundamental consequence of this strategy for liquidity management is certain. The futures being used to hedge were exchange-traded instruments requiring daily cash settlement. The long-term contracts with customers involved no such cash settlement. So no matter how effective the hedging strategy was, the consequence of a large downward move in gas and oil prices would be to require MGRM to pay cash against its futures positions that would be offset by money owed to MGRM by customers who would be paid in the future.

A properly designed hedge will reflect both the cash paid and the financing cost of that cash during the period until the customer payment is due and hence will be effective from a P&L standpoint. However, the funding must still be obtained, which can lead to funding liquidity risk. Such cash needs must be planned in advance. Limits need to be set on positions based on the amount of cash shortfall that can be funded.

It appears that MGRM did not communicate to its parent company the possible need for such funding. In 1993, when a large decrease in gas and oil prices had resulted in funding needs of around $900 million, the MG parent responded by closing down the futures positions, leaving unhedged exposure to gas and oil price increases through the customer contracts. Faced with this open exposure, MG negotiated unwinds of these contracts at unfavorable terms. It may be that MG, with lack of advance warning as to possible cash needs, responded to the demand for cash as a sign that the trading strategy was deeply flawed; if only Barings' management had reacted similarly.

As mentioned earlier, the MG incident spurred considerable debate as to whether MGRM's trading strategy was reasonable or fundamentally flawed. Most notably, Culp and Miller (1995a) wrote an article defending the reasonableness of the strategy, and Mello and Parsons (1995) wrote an article attacking the Culp and Miller conclusions, which were then defended by Culp and Miller (1995b). Although it is difficult to settle the factual arguments about the particular events in the MG case, I believe the following lessons can be drawn:

- It is often a key component of a market maker's business strategy to extend available liquidity in a market. This requires the use of shorter-term hedges against longer-term contracts. Experience shows that this can be successfully carried out when proper risk controls are applied.

- The uncertainty of roll cost is a key risk for strategies involving shorter-term hedges against longer-term risk. This requires the use of valuation reserves based on conservative assumptions of future roll cost. MGRM does not appear to have utilized valuation reserves; it just based its valuation on the historical averages of roll costs.

- A firm running short-term hedges against longer-term risk requires the flexibility to choose the shorter-term hedge that offers the best trade-off between risk and reward. It may legitimately choose to follow a hedging strategy other than a theoretical minimum variance hedge, or choose not to hedge with the longest future available, based on liquidity considerations, or take into account the expectation of positive roll cost as part of potential return. It is not reasonable to conclude, as Mello and Parsons (1995) do, that these choices indicate that the firm is engaged in pure speculation rather than hedging. At the same time, regardless of a firm's conclusions about probable return, its assessment of risk should include valuation reserves, as in the previous point, and volume limits based on reasonable stress testing of assumptions.

DISASTERS DUE TO THE CONDUCT OF CUSTOMER BUSINESS

In this section, we focus on disasters that did not involve any direct financial loss to the firm, but were completely a matter of reputational risk due to the conduct of customer business.

Bankers Trust (BT)

The classic case of this type is the Bankers Trust (BT) incident of 1994, when BT was sued by Procter & Gamble (P&G) and Gibson Greetings. Both P&G and Gibson claimed that they had suffered large losses in derivatives trades they had entered into with BT due to being misled by BT as to the nature of the positions. These were trades on which BT had little market or credit risk, since it had hedged the market risk on them with other derivatives and there was no credit issue of P&G or Gibson being unable to pay the amount they owed. However, the evidence uncovered in the course of legal discovery for these lawsuits was severely damaging to BT's reputation for fair business dealing, led to the resignation of the firm's CEO, and ultimately had such negative consequences for the bank's ability to do business that it was forced into an acquisition by Deutsche Bank, which essentially amounted to a dismemberment of the firm.

The exact terms of these derivative trades were quite complex and are not essential to understanding the incident. Interested readers are referred to Chew (1996, Chapter 2) for details. The key point is that the trades offered P&G and Gibson a reasonably probable but small reduction in funding expenses in exchange for a potentially large loss under some less probable circumstances. P&G and Gibson had been entering into such trades for several years prior to 1994 with good results. The derivatives were not tailored to any particular needs of P&G or Gibson in the sense that the circumstances under which the derivatives would lose them money were not designed to coincide with cases in which other P&G or Gibson positions would be making money. Their objective was just to reduce expected funding costs. Since the only way to reduce costs in some cases is to raise them in others, P&G and Gibson can be presumed to have understood that they could lose money under some economic circumstances. On what basis could they claim that BT had misled them?

One element that established some prima facie suspicion of BT was the sheer complexity of the structures. It was hard to believe that BT's clients started out with any particular belief about whether there was a small enough probability of loss in such a structure to be comfortable entering into it. BT would have had to carefully explain all the intricacies of the payoffs to the clients for them to be fully informed.

Since it was quite clear that the exact nature of the structures hadn't been tailored to meet client needs, why had BT utilized so complex a design? The most probable reason was that the structures were designed to be complex enough to make it difficult for clients to comparison shop the pricing to competitor firms. However, this also made the clients highly dependent on BT on an ongoing basis. If they wanted to unwind the position, they couldn't count on getting a competitive quote from another firm.

BT claimed that it had adequately explained all the payoffs and risks to P&G and Gibson. But then came the discovery phase of the lawsuit. BT, like all trading firms, recorded all phone lines of traders and marketers as a means of resolving disputes about verbal contracts. However, this recording also picked up internal conversations among BT personnel. When subpoenaed, they produced evidence of BT staff boasting of how thoroughly they had fooled the clients as to the true value of the trades and how little the clients understood the true risks. Further, the internal BT recordings showed that price quotes to P&G and Gibson were being manipulated to mislead them. At first, they were given valuations of the trades that were much too high to mask the degree of profit BT was able to book up front. Later, they were given valuations that were too low because this was BT's bid at which to buy back the trade or swap it into a new trade offering even more profit to BT. For more details on what was revealed in the recordings, see Holland and Himelstein (1995).

The BT scandal caused all financial firms to tighten up their procedures for dealing with customers, both in better controls on matching the degree of complexity of trades to the degree of financial sophistication of customers and in providing for customers to obtain price quotes from an area independent of the front office.

Another lesson that you would think would be learned is to be cautious about how you use any form of communication that can later be made public. BT's reputation was certainly hurt by the objective facts about its conduct, but it was even further damaged by the arrogant and insulting tone some of its employees used in referring to clients, which could be documented through recorded conversations. However, even with such an instructive example, we have seen Merrill Lynch's reputation being damaged in 2002 by remarks its stock analysts made in e-mails and tape-recorded conversations (see the article "Value of Trust" in the June 6, 2002, *Economist*) along with a number of similar incidents surrounding Wall Street's relations with Enron (see the article "Banks on Trial" in the July 25, 2002, *Economist*).

JPMorgan, Citigroup, and Enron

Following the Bankers Trust incident, investment banks put in controls to guard against exploitation of customers. But it was not seen as part of a bank's responsibility to safeguard others from actions by the customer. This has changed as part of the fallout from Enron's 2001 bankruptcy. As part of the process leading up to the bankruptcy, it was revealed that Enron had for years been engaging in dubious accounting practices to hide the size of its borrowings from investors and lenders (it was their part in these shenanigans that brought an end to the major accounting firm Arthur Andersen). One of the ploys that Enron had used was to disguise a borrowing as an oil futures contract.

As a major player in the energy markets, it was to be expected that Enron would be heavily engaged in futures contracts on oil. But these particular futures contracts did not involve taking any position on oil price movements. Enron sold oil for future delivery, getting cash, and then agreed to buy back the oil that it delivered for a fixed price. So, in effect, no oil was ever delivered. When you canceled out the oil part of the trades, what was left was just an agreement for Enron to pay cash later for cash it had received up front—in practice, if not in legal terms, a loan. The advantage to Enron was that it did not have to report this in its public statements as a loan, making the firm appear more desirable as an investment and as a borrower.

When this was finally disclosed, JPMorgan Chase and Citigroup, Enron's principal counterparties on these trades, justified their activities by saying that they had not harmed Enron, their client, in any way, and that they had no part in determining how Enron had accounted for the transactions on its books; that was an issue between Enron and Arthur Andersen. JPMorgan and Citigroup had treated these transaction as loans in their own accounting and reporting to regulators, so they had not deceived their own investors or lenders.

But both JPMorgan and Citigroup clearly knew what Enron's intent was in entering into the transaction. In the end, they agreed to pay a combined $286 million for "helping to commit a fraud" on Enron's shareholders. They also agreed to put new controls in place to ascertain that their clients were accounting for derivative transactions with them in ways that were transparent to investors.

The precedent of this successful legal action caused other investment banks to commit to similar new controls. And yet we have recently witnessed charges against Goldman Sachs for helping Greece hide its level of indebtedness from its European Union partners by disguising debt as an interest rate swap, a mechanism very similar to that in the Enron case. The details here are that the swap was deliberately done at an off-market rate, creating an up-front payment to Greece that would of course need to be paid back by Greece, with suitable interest, over the course of the swap's life. The only reason for creating the swap at an off-market rate would appear to be letting Greece take out a loan that didn't need to show up on its books.

Details on the Enron case can be found in McLean and Elkind (2003, 159–160, 407–408). Details on the Greek case can be found in Dunbar and Martinuzzi (2012).

Other Cases

The following are some examples of other cases in which firms damaged their reputations by the manner in which they dealt with customers:

- Prudential-Bache Securities was found to have seriously misled thousands of customers concerning the risk of proposed investments in limited partnerships. In addition to damaging its reputation, Prudential-Bache had to pay more than $1 billion in fines and settlements. An account of this incident can be found in Eichenwald (1995).

- In 1995, a fund manager at Morgan Grenfell Asset Management directed mutual fund investments into highly speculative stocks, utilizing shell companies to evade legal restrictions on the percentage of a firm's stock that could be owned by a single fund. In addition to damage to its reputation, Morgan Grenfell had to pay roughly $600 million to compensate investors for resulting losses. A brief case account can be found in Garfield (1998).

- JPMorgan's reputation was damaged by allegations that it misled a group of South Korean corporate investors as to the risk in derivative trades that lost hundreds of millions of dollars based on the precipitous decline in the Thai baht exchange rate against the dollar in 1997. An account of these trades and the ensuing lawsuits can be found in Gillen, Lee, and Austin (1999).

- Many investment banks had their reputations damaged in the events leading up to the large fall in value of technology stocks in 2001 and 2002. Evidence showed that some widely followed stock market analysts working at investment banks had issued favorable recommendations for companies as a quid pro quo for underwriting business, with analyst bonuses tied to underwriting business generated. Regulators responded with fines for firms, bans from the industry for some analysts, and requirements for separation of the stock analysis function from the underwriting business. A summary account with references can be found in Lowenstein (2004, 212–213).

References

Asiaweek. 1996. "Perils of Profit." July 5. www-cgi.cnn .com/ASIANOW/asiaweek/96/0705/ed2.html.

Broom, Giles. 2011. "UBS in 'Disarray.'" *Bloomberg News.* September 26. www.bloomberg.com/news/2011-09-25/ ubs-in-disarray-as-gruebel-quits-ermotti-named-interim-chief.html.

Chew, Lillian. 1996. *Managing Derivatives Risks.* New York: John Wiley & Sons.

Counterparty Risk Management Policy Group. 1999. "Improving Counterparty Risk Management Practices." www.defaultrisk.com/pp_other_08.htm.

Crouhy, Michel, Dan Galai, and Robert Mark. 2001. *Risk Management.* New York: McGraw-Hill.

Culp, Christopher, and Merton Miller. 1995a. "Hedging in the Theory of Corporate Finance: A Reply to Our Critics." *Journal of Applied Corporate Finance* (Spring): 121–127.

Culp, Christopher, and Merton Miller. 1995b. "Metallgesellschaft and the Economics of Synthetic Storage." *Journal of Applied Corporate Finance* (Winter): 62–75. www.rmcsinc .com/articles/JACF74.pdf.

Davies, Rob. 2008. "Genius or Blunder?" *Risk.* 3:22–27. www.risk.net/risk-magazine/feature/1498128/ genius-blunder.

Derivative Strategies. 1998. "What Really Happened at UBS?" October. www.derivativesstrategy.com/magazine/ archive/1998/1098fea1.asp.

Dunbar, Nicholas, and Elisa Martinuzzi. 2012. "Goldman Secret Greek Loan Shows Two Sinners as Client Unravels." *Bloomberg News,* March 5. www.bloomberg.com/ news/2012-03-06/goldman-secret-greece-loan-shows-two-sinners-as-client-unravels.html.

Dwyer, Paula. 1996. "Sumitomo's Descent into the Abyss." *Business Week,* July 1. www.businessweek.com/1996/27/ b348241.htm.

Eichenwald, Kurt. 1995. *Serpent on the Rock.* New York: HarperBusiness.

Fay, Stephen. 1996. *The Collapse of Barings.* London: Richard Cohen Books.

Garfield, Andrew. 1998. "Peter Young Charged with Morgan Grenfell Fraud." *The Independent.* October 20. www.independent.co.uk/news/business/peter-young-charged-with-morgan-grenfell-fraud-1179481.html.

Gillen, David, Yoolim Lee, and Bill Austin. 1999. "J.P. Morgan's Korean Debacle." *Bloomberg Magazine* 3:24–30.

Hansell, Saul. 1997. "Joseph Jett: A Scoundrel or a Scapegoat?" *New York Times,* April 6.

Holland, Kelley, and Linda Himelstein. 1995. "The Bankers Trust Tapes." *Business Week,* October 16. www .businessweek.com/1995/42/b34461.htm.

Jett, Joseph, with Sabra Chartrand. 1999. *Black and White on Wall Street.* New York: William Morrow.

Kooi, Mari. 1996. "Analyzing Sumitomo." http://riskinstitute .ch/134800.htm.

Leeson, Nick, with Edward Whitley. 1996. *Rogue Trader.* Boston: Little, Brown.

Lowenstein, Roger. 2000. *When Genius Failed.* New York: Random House.

Lowenstein, Roger. 2004. *Origins of the Crash.* New York: Penguin.

Ludwig, Eugene. 2002. "Report on Allied Irish Bank." www.aibgroup.com/servlet/ContentServer? pagename=AIB_Investor_Relations/AIB_Download/ aib_d_download&c=AIB_Download&cid=1015597173380& channel=IRHP.

Mayer, Martin. 1995. "Joe Jett: Did the Computer Make Him Do It?" *Institutional Investor* 3:7–11.

Mayer, Martin. 1997. *The Bankers: The Next Generation.* New York: Truman Talley Books.

McKay, Peter. 1999. "Merrill Lynch to Pay Fines of $25 Million for Scandal." *Dow Jones Newswires,* July 1.

McLean, Bethany, and Peter Elkind. 2003. *The Smartest Guys in the Room.* New York: Penguin.

Mello, Antonio, and John Parsons. 1995. "Maturity Structure of a Hedge Matters." *Journal of Applied Corporate Finance* (Spring): 106–120.

Perold, Andre. 1999a. Harvard Business School Case Study (9-200-007) of Long-Term Capital Management (A).

Perold, Andre. 1999b. Harvard Business School Case Study (9-200-009) of Long-Term Capital Management (C).

Rawnsley, Judith. 1995. *Total Risk.* New York: HarperCollins.

Schutz, Dirk. 2000. *The Fall of UBS.* New York: Pyramid Media Group.

Shirreff, David. 1998. "Another Fine Mess at UBS." *Euromoney* 11:41–43.

Shirreff, David. 2000. "Lessons from the Collapse of Hedge Fund, Long-Term Capital Management." http://elsa.berkeley.edu/users/webfac/craine/e137_f03/137lessons.pdf.

Stigum, Marcia. 1989. *The Repo and Reverse Markets.* Homewood, IL: Dow Jones-Irwin.

Weiss, Gary. 1994. "What Lynch Left Out." *BusinessWeek,* August 22. www.businessweek.com/stories/1994-08-21/what-lynch-left-out.

Wilson, Harry. 2011. "UBS Rogue Trader: Investigations Focus on Fictitious Hedges." *The Telegraph,* September 16. www.telegraph.co.uk/finance/financial-crime/8772540/Fictitious-hedges-see-UBS-rogue-trader-losses-climb-to-2.3bn.html.

Wolfe, Eric. 2001. "NatWest Markets: E-Risk." www.riskmania.com/pdsdata/NatWestCaseStudy-erisk.pdf.

The Credit Crisis of 2007

7

Learning Objectives

Candidates, after completing this reading, should be able to:

- Analyze various factors that contributed to the Credit Crisis of 2007 and examine the relationships between these factors.
- Describe the mechanics of asset-backed securities (ABS) and ABS collateralized debt obligations (ABS CDOs), and explain their role in the 2007 credit crisis.

- Explain the roles of incentives and regulatory arbitrage in the outcome of the crisis.
- Apply the key lessons learned by risk managers to the scenarios provided.

Excerpt is Chapter 6 of Risk Management and Financial Institutions, *Fourth Edition, by John C. Hull.*

Starting in 2007, the United States experienced the worst financial crisis since the 1930s. The crisis spread rapidly from the United States to other countries and from financial markets to the real economy. Some financial institutions failed. Many more had to be bailed out by national governments. The first decade of the twenty-first century was disastrous for the financial sector, and the risk management practices of financial institutions have been subjected to a great deal of criticism. The crisis led to a major overhaul of the way financial institutions are regulated.

This chapter examines the origins of the crisis, what went wrong, why it went wrong, and the lessons that can be learned. In the course of the chapter, we will find out about the U.S. housing market, asset-backed securities, and collateralized debt obligations.

THE U.S. HOUSING MARKET

A natural starting point for a discussion of the credit crisis of 2007 is the U.S. housing market. Figure 7-1 shows the S&P/Case-Shiller composite-10 index for house prices in the United States between January 1987 and March 2014. This tracks house prices for ten major metropolitan areas in the United States. In about the year 2000, house prices started to rise much faster than they had in the previous decade. The very low level of interest rates between 2002 and 2005 was an important contributory factor, but the bubble in house prices was largely fueled by mortgage lending practices.

The 2000 to 2006 period was characterized by a huge increase in what is termed subprime mortgage lending. Subprime mortgages are mortgages that are considered to be significantly more risky than average. Before 2000, most mortgages classified as subprime were second mortgages. After 2000, this changed as financial institutions became more comfortable with the notion of a subprime first mortgage.

The Relaxation of Lending Standards

Mortgage lenders in the United States started to relax their lending standards in about 2000. This made house purchases possible for many families that had previously been considered to be not sufficiently creditworthy to qualify for a mortgage. These families increased the demand for real estate and prices rose. To mortgage brokers and mortgage lenders, the combination of more lending and rising house prices was attractive. More lending meant higher profits. Rising house prices meant that the lending was well covered by the underlying collateral. If the borrower defaulted, the resulting foreclosure would lead to little or no loss.

How could mortgage brokers and mortgage lenders keep increasing their profits? Their problem was that, as house prices rose, it was more difficult for first-time buyers to afford a house. In order to continue to attract new entrants to the housing market, they had to find ways to relax their lending standards even more—and this is exactly what they did. The amount lent as a percentage of the house price increased. Adjustable rate mortgages (ARMs) were developed where there was a low teaser rate of interest that would last for two or three years and be followed by a rate that was liable to be much higher.[1] Lenders also became more cavalier in the way they reviewed mortgage applications. Indeed, the applicant's income and other information reported on the application were frequently not checked.

Why was the government not regulating the behavior of mortgage lenders? The answer is that the U.S. government had, since the 1990s, been trying to

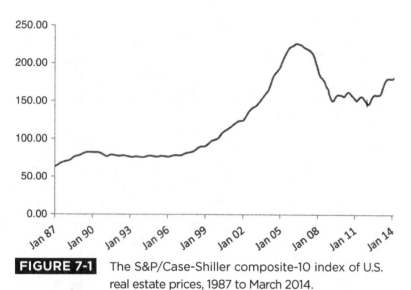

FIGURE 7-1	The S&P/Case-Shiller composite-10 index of U.S. real estate prices, 1987 to March 2014.

---

[1] A "2/28" ARM, for example, is an ARM where the rate is fixed for two years and then floats for the remaining 28 years. If real estate prices increased, lenders expected the borrowers to prepay and take out a new mortgage at the end of the teaser rate period. However, prepayment penalties, often zero on prime mortgages, were quite high on subprime mortgages.

expand home ownership, and had been applying pressure to mortgage lenders to increase loans to low and moderate income households. Some state legislators (such as those in Ohio and Georgia) were concerned about what was going on and wanted to curtail predatory lending.[2] However, the courts decided that national standards should prevail.

A number of terms have been used to describe mortgage lending during the period leading up to the credit crisis. One is "liar loans" because individuals applying for a mortgage, knowing that no checks would be carried out, sometimes chose to lie on the application form. Another term used to describe some borrowers is "NINJA" (no income, no job, no assets), Some analysts realized that the mortgages were risky, but pricing in the market for securities created from the mortgages suggests that the full extent of the risks and their potential impact on markets was not appreciated until well into 2007.

Mian and Sufi (2009) have carried out research confirming that there was a relaxation of the criteria used for mortgage lending.[3] Their research defines "high denial zip codes" as zip codes where a high proportion of mortgage applicants had been turned down in 1996, and shows that mortgage origination grew particularly fast for these zip codes between 2000 to 2007. (Zip codes are postal codes in the United States defining the area in which a person lives.) Moreover, their research shows that lending criteria were relaxed progressively through time rather than all at once because originations in high denial zip codes are an increasing function of time during the 2000 to 2007 period. Zimmerman (2007) provides some confirmation of this.[4] He shows that subsequent default experience indicates that mortgages made in 2006 were of a lower quality than those made in 2005 and these were in turn of lower quality than the mortgages made in 2004. Standard & Poor's has estimated that subprime mortgage origination in 2006 alone totaled $421 billion. AMP Capital

Investors estimate that there was a total of $1.4 trillion of subprime mortgages outstanding in July 2007.

The Bubble Bursts

The result of the relaxation of lending standards was an increase in the demand for houses and a bubble in house prices. Prices increased very fast during the 2000 to 2006 period. All bubbles burst eventually and this one was no exception. In the second half of 2006, house prices started to edge down. One reason was that, as house prices increased, demand for houses declined. Another was that some borrowers with teaser rates found that they could no longer afford their mortgages when the teaser rates ended. This led to foreclosures and an increase in the supply of houses for sale. The decline in house prices fed on itself. Individuals who had borrowed 100%, or close to 100%, of the cost of a house found that they had negative equity (i.e., the amount owed on the mortgage was greater than the value of the house). Some of these individuals chose to default. This led to more foreclosures, a further increase in the supply of houses for sale, and a further decline in house prices.

One of the features of the U.S. housing market is that mortgages are non-recourse in some states. This means that, when there is a default, the lender is able to take possession of the house, but other assets of the borrower are off-limits.[5] Consequently, the borrower has a free American-style put option. He or she can at any time sell the house to the lender for the principal outstanding on the mortgage. (During the teaser-interest-rate period this principal typically increased, making the option more valuable.) Market participants realized belatedly how costly the put option could be. If the borrower had negative equity, the optimal decision was to exchange the house for the outstanding principal on the mortgage. The house was then sold, adding to the downward pressure on house prices.

It would be a mistake to assume that all mortgage defaulters were in the same position. Some were unable to meet mortgage payments and suffered greatly when they had to give up their homes. But many of the defaulters were speculators who bought multiple homes as rental properties and chose to exercise their put options. It was

---

[2] Predatory lending describes the situation where a lender deceptively convinces borrowers to agree to unfair and abusive loan terms.

[3] See A. Mian and A. Sufi, "The Consequences of Mortgage Credit Expansion: Evidence from the US Mortgage Default Crisis," *Quarterly Journal of Economics* 124, no. 4 (November 2009): 1449–1496.

[4] See T. Zimmerman, "The Great Subprime Meltdown," *Journal of Structured Finance* (Fall 2007): 7–20.

---

[5] In some other states, mortgages are not non-recourse but there is legislation making it difficult for lenders to take possession of other assets besides the house.

their tenants who suffered. There are also reports that some house owners (who were not speculators) were quite creative in extracting value from their put options. After handing the keys to their house to the lender, they turned around and bought (sometimes at a bargain price) another house that was in foreclosure. Imagine two people owning identical houses next to each other. Both have mortgages of $250,000. Both houses are worth $200,000 and in foreclosure can be expected to sell for $170,000. What is the owners' optimal strategy? The answer is that each person should exercise the put option and buy the neighbor's house.

As foreclosures increased, the losses on mortgages also increased. Losses were high because houses in foreclosure were often surrounded by other houses that were also for sale. They were sometimes in poor condition. In addition, banks faced legal and other fees. In normal market conditions, a lender can expect to recover 75% of the amount owing in a foreclosure. In 2008 and 2009, recovery rates as low as 25% were experienced in some areas.

The United States was not alone in having declining real estate prices. Prices declined in many other countries as well. Real estate in the United Kingdom was particularly badly affected. As Figure 7-1 indicates, average house prices recovered somewhat in the United States between mid-2012 and March 2014.

SECURITIZATION

The originators of mortgages did not in many cases keep the mortgages themselves. They sold portfolios of mortgages to companies that created products for investors from them. This process is known as *securitization*. Securitization has been an important and useful tool for transferring risk in financial markets for many years. It underlies the originate-to-distribute model that was widely used by banks prior to 2007.

Securitization played a part in the creation of the housing bubble. The behavior of mortgage originators was influenced by their knowledge that mortgages would be securitized.[6] When considering new mortgage applications, the question was not: "Is this a credit we want to

assume?" Instead it was: "Is this a mortgage we can make money from by selling it to someone else?"

When mortgages were securitized, the only information received about the mortgages by the buyers of the products that were created from them was the loan-to-value ratio (i.e., the ratio of the size of the loan to the assessed value of the house) and the borrower's FICO (credit) score.[7] The reason why lenders did not check information on things such as the applicant's income, the number of years the applicant had lived at his or her current address, and so on, was that this information was considered irrelevant. The most important thing for the lender was whether the mortgage could be sold to others—and this depended primarily on the loan-to-value ratio and the applicant's FICO score.

It is interesting to note in passing that both the loan-to-value ratio and the FICO score were of doubtful quality. The property assessors who determined the value of a house at the time of a mortgage application sometimes inflated valuations because they knew that the lender wanted a low loan-to-value ratio. Potential borrowers were sometimes counseled to take certain actions that would improve their FICO scores.[8]

We now consider the products that were created from the mortgages and sold in the market.

Asset-Backed Securities

An *asset-backed security* (ABS) is a security created from the cash flows of financial assets such as loans, bonds, credit card receivables, mortgages, auto loans, and aircraft leases. Sometimes, cash flow streams such as royalties from the future sales of a piece of music are even used. The way the security works is illustrated by Figure 7-2. A portfolio of assets (such as subprime mortgages) is sold by the originators of the assets to a special purpose vehicle (SPV) and the cash flows from the assets are allocated to tranches. In Figure 7-2, there are three tranches. (This is a simplification. In reality there are usually many more than three tranches created.) These are the senior tranche, the mezzanine tranche, and the equity tranche. The portfolio has a principal of $100 million. This is divided as follows: $75 million to the senior tranche, $20 million to the

---

[6] Research by Keys et al. shows that there was a link between securitization and the lax screening of mortgages. See S. J. Keys, T. Mukherjee, A. Seru, and V. Vig, "Did Securitization Lead to Lax Screening? Evidence from Subprime Loans," *Quarterly Journal of Economics* 125, no. 1 (February 2010): 307–362.

[7] FICO is a credit score developed by the Fair Isaac Corporation and is widely used in the United States. It ranges from 300 to 850.

[8] One such action might be to make regular payments on a credit card for a few months.

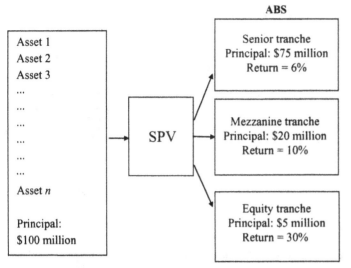

ABS

FIGURE 7-2 Creation of an asset-backed security from a portfolio of assets (simplified).

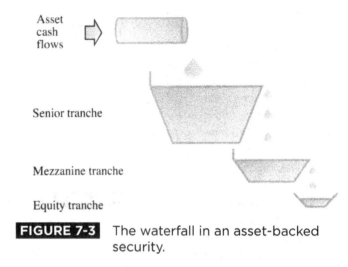

FIGURE 7-3 The waterfall in an asset-backed security.

mezzanine tranche, and $5 million to the equity tranche. The senior tranche is promised a return of 6%, the mezzanine tranche is promised a return of 10%, and the equity tranche is promised a return of 30%.

It sounds as though the equity tranche has the best deal, but this is not necessarily the case. The equity tranche is much less likely to realize its return than the other two tranches. Cash flows are allocated to tranches by specifying what is known as a waterfall. An approximation to the way a waterfall works is in Figure 7-3. There is a separate waterfall for interest and principal cash flows. Interest cash flows from the assets are allocated to the senior tranche until the senior tranche has received its promised return on its outstanding principal. Assuming that the promised return to the senior tranche can be made. cash flows are then allocated to the mezzanine tranche. If the promised return to the mezzanine tranche on its outstanding principal can be made and interest cash flows are left over, they are allocated to the equity tranche. Principal cash flows are used first to repay the principal of the senior tranche, then the mezzanine tranche, and finally the equity tranche.[9]

The structure in Figure 7-2 typically lasts several years. The extent to which the tranches get their principal back depends on losses on the underlying assets. The first 5%

of losses are borne by the principal of the equity tranche. If losses exceed 5%, the equity tranche loses all its principal and some losses are borne by the principal of the mezzanine tranche. If losses exceed 25%, the mezzanine tranche loses all its principal and some losses are borne by the principal of the senior tranche.

There are therefore two ways of looking at an ABS. One is with reference to the waterfall in Figure 7-3. Cash flows go first to the senior tranche, then to the mezzanine tranche, and then to the equity tranche. The other is in terms of losses. Losses of principal are first borne by the equity tranche, then by the mezzanine tranche, and then by the senior tranche.

The ABS is designed so that the senior tranche is rated AAA. The mezzanine tranche is typically rated BBB. The equity tranche is typically unrated. Unlike the ratings assigned to bonds, the ratings assigned to the tranches of an ABS are what might he termed "negotiated ratings." The objective of the creator of the ABS is to make the senior tranche as big as possible without losing its AAA credit rating. (This maximizes the profitability of the structure.) The ABS creator examines information published by rating agencies on how tranches are rated and may present several structures to rating agencies for a preliminary evaluation before choosing the final one. The creator of the ABS expects to make a profit because the weighted average return on the assets in the underlying portfolio is greater than the weighted average return offered to the tranches.

A particular type of ABS is a *collateralized debt obligation* (CDO). This is an ABS where the underlying assets are fixed-income securities.

___
[9] The priority rule described here is a simplification. The precise waterfall rules are somewhat more complicated and outlined in a legal document several hundred pages long.

ABS CDOs

Finding investors to buy the senior AAA-rated tranches created from subprime mortgages was not difficult. Equity tranches were typically retained by the originator of the mortgages or sold to a hedge fund. Finding investors for the mezzanine tranches was more difficult. This led financial engineers to be creative (arguably too creative). Financial engineers created an ABS from the mezzanine tranches of ABSs that

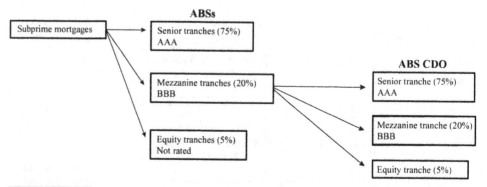

FIGURE 7-4 Creation of ABSs and an ABS CDO from subprime mortgages (simplified).

were created from subprime mortgages. This is known as an *ABS CDO* or *Mezz ABS CDO* and is illustrated in Figure 7-4. (Like the ABS in Figure 7-3, this is simplified.) The senior tranche of the ABS CDO is rated AAA. This means that the total of the AAA-rated instruments created in the example that is considered here is 90% (75% plus 75% of 20%) of the principal of the underlying mortgage portfolios. This seems high but, if the securitization were carried further with an ABS being created from the mezzanine tranches of ABS CDOs (and this did happen), the percentage would be pushed even higher.

In the example in Figure 7-4, the AAA-rated tranche of the ABS would probably be downgraded in the second half of 2007. However, it would receive the promised return if losses on the underlying mortgage portfolios were less than 25% because all losses of principal would then be absorbed by the more junior tranches. The AAA-rated tranche of the ABS CDO in Figure 7-4 is much more risky. It will get paid the promised return if losses on the underlying portfolios are 10% or less because in that case mezzanine tranches of ABSs have to absorb losses equal

to 5% of the ABS principal or less. As they have a total principal of 20% of the ABS principal, their loss is at most 5/20 or 25%. At worst this wipes out the equity tranche and mezzanine tranche of the ABS CDO but leaves the senior tranche unscathed.

The senior tranche of the ABS CDO suffers losses if losses on the underlying portfolios are more than 10%. Consider, for example, the situation where losses are 20% on the underlying portfolios. In this case, losses on the mezzanine tranches of the ABS CDO are 15/20 or 75% of their principal. The first 25% is absorbed by the equity and mezzanine tranches of the ABS CDO. The senior tranche of the ABS CDO therefore loses 50/75 or 67% of its value. These and other results are summarized in Table 7-1.

Many banks have lost money investing in the senior tranches of ABS CDOs. The investments typically promised a return quite a bit higher than the bank's funding cost. Because they were rated AAA, the capital requirements were minimal. Merrill Lynch is an example of a bank

TABLE 7-1 Losses to Tranches in Figure 7-4

Losses to Subprime Portfolios	Losses to Mezzanine Tranche of ABS	Losses to Equity Tranche of ABS CDO	Losses to Mezzanine Tranche of ABS CDO	Losses to Senior Tranche of ABS CDO
10%	25%	100%	100%	0%
15%	50%	100%	100%	33%
20%	75%	100%	100%	67%
25%	100%	100%	100%	100%

that lost a great deal of money from investments in ABS CDOs. In July 2008, Merrill Lynch agreed to sell senior tranches of ABS CDOs, that had previously been rated AAA and had a principal of $30.6 billion, to Lone Star funds for 22 cents on the dollar.[10]

CDOs and ABS CDOs in Practice

Figures 7-2 and 7-4 illustrate the nature of the securitizations that were done. In practice, many more tranches were created than those shown in Figures 7-2 and 7-4 and many of the tranches were thinner (i.e., corresponded to a narrower range of losses). Figure 7-5 shows a more realistic example of the structures that were created. This is adapted from an illustration by Gorton, which was taken from an article by UBS.[11]

In Figure 7-5, two ABS CDOs are created. One (referred to as a Mezz ABS CDO) is created from the BBB rated tranches of ABSs (similarly to the ABS CDO in Figure 7-4); the other (referred to as a high-grade ABS CDO) is from the AAA, AA, and A tranches of ABSs. The figure shows a third level of securitization based on the A and AA tranches of the Mezz ABS CDO. There was typically a small amount of *over-collateralization* with the face value of the mortgages being greater (by 1% or 2%) than the total face value of the ABS tranches. This created a cushion for investors, but by carrying our a similar analysis to that in Table 7-1 it is not difficult to see that investors in many of the tranches created will lose principal in situations where losses on the underlying subprime mortgage portfolios are moderately high.

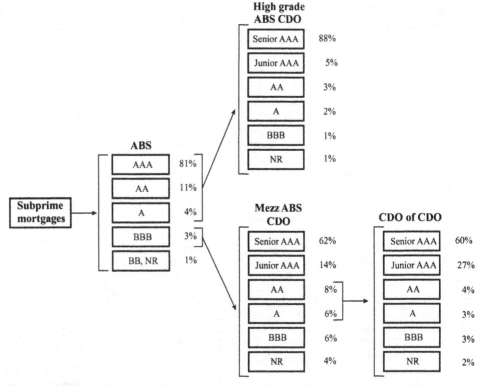

FIGURE 7-5 More realistic example of subprime securitizations with ABS, ABS CDOs, and a CDO of CDO being created.

---

[10] In fact the deal was worse than it sounds for Merrill Lynch because Merrill Lynch agreed to finance 75% of the purchase price. If the value of the tranches fell below 16.5 cents on the dollar, Merrill Lynch might find itself owning the assets again.

[11] G. Gorton, "The Subprime Panic," *European Financial Management* 15, no. 1 (2008): 10–46.

The risks in the AAA-rated tranches of ABSs and ABS CDOs were higher than either investors or rating agencies realized. One of the reasons for this involves correlation. The values of the tranches of ABSs depend on the default correlation of the underlying mortgages. The tranches of ABS CDOs are even more heavily dependent on these default correlations. If mortgages exhibit a fairly low default correlation (as they do in normal times), there is very little chance of a high overall default rate and the AAA-rated tranches of both ABSs and ABS CDOs are safe. But, many analysts overlooked the fact that correlations always increase in stressed market conditions. In 2005 to 2006, the models used by investors and rating agencies assumed correlations that were too low for the upheavals in the U.S. housing market that were considered likely by many observers. As explained in Box 7-1, another mistake made by analysts was to assume that the BBB-rated tranches of an ABS were equivalent in risk to BBB-rated bonds. There are important differences between the two and these differences can have a big effect on the valuation of the tranches of ABS CDOs.

Analysts tended to assume that the mezzanine tranche of an ABS, when rated BBB, can be considered to be identical to a BBB bond for the purposes of evaluating a CDO created from the mezzanine tranches. This is not a good assumption. The rating agency models attempted to ensure that the BBB tranche of an ABS had the same probability of loss, or the same expected loss, as a BBB bond. But the probability distribution of the loss is very different. Because the BBB tranches of ABSs were thin, it is much more likely that an investor in the BBB tranche of an ABS will lose everything, than that this will happen for an investor in a BBB-rated bond. (This is sometimes referred to as "cliff risk.") This means that the risk characteristics of ABS CDO tranches created from the BBB tranches of ABSs are quite different from the risk characteristics of similar tranches created from BBB bonds.

One lesson from this is that it is dangerous to interpret ratings for tranches of an ABS—or any other structured product—in the same way that ratings for bonds are interpreted. For similarly rated bonds and structured products, the probability distribution of losses are markedly different.

realized that they did not understand the tranches as well as they had previously thought and that they had placed too much reliance on credit ratings. This emphasizes the importance of transparency in financial markets. The products created during the period leading up to the crisis were very complicated.[12] Investors did not worry about this until problems emerged. They then found that the liquidity of the market was such that they could only trade at fire-sale prices.

Banks such as Citigroup, UBS, and Merrill Lynch suffered huge losses. There were many government bailouts of financial institutions. Lehman Brothers was allowed to fail. The world experienced the worst recession since the 1930s. Unemployment increased. Even people in remote parts of the world that had no connection with U.S. financial institutions were affected.

Banks are now paying a price for the crisis. They are required to keep more capital than before. They are also required to maintain certain liquidity ratios. Legislation such as Dodd-Frank in the United States increases the oversight of financial institutions and restricts their activities in areas such as proprietary trading and derivatives trading.

THE CRISIS

The defaults on mortgages in the United States had a number of consequences. Financial institutions and other investors who had bought the tranches of ABSs and ABS CDOs lost money. Losses were also incurred by some mortgage originators because they had provided guarantees as to the quality of the mortgages that were securitized and because they faced lawsuits over their lending practices.

As often happens when losses are experienced in one segment of the debt market, there was a "flight to quality." Investors became reluctant to take any credit risk and preferred to buy Treasury instruments and similarly safe investments. Credit spreads (the extra return required for taking credit risks) increased sharply. It was difficult for many non-financial companies to obtain loans from banks. Indeed, banks became reluctant to lend to each other at all and interbank lending rates increased sharply.

The tranches of ABSs and ABS CDOs were downgraded by rating agencies in the second half of 2007. The market for these tranches became very illiquid. Investors

WHAT WENT WRONG?

"Irrational exuberance" is a phrase coined by Alan Greenspan, Chairman of the Federal Reserve Board, to describe the behavior of investors during the bull market of the 1990s. It can also be applied to the period leading up to the credit crisis. Mortgage lenders, the investors in tranches of ABSs and ABS CDOs that were created from residential mortgages, and the companies that sold protection on the tranches assumed that the U.S. house prices would continue to increase—or at least not decrease. There might be declines in one or two areas, but the possibility of the widespread decline shown in Figure 7-1 was a scenario not considered by most people.

Many factors contributed to the crisis that started in 2007. Mortgage originators used lax lending standards. Products were developed to enable mortgage originators to

---

[12] Some of the products that were created were even more complicated than indicated by the description in the Securitization section. For example, sometimes ABS CDO tranches were included in the portfolios used to create other ABS CDOs.

profitably transfer credit risk to investors. Rating agencies moved from their traditional business of rating bonds, where they had a great deal of experience, to rating structured products, which were relatively new and for which there were relatively little historical data. The products bought by investors were complex and in many instances investors and rating agencies had inaccurate or incomplete information about the quality of the underlying assets. Investors in the structured products that were created thought they had found a money machine and chose to rely on rating agencies rather than forming their own opinions about the underlying risks. The return promised on the structured products rated AAA was high compared with the returns promised on bonds rated AAA.

Regulatory Arbitrage

Many of the mortgages were originated by banks and it was banks that were the main investors in the tranches that were created from the mortgages. Why would banks choose to securitize mortgages and then buy the securitized products that were created? The answer concerns what is termed *regulatory arbitrage*. The regulatory capital banks were required to keep for the tranches created from a portfolio of mortgages was less than the regulatory capital that would be required for the mortgages themselves. This is because the mortgages were kept in what is referred to as the "banking book" whereas the tranches were kept in what is referred to as the "trading book." Capital requirements were different for the banking book and the trading book.

Incentives

Economists use the term "agency costs" to describe the situation where incentives are such that the interests of two parties in a business relationship are not perfectly aligned. The process by which mortgages were originated, securitized, and sold to investors was unfortunately riddled with agency costs.

The incentive of the originators of mortgages was to make loans that would be acceptable to the creators of the ABS and ABS CDO tranches. The incentive of the individuals who valued houses on which the mortgages were written was to please the lender by providing as high a valuation as possible so that the loan-to-value ratio was as low as possible. (Pleasing the lender was likely to lead to more business from that lender.) The main concern of the creators of

ABSs and ABS CDOs was the profitability of the structures (i.e., the excess of the weighted average inflows over the weighted average outflows). They wanted the volume of AAA-rated tranches that they created to be as high as possible and found ways of using the published criteria of rating agencies to achieve this. The rating agencies were paid by the issuers of the securities they rated and about half their income came from structured products.

Another source of agency costs concerns financial institutions and their employees. Employee compensation falls into three categories: regular salary, the end-of-year bonus, and stock or stock options. Many employees at all levels of seniority in financial institutions, particularly traders, receive much of their compensation in the form of end-of-year bonuses. Traditionally, this form of compensation has focused employee attention on short-term performance. If an employee generates huge profits one year and is responsible for severe losses the next year, the employee will receive a big bonus the first year and will not have to return it the following year. The employee might lose his or her job as a result of the second year losses, but even that is not a disaster. Financial institutions seem to be surprisingly willing to recruit individuals with losses on their resumes.

Imagine you are an employee of a financial institution investing in ABS CDOs in 2006. Almost certainly you would have recognized that there was a bubble in the U.S. housing market and would expect that bubble to burst sooner or later. However, it is possible that you would decide to continue with your ABS CDO investments. If the bubble did not burst until after December 31, 2006, you would still get a nice bonus at the end of 2006!

LESSONS FROM THE CRISIS

Some of the lessons for risk managers from the crisis are as follows:

1. Risk managers should be watching for situations where there is irrational exuberance and make sure that senior management recognize that the good times will not last forever.

2. Correlations always increase in stressed markets. In considering how bad things might get, risk managers should not use correlations that are estimated from data collected during normal market conditions.

3. Recovery rates decline when default rates increase. This is true for almost all debt instruments, not just mortgages. In considering how bad things might get, risk managers should not use recovery rates that are estimated from data collected during normal market conditions.

4. Risk managers should ensure that the incentives of traders and other personnel encourage them to make decisions that are in the interests of the organization they work for. Many financial institutions have revised their compensation policies as a result of the crisis. Bonuses are now often spread out over several years rather than all being paid at once. If good performance in one year is followed by bad performance in the next, part of the bonus for the good-performance year that has not yet been paid may be clawed back.

5. If a deal seems too good to be true, it probably is. AAA-rated tranches of structured products promised returns that were higher than the returns promised on AAA bonds by 100 basis points, or more. A sensible conclusion from this for an investor would be that further analysis is needed because there are likely to be risks in the tranches that are not considered by rating agencies.

6. Investors should not rely on ratings. They should understand the assumptions made by rating agencies and carry out their own analyses.

7. Transparency is important in financial markets. If there is a lack of transparency (as there was for ABS CDOs), markets are liable to dry up when there is negative news.

8. Re-securitization, which led to the creation of ABS CDOs and CDOs of CDOs, was a badly flawed idea. The assets used to create ABSs in the first leg of the securitization should be as well diversified as possible. There is then nothing to be gained from further securitization.

Box 7-1 makes the point that many market participants incorrectly considered ABS tranches rated BBB to be equivalent to BBB bonds. Box 7-2 suggests a trading strategy that could be followed by people who realized that this was not so.

BOX 7-2   A Trading Opportunity?

A few traders made a huge amount of money betting against the subprime mortgage market. Suppose that you are analyzing markets in 2005 and 2006, but are uncertain about how subprime mortgages will perform. Is there a trading opportunity open to you?

The answer is that Mezz ABS CDOs do present a trading opportunity. Figure 7-5 is a simplification of how tranches were actually created. In practice, there were usually three ABS tranches rated BBB+, BBB, and BBB–. Each was very thin—about 1 % wide. Separate Mezz ABS CDOs were created from each of the three types of tranches. Consider the Mezz ABS CDO created from BBB+ tranches. A trader might reasonably conclude that the BBB+ tranches created from different pools of mortgages would either all be safe (because there would be no real estate crisis) or would all be wiped out. (Because the tranches are only 1% wide, it is unlikely that they would be only partially wiped out.) This means that all the Mezz ABS CDO tranches created from ABS tranches rated BBB+ are either safe or wiped out. The Mezz ABS CDO tranches are therefore much the same as each other and should have the same rating (BBB+ in the case we are considering).

Having recognized this, what should the trader do? He or she should buy junior ABS CDO tranches (which are inexpensive because of their rating) and short senior ABS CDO tranches (which are relatively expensive). If the underlying principal is the same for both trades, the trader can then relax knowing that a profit has been locked in.

This emphasizes the point in Box 7-1 that BBB tranches (particularly very thin BBB tranches) should not be considered equivalent to BBB bonds.

SUMMARY

The credit crisis starting in 2007 had a devastating effect on financial markets throughout the world. Its origins can be found in the U.S. housing market. The U.S. government was keen to encourage home ownership. Interest rates were low. Mortgage brokers and mortgage lenders found it attractive to do more business by relaxing their lending standards. Products for securitizing mortgages had been developed so that the investors bearing the credit risk were not necessarily the same as the original lenders. Rating agencies were prepared to give an AAA rating to senior tranches that were created by securitization. There was no shortage of buyers for these AAA-rated tranches because their yields were higher than the yields on AAA-rated bonds. The compensation arrangements in banks focused their employees' attention on short-term profits, and as a result they chose to ignore the housing bubble and its potential impact on some very complex products they were trading.

House prices rose as both first-time buyers and speculators entered the market. Some mortgages had included a low "teaser rate" for two or three years. After the teaser rate ended, some borrowers faced higher interest rates that they could not afford and had no choice but to default. This led to foreclosures and an increase in the supply of houses being sold. The price increases between 2000 and 2006 began to be reversed. Speculators and others who found that the amount owing on their mortgages was greater than the value of their houses (i.e., they had negative equity) defaulted. This accentuated the price decline.

Many factors played a part in creating the U.S. housing bubble and resulting recession. These include irrational exuberance on the part of market participants, poor incentives, too much reliance on rating agencies, not enough analysis by investors, and the complexity of the products that were created. The crisis has provided a number of lessons for risk managers. As we will see later in this book, it has also led to a major overhaul of bank regulation and bank legislation.

Further Reading

Gorton, G. "The Subprime Panic." *European Financial Management* 15, no. 1 (2008): 10–46.

Hull, J. C. "The Financial Crisis of 2007: Another Case of Irrational Exuberance." In *The Finance Crisis and Rescue: What Went Wrong? Why? What Lessons Can Be Learned?* University of Toronto Press, 2008.

Keys, B. J., T. Mukherjee. A. Seru, and V. Vig. "Did Securitization Lead to Lax Screening? Evidence from Subprime Loans." *Quarterly Journal of Economics* 125, no. 1 (February 2010): 307–362.

Krinsman, A. N. "Subprime Mortgage Meltdown: How Did It Happen and How Will It End?" *Journal of Structured Finance* (Summer 2007): 13–19.

Mian, A., and A. Sufi. "The Consequences of Mortgage Credit Expansion: Evidence from the US Mortgage Default Crisis." *Quarterly Journal of Economics* 124, no. 4 (November 2009): 1449–1496.

Sorkin, A. R. *Too Big to Fail.* New York: Penguin, 2009.

Tett, G. *Fool's Gold: How the Bold Dream of a Small Tribe at JPMorgan Was Corrupted by Wall Street Greed and Unleashed a Catastrophe.* New York: Free Press, 2009.

Zimmerman, T. "The Great Subprime Meltdown." *Journal of Structured Finance* (Fall 2007): 7–20.

Failures
What Are They and When Do They Happen?

8

Learning Objectives

Candidates, after completing this reading, should be able to:

- Explain how a large financial loss may not necessarily be evidence of a risk management failure.
- Analyze and identify instances of risk management failure.

- Explain how risk management failures can arise in the following areas: measurement of known risk exposures, identification of risk exposures, communication of risks, and monitoring of risks.
- Evaluate the role of risk metrics and analyze the shortcomings of existing risk metrics.

Excerpt is Risk Management Failures: What Are They and When Do They Happen?, *by René Stulz, Fisher College of Business Working Paper Series.*

ABSTRACT

A large loss is not evidence of a risk management failure because a large loss can happen even if risk management is flawless. I provide a typology of risk management failures and show how various types of risk management failures occur. Because of the limitations of past data in assessing the probability and the implications of a financial crisis, I conclude that financial institutions should use scenarios for credible financial crisis threats even if they perceive the probability of such events to be extremely small.

In commentaries on the financial crisis that started during the summer of 2007, a constant refrain is that somehow risk management failed and that there were risk management failures at financial institutions across the world. For instance, an article in the *Financial Times* states that "it is obvious that there has been a massive failure of risk management across most of Wall Street."[1] In this article, I want to examine what it means for risk management to fail. I show that the fact that an institution makes an extremely large loss does not imply that risk management failed or that the institution made a mistake. This article does not examine the subprime financial crisis or problems of financial institutions during that crisis directly. Rather, it is an attempt to make sure that if risk management is blamed, it is for the right reasons. Otherwise, changes in risk management that take place in response to the crisis might be counterproductive and top executives and investors could keep expecting more from risk management than what it can actually deliver. I therefore show when bad outcomes can be blamed on risk management and when they cannot. In the process of doing so, I provide a typology of risk management failures.

To examine risk management failures more concretely, I go back to the problems experienced by the hedge fund LTCM in 1998 to analyze how one might conclude that the failure of LTCM was a risk management failure or not. I then generalize from that example to describe what constitutes a risk management failure and what does not. I will show that some events considered in the financial press to be risk management failures actually are not risk management failures, but at the same time I will analyze many different ways in which risk management can fail. I then address the question of whether lessons from risk management failures can be used to help improve the practice of risk management. In the last part of this article, I discuss an approach to risk management that might enable institutions to better manage risks such as those that threatened them during the subprime financial crisis.

WAS THE COLLAPSE OF LONG-TERM CAPITAL MANAGEMENT A RISK MANAGEMENT FAILURE?

The story of Long-Term Capital Management (LTCM) is well-known.[2] In 1994, ex-Salomon Brothers traders and two future Nobel Prize winners started a hedge fund, the Long-Term Capital Fund. LTCM was the company that managed the fund. The fund performed superbly for most of its life: Investors earned 20% for ten months in 1994, 43% in 1995, 41% in 1996, and 17% in 1997. In August and September 1998, following the default of Russia on its ruble denominated debt, world capital markets were in crisis and the hedge fund LTCM lost most of its capital. Before its collapse, LTCM had capital close to $5 billion, assets in excess of $100 billion, and derivatives for a notional amount in excess of $1 trillion. By mid-September, LTCM's capital had fallen by more than $3.5 billion and the Federal Reserve Bank of New York coordinated a rescue by private financial institutions that injected $3.65 billion in the fund.

Does a loss of more than 70% of capital represent a risk management failure? Does a loss that requires a rescue by banks involving an injection of $3.65 billion of new capital show that risk management failed? It turns out that it is not easy to answer these questions. To define a risk management failure, one must first define the role of risk management.

In a typical firm, the role of risk management is first to assess the risks faced by the firm, communicate these

---

[1] "Wall Street dispatch: Imagination and common sense brew a safer culture," by David Wighton, Nov. 26, 2007, FT.com.

[2] The best public source for data on LTCM is a collection of four case studies by André Perold published in 1999, Long-Term Capital Management (A)—(D), available from Harvard Business School Publishing. Many books have been written on LTCM. Some of the numbers used in this article come from Roger Lowenstein, *When Genius Failed: The Rise and Fall of Long-Term Capital Management,* Random House, 2000.

risks to those who make risk-taking decisions for the firm, and finally manage and monitor those risks to make sure that the firm only bears the risks its management and board of directors want it to bear. In general, a firm will specify a risk measure that it focuses on together with additional risk metrics. When that risk measure exceeds the firm's tolerance for risk, risk is reduced. Alternatively, when the risk measure is too low for the firm's risk tolerance, the firm increases its risk. Because firms are generally more concerned about unexpected losses, a frequently used risk measure is value-at-risk or VaR, a measure of downside risk. VaR is the maximum loss at a given confidence level over a given period of time. Hence, if the 95% confidence level is used and a firm has a one-day VaR of $150 million, the firm has a 5% chance of making a loss in excess of $150 million over the next day if the VaR is correctly estimated. This measure might be estimated daily or over longer periods of time.

Even with our definition of the role of risk management, the returns of LTCM do not tell us anything about whether its risk management failed. To understand why, it is helpful to consider a very simple hypothetical example. Suppose that you stood in the shoes of the managers of LTCM in January 1998 and had the opportunity to invest in trades that, overall, had a 99% chance of producing a return for the fund before fees of 25% and a 1% chance of making a loss of 70% over the coming year. Though this example is hypothetical, it is plausible in light of the returns of LTCM and what LTCM was telling its investors. First, in its two best years the fund earned more than 50% before fees, so that a return of 25% does not sound implausible. Second, LTCM wrote to its investors to tell them that it expected that the fund would experience a loss in excess of 20% only in one year out of 50—here, instead, one year out of 100 can be expected to have a loss of 70%.[3] Let's assume that whether the fund had the high return or not depended on the flip of a weighted coin, so that the risk of the fund would have been completely diversifiable for its investors. With this hypothetical example, the expected return on the fund would then have been 24.05%. Such an expected return would have been a great expected return for a hedge fund or for any investment as this would have been the expected return for bearing diversifiable risk, given my assumptions. Had the managers had the

opportunity to keep repeating this investment, 99 years out of 100 they would have earned 25% before fees and would have been stars.

In my hypothetical example, when the managers of the funds (the partners) made their choice, they knew the true distribution of possible outcomes of the fund. Hence, they knew the distribution of gains and losses perfectly—the risk managers should have earned a gold medal for their work. Suppose, however, that the bad outcome occurs. In this case, the fund would have made headlines for having lost $3.5 billion. Some would argue that the risk of the fund was poorly managed. However, by construction, risk management could not have been improved in this case. The managers knew exactly the risks they faced—and they decided to take them. Therefore, there is no sense in which risk management failed. Ex post, the only argument one could make is that the managers took risks they should not have, but that is not a risk management issue as long as the risks were properly understood. Rather, it is an issue of assessing the costs of losses versus the gains from making large profits.

Deciding whether to take a known risk is not a decision for risk managers. The decision depends on the risk appetite of an institution. However, defining the risk appetite is a decision for the board and top management. That decision is at the heart of the firm's strategy and of how it creates value for its shareholders. A decision to take a known risk may turn out poorly even though, at the time it was made, the expectation was that taking the risk increased shareholder wealth and hence was in the best interest of the shareholders.

In the case of LTCM, it could be argued that the cost of losing $3.5 billion for the investors in LTCM was just that—namely, there were no additional costs beyond the direct monetary loss. For most firms, however, large losses have deadweight costs. These deadweight costs are at the foundation of financial theories of why risk management creates shareholder wealth.[4] If a financial institution makes a large loss, the institution may, for instance, have to scale back its investments because of being financially constrained, have to sell assets in unfavorable markets, lose valuable employees who become concerned for their bonuses, lose customers who are concerned about

---

[3] See Lowenstein, p. 63.

[4] See René M. Stulz, *Risk Management and Derivatives,* Thompson Publishing, 2003.

the institution being distracted or not having sufficient resources to help them, and face increased scrutiny from regulators. In any institution, the board and top management have to take into account these deadweight costs of large losses when making decisions that create the risk of large losses.

Risk managers can estimate whether an action is profitable for the firm given its risk appetite because they can evaluate how much capital is required to support that action.[5] However, an action that is not profitable for a given level of risk appetite can become profitable if the firm's risk appetite increases because less capital is required to support that action. Whether taking large risks is worthwhile for an institution ultimately depends on the firm's strategy. Risk managers do not set strategy. Suppose that a firm sets its risk appetite by choosing a target credit rating. Such an approach is well-established. Once the credit rating is chosen, there are multiple combinations of risk and capital that achieve the target rating. For a given choice of leverage, the firm does not have much choice in choosing its risk level if it wants to achieve its target rating. However, faced with good opportunities, the firm could choose to have less leverage so that it can bear more risk or it could choose to depart from its credit rating target.

LTCM provides a good example of such trade-offs. In the fall of 1997, the managers of LTCM concluded that they did not want to manage a business earning 17% for its investors, which is what their investors had earned for the year. Instead, they wanted the higher returns achieved in 1995 and 1996. At the end of 1997, LTCM had capital of $7.4 billion but decided to return roughly 36% of the capital to its investors. With less capital, LTCM could still execute the same trades. However, now, to implement them it had to borrow more and hence had to increase its leverage. By increasing its leverage, it could boost the return to its shareholders if things went well at the expense of making more losses if things went poorly. Was increasing leverage a poor risk management decision? In my example, the partners of LTCM knew the risks and the rewards from

doing so. In the well-worn language of financial economics, increasing leverage was a positive NPV decision when it was made, but obviously ex post it was a costly decision as it meant that when assets fell in value, the fund's equity fell in value faster than it would have with less leverage.

There has been much discussion of incentives of top management during the credit crisis, with various commentators arguing that part of the problem has been that top management had incentives to take too much risk. This may well be so, but before reaching conclusions one should not forget that financial economists have argued for decades that incentives of management become better aligned with those of shareholders when management has a large stake in the firm's equity. Top management owned hundreds of millions of dollars of equity in Bear Stearns and Lehman at the peak of the valuation of these firms. Similarly, the partners of LTCM collectively had almost $2 billion invested in the fund at the beginning of 1998. If such equity stakes do not incentivize managers to make the right decisions for their shareholders, what would?

In summary, risk management does not prevent losses. With good risk management, large losses can occur when those making the risk-taking decisions conclude that taking large, well-understood risks creates value for their organization.

A TYPOLOGY OF RISK MANAGEMENT FAILURES

How can risk management go wrong? The way we describe the role of risk management suggests important ways in which risk management can go wrong. We started by saying that the first step in risk management is to measure risk. Let's assume, for now, that the right risk measure is used given the situation of the firm. This measure could be VaR or could be some other measure. Two types of mistakes can be made in measuring risk: Known risks can be mismeasured and some risks can be ignored, either because they are unknown or viewed as not material. Once risks are measured, they have to be communicated to the firm's leadership. A failure in communicating risk to management is a risk management failure as well. After management decides what kind of risks to take, risk management has to make sure that the firm takes these risks. In other words, risk managers

---

[5] My article with Brian Nocco, Enterprise Risk Management: Theory and Practice, *Journal of Applied Corporate Finance,* Fall 2006, v18(8), 8–20, describes the key principles of enterprise risk management, issues that arise in its implementation, and the role of capital allocation.

must then manage the firm's risk, a task that may involve identifying appropriate risk mitigating actions, hedging some risks, and rejecting some proposed trades or projects. Lastly, a firm's risk managers may fail to use appropriate risk metrics.

With this perspective, there are six types of risk management failures:

1. Mismeasurement of known risks.
2. Failure to take risks into account.
3. Failure in communicating the risks to top management.
4. Failure in monitoring risks.
5. Failure in managing risks.
6. Failure to use appropriate risk metrics.

We discuss each one of these types of failures in turn.

Mismeasurement of Known Risks

In the LTCM example, risk mismeasurement could have taken a number of different forms. When measuring risk, risk managers attempt to understand the distribution of possible returns. With our simple example, the distribution was a binomial distribution—the outcome of the toss of a weighted coin. Risk managers could make a mistake in assessing the probability of a large loss or the size of the large loss if it occurs. However, in addition, they could use the wrong distribution altogether. Further, financial institutions have many positions, each position has a return from a given distribution, but these returns are related across positions, and that relation may be assessed incorrectly—a simple way to put this is that correlations may be mismeasured. Correlations are extremely important in risk management because the benefit of diversification falls as correlations increase.

With the LTCM example, it could be that the true probability of a loss of 70% was higher than 1%, say 25%. In this case, the expected return of LTCM in my hypothetical example would have been a paltry 1.25%. At the time, investors could have earned a higher expected return by investing in T-bills. In this case, the risk management mistake—assessing the probability of the bad outcome at 1% instead of 25%—would have had disastrous consequences for the fund because it would have led it to make trades that would have destroyed value.

Suppose that LTCM had made the mistake we just discussed. How would we know? We cannot identify such a mistake ex post because LTCM lost 70% only once. Having lost 70%, it could have done so whether the true probability of that loss was 1% or 25%. In fact, under the hypothetical conditions of my example, we can learn nothing from the fact that LTCM lost 70% about whether it made a risk management mistake of that type. It could have been that, as of January 1998, the probability of such a loss was infinitesimal or extremely large. It could have been a one in one hundred year event or a one in four year event for the portfolio of trades they had assembled.

Another risk management mistake would occur if the distribution is not binomial, but a different distribution altogether. For instance, it could be, keeping with the hypothetical example, that there was a 1% chance of a 70% loss and additionally a 9% chance of a 100% loss. In this case, the expected return would have been 12.8%, but there would also have been a nontrivial probability of a total wipeout.

When an institution has many positions or projects, the risk of the institution depends on how the risks of the different positions or projects are related. If the correlation between the positions or projects is high, it is more likely that all the firm's activities perform poorly at the same time, which leads to a higher probability of a large loss. These correlations can be difficult to assess and they change over time, at times abruptly. A partner of LTCM described the problem they faced in August and September as being one where correlations that they thought were extremely small suddenly became large. With this perspective, correlations would have been misestimated. It is well-known in finance that correlations increase in periods of crisis. Failure to assess correlations correctly would lead to the wrong assessment of the risk of a portfolio or of a firm. The problem of mismeasurement of correlations is more subtle, however, if correlations are random and sometimes turn out to be unexpectedly large ex post. In this case, risk managers could not be expected to know what correlations will be, but their assessment of the risk of a portfolio or of the firm would depend on their estimates of the distribution of the correlations. In this case, it would be possible for realized correlations to be different from their expected value and yet there would be no risk management failure.

When risks are known, statistical techniques are generally brought to bear to estimate the distribution of risks.

Such approaches work well when there is a lot of data and when it is reasonable to believe that the returns will have the same statistical distribution in the future as they had in the past. For instance, suppose that a risk manager wants to estimate the volatility of the return of a liquid stock. She will have hundreds of data points to fit a model. In most cases, the risk manager will have a model of the volatility of the stock that will perform reasonably well.

Historical data is at times of little use, because a known risk has not manifested itself in the past. For instance, with the subprime crisis, there was no historical data of a downturn in the real estate market during which a large amount of securitized subprime mortgages was outstanding. In such a situation, risk measurement cannot be done by simply using historical data since there is a risk of a decrease in real estate prices that has not manifested itself in a comparable historical period. With such a case, statistical risk measurement reaches its limits and risk management goes from science to art. Proper understanding of risks involves an assessment of the likelihood of a decrease in real estate prices and of the economic impact of such a decrease on the prices of securities. Such probability assessments have a significant element of subjectivity. Different risk managers can reach very different conclusions.

There is a fundamental problem with the performance of risk measurement when assessments become subjective. Suppose that all parties agree that an established statistical model works well. There is then little room for people to disagree. However, subjective forecasts are easily questioned. Why would a risk manager have a better understanding of the probability of a drop in real estate prices than experts in real estate? If experts in real estate conclude that a sharp drop in prices is unlikely, why would an organization then listen to a risk manager who wants to spend a large amount of money on a stress test to figure out the impact of such a large drop? As risk management moves away from established quantitative models, it becomes easily embroiled in intra-firm politics. At that point, the outcome for the firm depends much more on the firm's risk appetite and on its culture than on its risk management models.

Mismeasurement Due to Ignored Risks

Ignored risks can take three different forms that have different implications for a firm. First, a firm may ignore a risk even though that risk is known. Second, somebody in the firm knows about a risk, but that risk is not captured by the risk models. Third, there is a realization of a truly unknown risk. We examine these possibilities in turn.

Ignored Known Risks

Consider again the case of LTCM. LTCM could have failed to take into account a risk that, if realized, would have led to a large loss. A good example of this possibility is as follows. Before Russia defaulted on its domestic debt in August 1998, many hedge funds took positions where they bought high-yielding Russian debt, hedged the debt against default risk, and finally hedged the debt against exchange rate risk. It was easy to believe that the resulting position had no risk. However, to hedge the currency risk, the funds had to sell rubles forward against dollars. The banks willing to stand on the other side of those trades were often Russian banks. When Russia defaulted, it imposed a moratorium on these banks and many collapsed, as a result, the hedge funds ended up having exchange rate risk because their counterparties did not honor the hedges. Had they taken into account counterparty risk properly, they would have understood that their positions had substantial risk in the event of an adverse shock to the Russian banking system.

I have no reason to believe that LTCM behaved like these other hedge funds. Further, LTCM's Russian exposures were relatively small. However, suppose that it made losses because it did not correctly account for the risks of counterparties. Ex post, just knowing that LTCM lost 70% would not be sufficient to conclude that LTCM missed the counterparty risk in its risk models because it could have made a similar loss without missing that risk. Consequently, to assess whether LTCM made mistakes, one would have to look at the information it had when it made decisions, whether that information was flawed, and whether its use of that information was wrong.

Mistakes in Information Collection

The consequences of a risk management mistake are the same whether the risk was ignored because nobody in the firm knew about it or because somebody knew about it but it did not enter the relevant risk models. One of the benefits of implementing properly firm-wide risk management is that all risks are accounted for. If some risks are not accounted for when risk is measured for a firm, the risks left out are not adequately monitored and they can become large because organizations have a tendency to expand unmonitored risks. For instance, consider a trader whose risks are only partly monitored. Typically, traders have a compensation formula that involves an option payoff—they receive a significant share of the profits they generate, but they do not have to give back the losses. If only some of the risks of a trader are monitored, he can increase his expected compensation by increasing the risks that are not monitored, without suffering any of the consequences.

It is common practice in risk management to divide risks into market, credit, and operational risks. This distinction is partly artificial and driven by regulatory considerations. Typically, firms have trading books that are marked to market, while the credit book uses accrual accounting. However, this division of risk may be implemented in a way that ignores large chunks of risk. For instance, a firm has funding risks. Funding may become more expensive and/or less available precisely when the firm experiences bad market outcomes. To wit, an important factor contributing to the failure of Bear Stearns was the limitations it faced in accessing the repo market in its last week. Similarly, while Basel II rules have a rather restricted view of operational risk, business risks are often of critical importance and have to be carefully assessed as part of the evaluation of a firm's risk even though they are not part of the regulatory definition of operational risk. These risks may be highly correlated with both credit and market risks for financial institutions. For instance, for many banks, the loss of income from securitizations was the realization of a business risk that was correlated with a market risk, namely the loss in value of securities issued through securitizations, and with credit risks, namely the inability to use securitization to lay off the risks associated with loans.

Accounting for all the risks in risk measurement is a difficult and costly task. However, not performing that task for an organization means that the firm's top executives are managing the company with blinders on—they see only part of the big picture they have to understand to manage effectively. There are well-known examples of incomplete risk aggregation leading to large losses from risks that were not accounted for. Perhaps one of the best examples is the one of a bank that no longer exists, the Union Bank of Switzerland. In the second half of the 1990s, the bank was putting together risk management systems that would aggregate risks within its trading operations. One group of traders that focused on equity derivatives was extremely successful. However, this group of traders was using different computers from the rest of the bank, so that integrating their systems into the bank's systems would have required them to change computers. Eventually, the bank decided, at the top level, that it was more important to let the traders make money than disrupt what they were doing through changes of computers. Soon thereafter, this group of traders lost a large amount of money for the bank. The loss was partly responsible for the bank having to merge with another Swiss bank.[6]

Problems of aggregation were important at various stages of the subprime crisis as well. In particular, the management of UBS sent a report to its shareholders explaining why the bank had such large write-downs. In this report, UBS explains that "Efforts were made to capture Subprime holdings by mid-February 2007, however, materials did not effectively include the Super Senior and Negative Basis positions." (p. 39). It is interesting to note that, according to the report, the Super Senior positions were not included because they were hedged and hence were assigned no risk by the risk models—an evaluation which was consistent with past data used by many risk managers.

Unknown Risks

Most unknown risks do not create risk management problems. To see this, we can go back to the statistical model of risk measurement for a stock. Suppose that a risk manager models the return of a stock using the normal distribution and that he has no reason to believe that future returns will come from a different distribution than the one that held in the past. With this model, each period, the stock return will be random. It will come from a known distribution. The risk manager does not need to know why the return of the stock in one period is 10% and in another period it is −15%. He has captured the relevant risk characteristics of the stock through his estimation of the statistical distribution of the returns of the stock. With his work, he knows that the volatility is 20% and that

---

[6] See Dirk Schütz, *La Chute de l'UBS: Les raisons du declin de l'Union de Banques Suisses,* Bilan, 1998.

there is a 5% chance of a loss of say 30% or higher over a period. He does not need to be in a position to explain what events are associated with various losses.

Other unknown risks may not matter simply because they have a trivially low probability. There is some probability that a building will be hit by an asteroid. That risk does not affect any management decisions. Ignoring that risk has no implications for risk management.

The unknown risks that represent risk management failures are risks that, had the firm's managers known about them, their actions would have been different. Risk managers have to look out for unknown risks, but once everything is said and done, some risks will remain unknown. Because of this, they have to conclude that they do not capture all risks in their models and, therefore, some capital has to be made available to cope with unknown risks.

Communication Failures

Risk management is not an activity undertaken by risk managers for risk managers. Rather, it is an activity undertaken to enable the firm to maximize shareholder value by taking optimal decisions across the firm. In particular, the firm has to choose the level of risk it is exposed to and has to make sure that risks taken throughout the organization are valuable for shareholders. Therefore, risk management has to provide timely information to the board and top management that enables them to make decisions concerning the firm's risk and to factor the firm's risk in their decisions. In order for the board and the top management to understand the risk situation of the firm, this situation has to be communicated to them in a way that they can understand properly. If a firm has perfect risk systems, but the board and the top management cannot understand the output of these systems because the risk manager cannot communicate this output properly, the firm's systems may do more harm than good by inspiring false confidence in the performance of risk management. Even worse, information can arrive to top management too late or too distorted by intermediaries.

Communication failures seem to have played a role in the most recent crisis. For example, the UBS report to its shareholders explains that "A number of attempts were made to present Subprime or housing related exposures. The reports did not, however, communicate an effective

message for a number of reasons, in particular because the reports were overly complex, presented outdated data or were not made available to the right audience." (p. 39). An industry commission that drew lessons from the crisis emphasized communication issues as well. It concluded that "risk monitoring and management reduces to the basis of getting the right information, at the right time, to the right people, such that those people can make the most informed judgments possible."[7] Finally, a report from the Senior Supervisors Group, which includes top regulators from the U.S., England, and Germany as well as other countries, also emphasized communication issues, stating for instance that "In some cases, hierarchical structures tended to serve as filters when information was sent up the management chain, leading to delays or distortions in sharing important data with senior management."[8]

Failures in Monitoring and Managing Risks

Risk management is responsible for making sure that the firm takes the risks that it wants to take and not others. As a result, risk managers must constantly monitor the risks the firm is taking. Further, they have to hedge and mitigate known risks to meet the objectives of top management.

We have already discussed the problem that a firm may be taking risks that it does not know about. When we discussed that problem, we focused on it as an inventory issue. However, there is a different perspective on this problem which is particularly relevant in financial firms. For the typical non-financial firm, risks often change slowly. Not so for financial firms. For a financial firm, risks can change sharply even if the firm does not take new positions. The problem arises from the fact that financial firms have many derivatives positions and positions with embedded derivatives. Over time, these positions have become more complex.

---

[7] "Containing systemic risk: The road to reform," The Report of the CRMPG III, August 6, 2008.

[8] Senior Supervisors Group, "Observations on Risk Management Practices during the Recent Market Turbulence," March 6, 2008, p. 9.

The risk properties of portfolios of derivatives can change very rapidly with no trading whatsoever. This is because complex derivatives often have exposures to risk factors that are extremely sensitive to market conditions. Strikingly, it is perfectly possible with some products to see changes such that, during the same day, a security could have an exposure to interest rates so that it gains substantially if interest rates increase and later in the day have an exposure such that it loses substantially if interest rates increase. For such a product, hedges adjusted daily could end up creating large losses because the hedge that is optimal at the start of the day could end up aggravating the risk exposure at the end of the day.

One of the most obvious demonstrations of how risk exposures can change is the pricing of subprime derivatives. The ABX indices have been the most readily available data on the value of securities issued against subprime mortgage collateral. The indices are equally-weighted averages of credit-default swaps on securitization tranches. New indices were created every six months, reflecting new securitizations. Initially, the AAA indices, which represent the pricing of credit default swaps on AAA-rated tranches of securitizations, exhibited almost no variation, so that reasonable assessments of the risk of the AAA-rated tranches of securitizations using historical data would have been that they had little risk. Yet, suddenly, the value of these securities fell off a cliff as shown on Figure 8-1. Holders of AAA-rated tranches of subprime securities made sudden large losses if they chose to use the ABX indices as proxies for the value of their holdings.

When the risk characteristics of securities can change very rapidly, it is challenging for risk monitors to capture these changes and for risk managers to adjust hedges appropriately. This challenge is especially great when risk characteristics can change dramatically for small changes

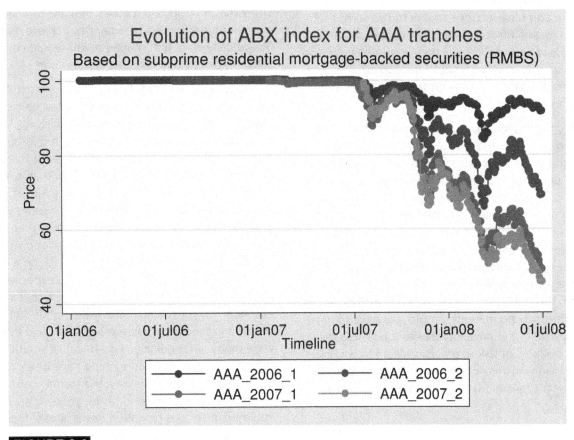

FIGURE 8-1

in the determinants of security prices. As a result, risk managers may fail to adequately measure risks or hedge risks simply because risk characteristics of securities may change too quickly to enable these managers to assess these characteristics properly or to put on correct hedges.

An important component of risk management is to identify possible solutions that can be implemented quickly if a firm has to reduce its risk over a short period of time. Contingency hedging plans are therefore critical. Lack of such plans could make it impossible for a firm to cope with unexpected difficulties. At the same time, however, when liquidity dries up in the markets, many risk-mitigating options that can be used easily outside of crisis periods can no longer be used.

Paradoxically, the introduction of mark-to-market accounting makes it even harder for risk managers to estimate risk and put on adequate hedges.[9] In many ways, mark-to-market has introduced the Heisenberg Principle into financial markets: For large organizations, observing the value of a complex security affects the value of that security. The reason for this is straightforward: As mark-to-market losses become known, they start a chain reaction of adjustments at other institutions and affect prices of possible trades as the market understands the capital positions of institutions better.

In large complex organizations, it is also possible for individuals to take risks that remain hidden for a while. A trader might have constructed a complicated position that only he understands. This position might be such that under some circumstances it could lead to large losses. The position might use securities that are not incorporated in the risk management systems. At all times, organizations face trade-offs. Risk management might be structured to know everything at all times. However, if risk management were organized that way, it would stifle innovation within the firm and hamper the competitiveness of the firm. In fast moving markets, employees have to have flexibility. However, that flexibility makes it possible for unobserved pockets of risk to emerge. When these risks manifest themselves, it is not clear that they represent a risk management failure. Risk management could have

made sure that these risks were not taken, but ex ante shareholders would have been worse off. Besides eliminating flexibility within the firm, risk monitoring is costly so that at some point, tighter risk monitoring is not efficient.

The effectiveness of risk monitoring and control depends crucially on an institution's culture and incentives. If risk is everybody's business in an organization, it is harder for pockets of risk to be left unobserved. If employees' compensation is affected by how they take risks, they will take risk more judiciously. The best risk models in a firm with poor culture and poor incentives will be much less effective than in a firm where the incentives of employees are better aligned with the risk-taking objectives of the firm.

Risk Measures and Risk Management Failures

So far, we have taken the risk metrics as given. We now show that focusing on metrics that are too narrow may make it harder for management to achieve its objectives. Specifically, risks that management would consider important can be left unmeasured and ignored.

A widely used risk measure in financial institutions is a daily VaR measure for trading activities. Large banks usually disclose data on that measure quarterly. They will generally say the number of times in a quarter the P&L had a loss that exceeds the daily VaR. For instance, UBS reported in its annual report for 2006 that it never had a loss that exceeded its daily VaR. In contrast, in 2007, it reported in its annual report that it exceeded its daily VaR 29 times. The results for 2007 show that fundamental changes were taking place in the economy that made it difficult for risk managers to track risk on a daily basis. However, such a large number of VaR exceedances provide little or no information about the implication of these exceedances for the financial health of UBS. It could be that the exceedances were really small and that there were many large gains as well because volatility increased rapidly. Alternatively, there could have been very large losses and few large gains. In the former case, the firm could be ahead at the end of the year. In the latter case, it could be in serious trouble. Consequently, focusing on the daily market VaR, though intellectually satisfying for risk managers because the most up-to-date quantitative techniques can be brought to bear on the problem, can only be one part of risk management and not the one that top

---

[9] For a discussion of some of the issues concerning mark-to-market accounting that accounts for possible feedback effects, see Guillaume Plantin, Haresh Sapra, and Hyun Song Shin, Marking to Market: Panacea or Pandora's Box?, 2008, *Journal of Accounting Research* 46, 435–460.

management should focus on. Top management has to focus on the longer-run implications of risk.

Short-run VaR measures can be low and the firm can appear to do an extremely good job with them, yet it can fail. I have not seen monthly VaR estimates from LTCM. However, from March 1994 to December 1997, LTCM had only eight months with losses and the worst monthly loss was 2.9%. In contrast, it had 37 months with gains.[10] As a result, one would have a hard time using historical monthly returns to conclude that its risk management was flawed. Consider a firm that has a one-day VaR of $100 million for its trading book at the 1% probability level. This means that the firm has a one percent chance of losing more than $100 million. If this firm exceeded its VaR once over 100 trading days and lost $10 billion, all existing statistical tests of risk management performance based on VaR exceedances would indicate that the firm has excellent risk management. VaR does not capture catastrophic losses that have a small probability of occurring.

Daily VaR measures assume that assets can be sold quickly or hedged, so that a firm can limit its losses essentially within a day. However, both in 1998 and over the last year, we have seen that markets can become suddenly less liquid, so that daily VaR measures lose their meaning. If a firm sits on a portfolio that cannot be traded, a daily VaR measure is not a measure of the risk of the portfolio because the firm is stuck with the portfolio for a much longer period of time.

To assess risk, firms have to look at longer horizons and have to take a comprehensive view of their risks. A one-year horizon is widely used in enterprise risk management for measures of firm-wide risk. Generally, financial institutions that focus on firm-wide risk at a one-year horizon aim for credit ratings that imply an extremely small probability of default. Such approaches are useful in assessing a firm's risk, in estimating the optimal amount of capital for a firm, and estimating the profitability of projects and lines of business through a careful evaluation of the cost of the capital required to bear their risks. However, at the same time, such approaches are not sufficient.

A high target credit rating effectively means that the firm tries to avoid default in all but the most extreme circumstances. If a firm aims for an AA credit rating, it

effectively chooses a probability of default which is such that it would default less frequently than one year out of a thousand. Crises occur much more often than that, so that the firm has to have a strategy which allows it to survive crises. Further, the probability of a crisis is difficult to estimate precisely, so that even if the estimate of the probability is very small, estimation error could be such that the true, unknown, probability is much higher. Consequently, the firm has to focus on crisis events in its risk measurement and management.

Existing risk models are generally not designed to capture risks associated with crises and to help firms manage them. These models use historical data and are most precise for short horizons—like days. With short horizons, crises are extremely rare events. Yet, when we consider years, crises are not extremely rare events. Months and years are a better horizon to evaluate risk when it comes to crises for at least two reasons. First, as evidenced since the summer of 2007, crises involve a dramatic withdrawal of liquidity from the markets. The withdrawal of liquidity means that firms are stuck with positions that they never expected to hold for a long time because price pressure costs involved in trading out of these positions are extremely high. Positions whose risk was evaluated over one day because the firm thought it could trade out of these positions suddenly became positions that had to be held for weeks or months. Second, during crisis periods, firms will make multiple losses that exceed their daily VaRs and these losses can be large enough to substantially weaken them. As a result, risk measures have to contemplate the distribution of large losses over time rather than over one day.

Crises involve complicated interactions across risks and across institutions. Statistical risk models typically take returns to be exogenous to the firm and ignore risk concentrations across institutions. Such an approach is appropriate for many institutions, but it is insufficient for institutions that, for whatever reasons, are important in specific markets and whose actions affect security prices. For instance, it is well-known that LTCM had extremely large positions in the index option market where it was short. During the crisis, it had little ability to change these positions because it was so large in that market. Further, a large institution can be exposed to predatory trading—i.e., of trades made by others designed to exploit its problems. An example of predatory trading is a situation where traders from other institutions benefit from pushing a

---

[10] These monthly returns are for Long-Term Capital Management, L.P. (B), prepared by André Perold, Harvard Business School, 1999.

price down if they can because it might force a fire sale. Typical risk management models would not account for this. They would not account for the fact that if the institution is large in a market, its losses can lead to more losses. As a firm makes a loss, it may drag down prices for other institutions and make funding more costly across institutions, which can have feedback effects for the institution. Ignoring these potential feedback effects may lead to an understatement of the risk of positions in the event of a crisis.

There is little hope for statistical risk models relying on historical data to capture such complicated situations. Rather, a firm has to augment these models with scenario analysis that investigates how crises can unfold and how they will affect it under various assumptions about how it reacts to the crisis. With such scenarios in hand, top management can then understand how crises can endanger the franchise of their institution and how to manage risks before they occur so that they can survive them. Such a scenario approach requires economic and financial analysis. It cannot be done by risk management departments populated by physicists and mathematicians. Such an approach also cannot be successful unless top management believes that the scenarios considered represent legitimate threats to the institution and that the institution has to protect itself against such threats.

SUMMARY

Risk management has made considerable progress since 1998. The difficulties of the last year have convinced many observers that somehow there are deep flaws in risk management and that the problems of the last year are partly explained by risk management failures. In this paper, I show that one ought to distinguish carefully between risk-taking decisions that unexpectedly lead to losses and risk management assessments of risk. There are many ways that risk management failures can occur, but not every loss reflects a risk management failure. However, risk management practice can be improved by taking into account the lessons from financial crises.

These crises happen often enough that they have to be carefully modeled and institutions have to focus on scenario analyses that assess the implications of crises for their financial health and survival. Such scenario analyses cannot be built from quantitative models using past data, but instead they must use economic analysis to evaluate the impact of the withdrawal of liquidity and the feedback effects that are common in financial crises. To successfully impact firm strategy, such analyses have to be deeply rooted in a firm's culture and in the strategic thinking of top management.

The Standard Capital Asset Pricing Model

9

Learning Objectives

Candidates, after completing this reading, should be able to:

- Understand the derivation and components of the CAPM.
- Describe the assumptions underlying the CAPM.
- Interpret the capital market line.

- Apply the CAPM in calculating the expected return on an asset.
- Interpret beta and calculate the beta of a single asset or portfolio.

Excerpt is Chapter 13 of Modern Portfolio Theory and Investment Analysis, *Ninth Edition, by Edwin J. Elton, Martin J. Gruber, Stephen J. Brown, and William N. Goetzmann.*

Consider how an individual or institution, acting on a set of estimates, selects an optimum portfolio, or set of portfolios. If investors all act in a prescribed manner, then we should be able to draw on the analysis to determine how the aggregate of investors will behave and how prices and returns at which markets will clear are set. The construction of general equilibrium models will allow us to determine the relevant measure of risk for any asset and the relationship between expected return and risk for any asset when markets are in equilibrium. Furthermore, though the equilibrium models are derived from models of how portfolios should be constructed, the models themselves have major implications for the characteristics or optimum portfolios.

In this chapter we develop the simplest form of an equilibrium model, called the *standard capital asset pricing model* (CAPM), or the *one-factor capital asset pricing model*. This was the first general equilibrium model developed, and it is based on the most stringent set of assumptions.

It is worthwhile pointing out at this time that the final test of a model is not how reasonable the assumptions behind it appear but how well the model describes reality. As readers proceed with this chapter, they will, no doubt, find many of its assumptions objectionable. Furthermore, the final model is so simple that readers may well wonder about its validity. As we will see, despite the stringent assumptions and the simplicity of the model, it does an amazingly good job of describing prices in the capital markets.

THE ASSUMPTIONS UNDERLYING THE STANDARD CAPITAL ASSET PRICING MODEL (CAPM)

The real world is sufficiently complex that to understand it and construct models of how it works, one must assume away those complexities that are thought to have only a small (or no) effect on its behavior. As the physicist builds models of the movement of matter in a frictionless environment, the economist builds models where there are no institutional frictions to the movement of stock prices.

The first assumption we make is that there are no transaction costs. There is no cost (friction) of buying or selling any asset. If transaction costs were present, the return

from any asset would be a function of whether the investor owned it before the decision period. Thus to include transaction costs in the model adds a great deal of complexity. Whether it is worthwhile introducing this complexity depends on the importance of transaction costs to investors' decisions. Given the size of transaction costs, they are probably of minor importance.

The second assumption behind the CAPM is that assets are infinitely divisible. This means that investors could take any position in an investment, regardless of the size of their wealth. For example, they can buy one dollar's worth of IBM stock.

The third assumption is the absence of personal income tax.[1] This means, for example, that the individual is indifferent to the form (dividends or capital gains) in which the return on the investment is received.

The fourth assumption is that an individual cannot affect the price of a stock by his buying or selling action. This is analogous to the assumption of perfect competition. Although no single investor can affect prices by an individual action, investors in total determine prices by their actions.

The fifth assumption is that investors are expected to make decisions solely in terms of expected values and standard deviations of the returns on their portfolios.

The sixth assumption is that unlimited short sales are allowed. The individual investor can sell short any number of any shares.

The seventh assumption is unlimited lending and borrowing at the riskless rate. The investor can lend or borrow any amount of funds desired at a rate of interest equal to the rate for riskless securities.

The eighth and ninth assumptions deal with the homogeneity of expectations. First, investors are assumed to be concerned with the mean and variance of returns (or prices over a single period), and all investors are assumed to define the relevant period in exactly the same manner. Second, all investors are assumed to have identical expectations with respect to the necessary inputs to the portfolio decision. As we have said many times, these inputs are expected returns, the variance of returns, and the

---

[1] The major results of the model would hold if income tax and capital gains taxes were of equal size.

correlation matrix representing the correlation structure between all pairs of stocks.

The tenth assumption is that all assets are marketable. All assets, including human capital, can be sold and bought on the market.

Readers can now see the reason for the earlier warning that they might find many of the assumptions behind the CAPM untenable. It is clear that these assumptions do not hold in the real world, just as it is clear that the physicist's frictionless environment does not really exist. The relevant questions are, How much is reality distorted by making these assumptions? What conclusions about capital markets do they lead to? Do these conclusions seem to describe the actual performance of the capital market?

THE CAPM

The standard form of the general equilibrium relationship for asset returns was developed independently by Sharpe, Lintner, and Mossin. Hence it is often referred to as the *Sharpe-Lintner-Mossin form* of the capital asset pricing model. This model has been derived in several forms involving different degrees of rigor and mathematical complexity. There is a trade-off between these derivations. The more complex forms are more rigorous and provide a framework within which alternative sets of assumptions can be examined. However, because of their complexity, they do not convey the economic intuition behind the CAPM as readily as some of the simpler forms. Because of this, we approach the derivation of the model at two distinct levels. The first derivation consists of a simple, intuitively appealing derivation of the CAPM. This is followed by a more rigorous derivation.

Deriving the CAPM—A Simple Approach

Recall that in the presence of short sales, but without riskless lending and borrowing, each investor faced an efficient frontier such as that shown in Figure 9-1. In this figure, *BC* represents the efficient frontier, while *ABC* represents the set of minimum-variance portfolios. In general the efficient frontier will differ among investors because of differences in expectations.

When we introduced riskless lending and borrowing, we showed that the portfolio of risky assets that any investor would hold could be identified without regard to the

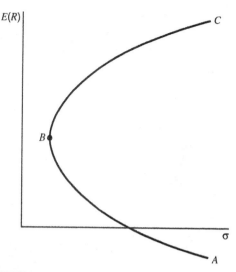

FIGURE 9-1 The efficient frontier—no lending and borrowing.

investor's risk preferences. This portfolio lies at the tangency point between the original efficient frontier of risky assets and a ray passing through the riskless return (on the vertical axis). This is depicted in Figure 9-2, where P_i denotes investor i's portfolio of risky assets.[2] The investors satisfy their risk preferences by combining portfolio P_i with lending or borrowing.

If all investors have homogeneous expectations and they all face the same lending and borrowing rate, then they will each face a diagram such as in Figure 9-2 and, furthermore, all of the diagrams will be identical. The portfolio of risky assets P_i held by any investor will be identical to the portfolio of risky assets held by any other investor. If all investors hold the same risky portfolio, then, in equilibrium, it must be the market portfolio. The market portfolio is a portfolio comprising all risky assets. Each asset is held in the proportion that the market value of that asset represents of the total market value of all risky assets. For example, if IBM stock represents 3% of all risky assets, then the market portfolio contains 3% IBM stock, and each investor will take 3% of the money that will be invested in all risky assets and place it in IBM stock.

---

[2] We have subscripted P because each individual can face a different efficient frontier and thus select a different P_i. This is true, though the composition of P_i does not depend on investor i's risk preference.

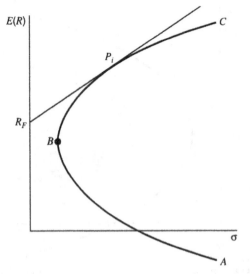

FIGURE 9-2 The efficient frontier with lending and borrowing.

Notice that we have already learned something important. All investors will hold combinations of only two portfolios: the market portfolio (*M*) and a riskless security. This is sometimes referred to as the *two mutual fund theorem* because all investors would be satisfied with a market fund, plus the ability to lend or borrow a riskless security.

The straight line depicted in Figure 9-2 is usually referred to as the *capital market line*. All investors will end up with portfolios somewhere along the capital market line, and all *efficient portfolios* would lie along the capital market line. However, not all securities or portfolios lie along the capital market line. In fact, from the derivation of the efficient frontier, we know that all portfolios of risky and riskless assets, except those that are efficient, lie below the capital market line. By looking at the capital market line, we can learn something about the market price of risk. The equation of a line connecting a riskless asset and a risky portfolio (the line we now call the capital market line) is

$$\bar{R}_e = R_F + \frac{\bar{R}_M - R_F}{\sigma_M} \sigma_e.$$

where the subscript *e* denotes an efficient portfolio.

The term $\left[(\bar{R}_M - R_F)/\sigma_M\right]$ can be thought of as the market price of risk for all efficient portfolios.[3] It is the extra

---

[3] The reader should be alerted to the fact that many authors have defined $(\bar{R}_M - R_F)/\sigma_M^2$ as the market price of risk. The reason we have selected $(\bar{R}_M - R_F)/\sigma_M$ will become clear as you proceed with this chapter.

return that can be gained by increasing the level of risk (standard deviation) on an efficient portfolio by one unit. The second term on the right-hand side of this equation is simply the market price of risk times the amount of risk in a portfolio. The second term represents that element of required return that is due to risk. The first term is simply the price of time or the return that is required for delaying potential consumption, one period given perfect certainty about the future cash flow. Thus the expected return on an efficient portfolio is

(Expected return) = (Price of time) + (Price of risk)
× (Amount of risk)

Although this equation establishes the return on an efficient portfolio, it does not describe equilibrium returns on nonefficient portfolios or on individual securities. We now turn to the development of a relationship that does so.

For very well-diversified portfolios, beta was the correct measure of a security's risk. For *very* well-diversified portfolios, nonsystematic risk tends to go to zero, and the only relevant risk is systematic risk measured by beta. As we have just explained, given the assumptions of homogeneous expectations and unlimited riskless lending and borrowing, all investors will hold the market portfolio. Thus the investor will hold a *very* well-diversified portfolio. Because we assume that the investor is concerned only with expected return and risk, the only dimensions of a security that need be of concern are expected return and beta.

Let us hypothesize two portfolios with the characteristics shown here:

Investment	Expected Return	Beta
A	10	1.0
B	12	1.4

We know that the expected return from portfolio *A* is simply the sum of the products of the proportion invested in each stock and the expected return on each stock. We also know that the beta on a portfolio is simply the sum of the product of the proportion invested in each stock times the beta on each stock. Now consider a portfolio *C* made up of one-half of portfolio *A* and one-half of portfolio *B*. From the facts stated earlier, the expected return on this portfolio is 11, and its beta is 1.2. These three potential investments are plotted in Figure 9-3. Notice they lie on a straight line. This is no accident. All portfolios composed of different fractions of investments A and B will lie along a straight line in expected return beta space.[4]

Now hypothesize a new investment D that has a return of 13% and a beta of 1.2. Such an investment cannot exist for very long. All decisions are made in terms of risk and return. This portfolio offers a higher return and the same risk as portfolio C. Hence it would pay all investors to sell C short and buy D. Similarly, if a security were to exist with a return of 8% and a beta of 1.2 (designated by E), it would pay arbitrageurs to step in and buy portfolio C while selling security E short. Such arbitrage would take place until C, D, and E all yielded the same return. This is just another illustration of the adage that two things that are equivalent cannot sell at different prices. We can demonstrate the arbitrage discussed earlier in a slightly more formal manner. Let us return to the arbitrage between portfolios C and D. An investor could sell $100 worth of portfolio C short and with the $100 buy portfolio D. If the investor were to do so, the characteristics of this arbitraged portfolio would be as follows:

	Cash Invested	Expected Return	Beta
Portfolio C	−$100	−$11	−1.2
Security D	+$100	$13	1.2
Arbitrage portfolio	0	$ 2	0

From this example it is clear that as long as a security lies above the straight line, there is a portfolio involving zero risk and zero net investment that has a positive expected profit. An investor will engage in this arbitrage as long as any security or portfolio lies above the straight line depicted in Figure 9-3. A similar arbitrage will exist if any amount lies below the straight line in Figure 9-3.

---

[4] If we let X stand for the fraction of funds invested in portfolio A, then the equation for return is

$$\bar{R}_P = X\bar{R}_A + (1-X)\bar{R}_B$$

The equation for beta is

$$\beta_P = X\beta_A + (1-X)\beta_B$$

Solving the second equation for X and substituting in the first equation, we see that we are left with an equation of the form

$$\bar{R}_P = a + b\beta_P$$

or the equation of a straight line.

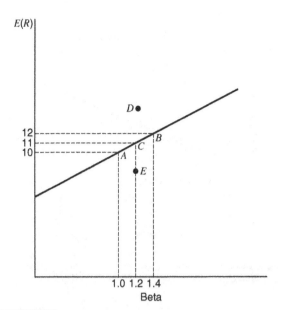

FIGURE 9-3 Combinations of portfolios.

We have now established that all investments and all portfolios of investments must lie along a straight line in return-beta space. If any investment were to lie above or below that straight line, then an opportunity would exist for riskless arbitrage. This arbitrage would continue until all investments converged to the line. There are many different ways that this straight line can be identified, for it takes only two points to identify a straight line. Because we have shown that, under the assumptions of the CAPM, everybody will hold the market portfolio because all portfolios must lie on the straight line, we will use this as one point. The market portfolio must have a beta of 1.

Thus, in Figure 9-4, the market portfolio is point M with a beta of 1 and an expected return of $\bar{R}_M$. It is often convenient to choose the second point to identify a straight line as the intercept. The intercept occurs when beta equals zero, or when the asset has zero systematic risk. One asset with zero systematic risk is the riskless asset. Thus we can treat the intercept as the rate of return on a riskless asset. These two points identify the straight line shown in Figure 9-4. The equation of a straight line has the form

$$\bar{R}_i = a + b\beta_i \tag{9.1}$$

One point on the line is the riskless asset with a beta of zero. Thus

$$R_F = a + b(0)$$

or

$$R_F = a$$

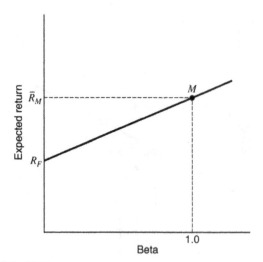

FIGURE 9-4   The security market line.

A second point on the line is the market portfolio with a beta of 1. Thus

$$\bar{R}_M = a + b(1)$$

or

$$(\bar{R}_M - a) = b$$

Putting these together and substituting into Equation (9.1) yields

$$\bar{R}_i = R_F + \beta_i(\bar{R}_M - R_F) \qquad \textbf{(9.2)}$$

Think about this relationship for a moment. It represents one of the most important discoveries in the field of finance. Here is a simple equation, called the *security market line*, that describes the expected return for all assets and portfolios of assets in the economy. The expected return on any asset, or portfolio, whether it is efficient or not, can be determined from this relationship. Notice that $\bar{R}_M$ and R_F are not functions of the assets we examine. Thus the relationship between the expected return on any two assets can be related simply to their difference in beta. The higher beta is for any security, the higher must be its equilibrium return. Furthermore, the relationship between beta and expected return is linear. One of the greatest insights that comes from this equation arises from what it states is unimportant in determining return. The risk of any stock could be divided into systematic and unsystematic risk. Beta was the index of systematic risk. This equation validates the conclusion that systematic risk is the only important ingredient in determining expected returns and that

nonsystematic risk plays no role.[5] Put another way, the investor gets rewarded for bearing systematic risk. It is not total variance of returns that affects expected returns but only that part of the variance in returns that cannot be diversified away. This result has great economic intuition for, if investors can eliminate all nonsystematic risk through diversification, there is no reason they should be rewarded, in terms of higher return, for bearing it. All of these implications of the CAPM are empirically testable. Provided the tests hold, we have, with a simple model, gained great insight into the behavior of the capital markets.

We digress for a moment and point out one seeming fallacy in the potential use of the CAPM. Invariably, when a group of investors is first exposed to the CAPM, one or more investors will find a high-beta stock that last year produced a smaller return than low-beta stocks. The CAPM is an equilibrium relationship. High-beta stocks are expected to give a higher return than low-beta stocks because they are more risky. This does not mean that they will give a higher return over all intervals of time. In fact, if they always gave a higher return, they would be less risky, not more risky, than low-beta stocks. Rather, because they arc more risky, they will sometimes produce lower returns. However, over long periods of time, they should on the average produce higher returns.

We have written the CAPM model in the form

$$\bar{R}_i = R_F + \beta_i(\bar{R}_M - R_F)$$

This is the form in which it is most often written and the form most amenable to empirical testing. However, there are alternative forms that give added insight into its meaning. Recall that

$$\beta_i = \frac{\sigma_{iM}}{\sigma_M^2}$$

We could then write the security market line as

$$\bar{R}_i = R_F + \left(\frac{\bar{R}_M - R_F}{\sigma_M}\right)\frac{\sigma_{iM}}{\sigma_M} \qquad \textbf{(9.3)}$$

This, in fact, is the equation of a straight line located in expected return σ_{iM}/σ_M space. Recall that earlier in our

---

[5] This result is somewhat circular for, in this proof, we assumed that beta was the relevant risk measure. In the more rigorous proof that follows, we make no such assumption, yet we end up with the same equation for the security market line.

discussion of the capital market, line $(R_m - R_F)/\sigma_M$ was described as the market price of risk. Because σ_{iM}/σ_M is a definition of the risk of any security, or portfolio, we would see that the security market line, like the capital market line, states that the expected return on any security is the riskless rate of interest plus the market price of risk times the amount of risk in the security or portfolio.[6]

Many authors write the CAPM equation as

$$\bar{R}_i = R_F + \left(\frac{\bar{R}_M - R_F}{\sigma_M^2} \right) \sigma_{iM}$$

They define $(\bar{R}_M - R_F)/\sigma_M^2$ as the market price of risk and σ_{iM} as the measure of the risk of security i. We have chosen the form we used because σ_{iM}/σ_M is the measure of how the risk on a security affects the risk of the market portfolio. It seems to us that this is the appropriate way to discuss the risk of a security.

We have now completed our intuitive proof of the CAPM. We are about to present a more complex mathematical proof. There are two reasons for presenting this mathematical proof. The first is that it is more rigorous. The second, and more important, reason is that one needs a richer framework to incorporate modifications of the assumptions of the standard CAPM. The method of proof just presented is too restrictive to allow forms of general

___

[6] In the following we offer theoretical justification that σ_{iM}/σ_M is the relevant measure of the risk of any security in equilibrium. Recall that the standard deviation of the market portfolio is given by

$$\sigma_M = \left[\sum_{i=1}^{N} X_i^2 \sigma_i^2 + \sum_{i=1}^{N} \sum_{\substack{j=1 \\ j \neq i}}^{N} X_i X_j \sigma_{ij} \right]^{1/2}$$

$\left(\begin{array}{c} SD \\ variance \end{array} \right)$

where all Xs are market proportions. Because all investors hold the market portfolio, the relevant definition of the risk of a security is the change in the risk of the market portfolio, as the holdings of that security are varied. This can be found as follows:

$$\frac{d\sigma_M}{dX_i} = \frac{d\left[\sum_{i=1}^{N} X_i^2 \sigma_i^2 + \sum_{i=1}^{N} \sum_{\substack{j=1 \\ j \neq i}}^{N} X_i X_j \sigma_{ij} \right]^{1/2}}{dX_i}$$

$$= \frac{\left(\frac{1}{2} \right) \left[2X_i \sigma_i^2 + (2) \sum_{\substack{j=1 \\ j \neq i}}^{N} X_j \sigma_{ij} \right]}{\left[\sum_{i=1}^{N} X_i^2 \sigma_i^2 + \sum_{i=1}^{N} \sum_{\substack{j=1 \\ j \neq i}}^{N} X_i X_j \sigma_{ij} \right]^{1/2}} = \frac{X_i^2 \sigma_i^2 + \sum_{\substack{j=1 \\ j \neq i}}^{N} X_j \sigma_{ij}}{\sigma_M} = \frac{\sigma_{iM}}{\sigma_M}$$

Therefore the relevant risk of security is equal to σ_{iM}/σ_M.

equilibrium equations that make more realistic assumptions about the world to be derived. The framework presented subsequently can be used to derive equilibrium models under alternative assumptions.

. . .

Deriving the CAPM—A More Rigorous Approach

We solved for the optimal portfolio when short sales were allowed and the investor could lend and borrow unlimited amounts of money at the riskless rate of interest. The solution involved finding the composition of the portfolio that maximized the slope of a straight line passing through the riskless rate of interest on the vertical axes and the portfolio itself. This involved maximizing the function

$$\theta = \left(\frac{\bar{R}_P - R_F}{\sigma_P} \right)$$

When the derivative of θ was taken with respect to all securities in the portfolio and each equation was set equal to zero, a set of simultaneous equations of the following form was derived:

$$\lambda \left(X_1 \sigma_{1k} + X_2 \sigma_{2k} + \cdots + X_k \sigma_k^2 + \cdots + X_N \sigma_{Nk} \right) = \bar{R}_k - R_F \quad \textbf{(9.4)}$$

This equation held for each security, and there is one such equation for each security in the market. If there are homogeneous expectations, then all investors must select the same optimum portfolio. If all investors select the same portfolio, then, in equilibrium, that portfolio must be a portfolio in which all securities are held in the same percentage that they represent of the market. In other words, in equilibrium, the proportion invested in security 1 must be that fraction of the total market value of all securities that security 1 represents. To get from Equation (9.4) to the CAPM involves simply recognizing that the left-hand side of Equation (9.4) is $\lambda \, \text{cov}(R_k R_M)$. To see this, first note that

$$R_M = \sum_{i=1}^{N} R_i X_i'$$

where the prime indicates market proportions. Thus

$$\text{cov}\left(R_k R_M \right) = E \left[\left(R_k - \bar{R}_k \right) \left(\sum_{i=1}^{N} R_i X_i' - \sum_{i=1}^{N} \bar{R}_i X_i' \right) \right] \quad \textbf{(9.5)}$$

Rearranging the second term,

$$\text{cov}\left(R_k R_M \right) = E \left[\left(R_k - \bar{R}_k \right) \left(\sum_{i=1}^{N} X_i' \left(R_i - \bar{R}_i \right) \right) \right]$$

Multiplying out the terms,

$$\operatorname{cov}(R_k R_M) = E[\, X_1'(R_k - \bar{R}_k)(R_1 - \bar{R}_1)$$
$$+ X_2'(R_k - \bar{R}_k)(R_2 - \bar{R}_2) + \cdots$$
$$+ X_k'(R_k - \bar{R}_k)(R_k - \bar{R}_k) + \cdots$$
$$+ X_N'(R_k - \bar{R}_k)(R_N - \bar{R}_N)\,]$$

Because the expected value of the sum of random variables is the sum of the expected values, factoring out the Xs yields

$$\operatorname{cov}(R_k R_M) = X_1' E(R_k - \bar{R}_k)(R_1 - \bar{R}_1) + X_2' E(R_k - \bar{R}_k)(R_2 - \bar{R}_2) +$$
$$\cdots + X_k' E(R_k - \bar{R}_k)^2 + X_N' E(R_k - \bar{R}_k)(R_N - \bar{R}_N)$$

Earlier we argued that the Xs in Equation (9.4) were market proportions. Comparing Equation (9.5) with the left-hand side of Equation (9.4) shows that they are, indeed, equal. Thus Equation (9.4) can be written as

$$\lambda \operatorname{cov}(R_k R_M) = \bar{R}_k - R_F \qquad \textbf{(9.6)}$$

Because this must hold for all securities (all possible values of k), it must hold for all portfolios of securities. One possible portfolio is the market portfolio. Writing Equation (9.6) for the market portfolio involves recognizing that $\operatorname{cov}(R_M R_M) = \sigma_M^2$:

$$\lambda \sigma_M^2 = \bar{R}_M - R_F$$

or

$$\lambda = \frac{\bar{R}_M - R_F}{\sigma_M^2}$$

Substituting this value for λ in Equation (9.6) and rearranging yields

$$\bar{R}_k = R_F + \frac{\bar{R}_M - R_F}{\sigma_M^2} \operatorname{cov}(R_k R_M) = R_F + \beta_k(\bar{R}_M - R_F)$$

This completes the more rigorous derivation of the security market line.

The advantages of this proof over that presented earlier are that we have not had to assume that beta is the relevant measure of risk, and we have established a framework that, as we see in the next chapter, can be used to derive general equilibrium solutions when some of the present assumptions are relaxed.

PRICES AND THE CAPM

Up to now, we have discussed equilibrium in terms of rate of return. In the introduction to this chapter, we mentioned that the CAPM could be used to describe equilibrium in terms of either return or prices. The latter is of importance in certain situations, for example, the pricing of new assets. It is very easy to move from the equilibrium relationship in terms of rates of return to one expressed in terms of prices. All that is involved is a little algebra.

Let us define

P_i as the present price of asset i.

P_M as the present price of the market portfolio (all assets).

Y_i as the dollar value of the asset one period hence. It is market value plus any dividends.

Y_M as the dollar value of the market portfolio one period hence, including dividends.

$\operatorname{cov}(Y_i Y_M)$ as the covariance between Y_i and Y_M.

$\operatorname{var}(Y_M)$ as the variance in Y_M.

r_F as $(1 + R_F)$.

The return on asset i is

$$R_i = \frac{\text{Ending value} - \text{Beginning value}}{\text{Beginning value}}$$

In symbols,

$$R_i = \frac{Y_i - P_i}{P_i} = \frac{Y_i}{P_i} - 1$$

Similarly,

$$R_M = \frac{Y_M - P_M}{P_M} = \frac{Y_M}{P_M} - 1$$

Substituting these expressions into Equation (9.3) yields

$$\frac{\bar{Y}_i}{P_i} - 1 = R_F + \left(\frac{\bar{Y}_M}{P_M} - 1 - R_F\right)\frac{\operatorname{cov}(R_i R_M)}{\sigma_M^2} \qquad \textbf{(9.7)}$$

Now we can rewrite $\operatorname{cov}(R_i R_M)$ as

$$\operatorname{cov}(R_i R_M) = E\left[\left(\frac{Y_i - P_i}{P_i} - \frac{\bar{Y}_i - P_i}{P_i}\right)\left(\frac{Y_M - P_M}{P_M} - \frac{\bar{Y}_M - P_M}{P_M}\right)\right]$$
$$= E\left[\left(\frac{Y_i}{P_i} - \frac{\bar{Y}_i}{P_i}\right)\left(\frac{Y_M}{P_M} - \frac{\bar{Y}_M}{P_M}\right)\right] = \frac{1}{P_i P_M}\operatorname{cov}(Y_i Y_M)$$

Similarly,

$$\sigma_M^2 = \frac{1}{P_M^2} \text{var}(Y_M)$$

Substituting these into Equation (9.7), adding 1 to both sides of the equation, and recalling that $r_F = 1 + R_F$,

$$\frac{\bar{Y}_i}{P_i} = r_F + \left(\frac{\bar{Y}_M}{P_M} - r_F\right) \frac{\frac{1}{P_i}\frac{1}{P_M}\text{cov}(Y_iY_M)}{\frac{1}{P_M^2}\text{var}(Y_M)}$$

Multiplying both sides of the equation by P_i and simplifying the last term on the right-hand side,

$$\bar{Y}_i = r_F P_i + \left(\bar{Y}_M - r_F P_M\right) \frac{\text{cov}(Y_iY_M)}{\text{var}(Y_M)}$$

Solving this expression for P_i,

$$P_i = \frac{1}{r_F}\left[\bar{Y}_i - \left(\bar{Y}_M - r_F P_M\right)\frac{\text{cov}(Y_iY_M)}{\text{var}(Y_M)}\right]$$

Valuation formulas of this type have often been suggested in the security analysis literature. The equation involves taking the expected dollar return next year, $(\bar{Y}_i)$, subtracting off some payment as compensation for risk taking, and then taking the present value of the net result. The term in square brackets can be thought of as the certainty equivalent of the horizon cash payment, and to find the present value of the certainty equivalent, we simply discount it at the riskless rate of interest. Although this general idea is not new, the explicit definition of how to find the certainty equivalent is one of the fundamental contributions of the CAPM. It can be shown that

$$\frac{\bar{Y}_M - r_F P_M}{\left[\text{var}(Y_M)\right]^{1/2}}$$

is equal to a measure of the market price of risk and that

$$\frac{\text{cov}(Y_iY_M)}{\left[\text{var}(Y_M)\right]^{1/2}}$$

is the relevant measure of risk for any asset.

CONCLUSION

In this chapter we have discussed the Sharpe-Lintner-Mossin form of a general equilibrium relationship in the capital markets. This model, usually referred to as the

capital asset pricing model or standard CAPM, is a fundamental contribution to understanding the manner in which capital markets function. It is worthwhile highlighting some of the implications of this model.

First, we have shown that, under the assumptions of the CAPM, the only portfolio of risky assets that any investor will own is the market portfolio. Recall that the market portfolio is a portfolio in which the fraction invested in any asset is equal to the market value of that asset divided by the market value of all risky assets. Each investor will adjust the risk of the market portfolio to her preferred risk-return combination by combining the market portfolio with lending or borrowing at the riskless rate. This leads directly to the two mutual fund theorem. The two mutual fund theorem states that all investors can construct an optimum portfolio by combining a market fund with the riskless asset. Thus all investors will hold a portfolio along the line connecting R_F with $\bar{R}_M$ in expected return, standard deviation of return space. See Figure 9-5.

This line, usually called the capital market line, which describes all efficient portfolios, is a pictorial representation of the equation

$$\bar{R}_e = R_F + \frac{\bar{R}_M - R_F}{\sigma_M}\sigma_e$$

Thus we can say that the return on an efficient portfolio is given by the market price of time plus the market price of risk times the amount of risk on an efficient portfolio.

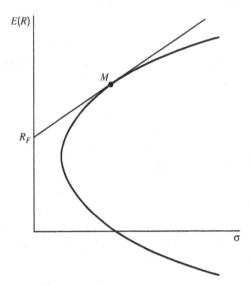

FIGURE 9-5 The efficient frontier.

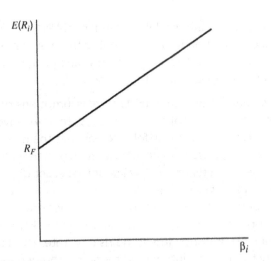

$E(R_i)$

R_F

β_i

FIGURE 9-6 The security market line.

Note that risk is defined as the standard deviation of return on any efficient portfolio.

From the equilibrium relationship for efficient portfolios we were able to derive the equilibrium relationship for any security or portfolio (efficient or inefficient). This relationship, presented in Figure 9-6, is given by

$$\bar{R}_i = R_F + \left(\frac{\bar{R}_M - R_F}{\sigma_M}\right)\frac{\sigma_{iM}}{\sigma_M}$$

or

$$\bar{R}_i = R_F + \beta_i\left(\bar{R}_M - R_F\right)$$

This relationship is usually called the security market line. Notice that it might have been called the security-portfolio market line, for it describes the equilibrium return on all portfolios as well as all securities.

Examination of the first form of the security market line shows that it is analogous in many ways to the capital market line. As we have shown, the impact of a security on the risk of the market portfolio is given by σ_{iM}/σ_M. Thus we can state that the equilibrium return on any security is equal to the price of time plus the market price of risk times the relevant definition of risk for the security.

The security market line clearly shows that return is an increasing function, in fact, a linearly increasing function, of risk. Furthermore, it is only market risk that affects return. The investor receives no added return for bearing diversifiable risk.

The capital asset pricing model has been derived under a set of very restrictive assumptions. The test of a model

is how well it describes reality. The key test is: Does it describe the behavior of returns in the capital markets? Before we turn to these tests, however, it is logical to examine forms of the general equilibrium relationship that exist under less restrictive assumptions. Even if the standard CAPM model explains the behavior of security returns, it obviously does not explain the behavior of individual investors. Individual investors hold nonmarket and, in fact, quite often, very small portfolios. Furthermore, by developing alternative forms of the general equilibrium relationship, we can test whether observed returns are more consistent with one of these than they are with the standard CAPM.

. . .

Bibliography

1. Aivazian, Varouj. "The Demand for Assets under Conditions of Risk: Comment," *Journal of Finance*, XXXII, No. 3 (June 1976), pp. 927–929.

2. Bawa, Vijay, and Lindenburg, Eric. "Capital Market Equilibrium in a Mean-Lower Partial Moment Framework," *Journal of Financial Economics*, 5 (1977), pp. 189–200.

3. Benninga, Simon, and Protopapadakis, Aris. "The Stock Market Premium, Production, and Relative Risk Aversion," *The American Economic Review*, 81, No. 3 (June 1991), pp. 591–599.

4. Bernstein, Peter L. "What Rate of Return Can You 'Reasonably' Expect?" *Journal of Finance*, XXVIII, No. 2 (May 1973), pp. 273–282.

5. Breeden, Douglas. "An Intertemporal Asset Pricing Model with Stochastic Consumption and Investment Opportunities," *Journal of Financial Economics*, 7 (1999), pp. 265–296.

6. Chen, Nai-Fu, Grundy, Bruce, and Stambaugh, Robert F. "Changing Risk, Changing Risk Premiums. and Dividend Yield Effects." *The Journal of Business*, 63, No. I (Jan. 1990), pp. 551–570.

7. Cochrane, John. *Asset Pricing* (Princeton, NJ: Princeton University Press, 2001).

8. Elton, Edwin J., and Gruber, Martin J. "The Multiperiod Consumption Investment Decision and Single-Period Analysis," *Oxford Economic Paper*, 26 (Sept. 1974). pp. 180–195.

9. Elton, Edwin J., and Gruber, Martin J. *Finance as a Dynamic Process* (Englewood Cliffs, NJ: Prentice Hall, 1975).

10. Fama, Eugene. "Risk. Return and Equilibrium: Some Clarifying Comments," *Journal of Finance,* XXIII, No. 1 (March 1968), pp. 29-40.

11. Fama, Eugene. "Multi-period Consumption Investment Decision." *American Economic Review,* 60 (March 1970), pp. 163-174.

12. ———. "Risk. Return and Equilibrium," *Journal of Political Economy,* 79, No. 1 (Jan./Feb. 1971), pp. 30-55.

13. ———. "Risk. Return and Portfolio Analysis: Reply to [20]." *Journal of Political Economy,* 81, No. 3 (May/June 1973), pp. 753-755.

14. Fama, Eugene F. "Determining the Number of Priced State Variables in the ICAPM." *Journal of Financial and Quantitative Analysis,* 33, No. 2 (June 1998), pp. 217-231.

15. Ferson, Wayne E., Harvey. C., and Campbell, R. "The Variation of Economic Risk Premiums." *The Journal of Political Economy,* 99, No. 2 (April 1991), pp. 385-416.

16. Ferson, Wayne E., Kandel, Shmuel, and Stambaugh, Robert F. "Tests of Asset Pricing with Time-Varying Expected Risk Premiums and Market Betas." *The Journal of Finance,* 42, No. 2 (June 1987), pp. 201-220.

17. Green, Richard C. "Benchmark Portfolio Inefficiency and Deviations from the Security Market Line." *The Journal of Finance,* 41, No. 2 (June 1986), pp. 295-312.

18. Hansen, Lars Peter, and Jagannathan, Ravi. "Implications of Security Market Data for Models of Dynamic Economics," *Journal of Political Economy,* 99 (1991), pp. 225-262.

19. Hietala, Pekka T. "Asset Pricing in Partially Segmented Markets: Evidence from the Finnish Market," *The Journal of Finance,* 44, No. 3 (July 1989), pp. 697-718.

20. Kroll, Yoram, and Levy, Haim. "Further Tests of the Separation Theorem and the Capital Asset Pricing Model," *The American Economic Review,* 82, No. 3 (June 1992), pp. 664-670.

21. Kroll, Yoram, Levy, Haim, and Rapoport, Amnon. "Experimental Tests of the Separation Theorem and the Capita," *The American Economic Review,* 78, No. 3 (June 1988), pp. 500-519.

22. Levy, Haim. "The Demand for Assets under Conditions of Risk," *Journal of Finance,* XXVIII, No. 1 (March 1973), pp. 79-96.

23. ———. "The Demand for Assets under Conditions of Risk: Reply to [1]," *Journal of Finance,* XXXII, No. 3 (June 1976), pp. 930-932.

24. Lintner, John. "Security Prices, Risk, and Maximal Gains from Diversification," *Journal of Finance* (Dec. 1965), pp. 587-615.

25. ———. "The Aggregation of Investor's Diverse Judgments and Preferences in Purely Competitive Security Markets," *Journal of Financial and Quantitative Analysis,* IV, No. 4 (Dec. 1969), pp. 347-400.

26. ———. "The Market Price of Risk, Size of Market and Investor's Risk Aversion," *Review of Economics and Statistics,* LII, No. 1 (Feb. 1970), pp. 87-99.

27. Markowitz, Harry M. "Nonnegative or Not Nonnegative: A Question about CAPMs," *The Journal of Finance,* 38, No. 2 (May 1983), pp. 283-296.

28. Modigliani, Franco, and Pogue, Jerry. "An Introduction to Risk and Return," *Financial Analysts Journal,* 30, No. 2 (Mar./Apr. 1974), pp. 68-80.

29. ———. "An Introduction to Risk and Return: Part II," *Financial Analysts Journal,* 30, No. 3 (May/June 1974), pp. 69-86.

30. Mossin, Jan. "Equilibrium in a Capital Asset Market," *Econometrica,* 34 (Oct. 1996), pp. 768-783.

31. Ng, Lilian. "Tests of the CAPM with Time-Varying Covariances: A Multivariate GARCH Approach," *The Journal of Finance,* 46, No. 4 (Sept. 1991), pp. 1507-1521.

32. Ross, Stephen. "A Simple Approach to the Valuation of Risky Streams," *Journal of Business,* 51, No. 3 (July 1978), pp. 453-475.

33. Rubinstein, Mark. "An Aggregation Theorem for Securities Markets," *Journal of Financial Economy,* 1, No. 3 (Sept. 1974), pp. 225-244.

34. Rubinstein, Mark E. "A Mean–Variance Synthesis of Corporate Financial Theory," *Journal of Finance,* XXXVIII, No. 1 (March 1973), pp. 167-181.

35. Sharpe, W. F. "Capital Asset Prices: A Theory of Market Equilibrium under Conditions of Risk," *Journal of Finance* (Sept. 1964), pp. 425-442.

36. ———. "Bonds versus Stocks: Some Lessons from Capital Market Theory," *Financial Analysts Journal,* 29, No. 6 (Nov./Dec. 1973), pp. 74-80.

37. ———. "Capital Asset Prices with and without Negative Holdings," *The Journal of Finance,* 46, No. 2 (June 1991), pp. 489-509.

38. Stapleton, C. Richard. "Portfolio Analysis, Stock Valuation and Capital Budgeting Decision Rules for Risky Projects." Journal of Finance, XXVI, No. 1 (March 1971), pp. 95–1 17.

39. Tinic, Seha M., and West, Richard R. "Risk, Return, and Equilibrium: A Revisit." *The Journal of Political Economy,* 94, No. 1 (Feb. 1986), pp. 126–147.

40. Tsiang, S. C. "Risk, Return and Portfolio Analysis: Comment on [4]," *Journal of Political Economy,* 81, No. 3 (May/June 1973), pp. 748–752.

41. Turnbull, Stuart. "Market Value and Systematic Risk," *Journal of Finance,* XXXII, No. 4 (Sept. 1977), pp. 1125–1142.

Applying the CAPM to Performance Measurement

10

Learning Objectives

Candidates, after completing this reading, should be able to:

- Calculate, compare, and evaluate the Treynor measure, the Sharpe measure, and Jensen's alpha.

- Compute and interpret tracking error, the information ratio, and the Sortino ratio.

Excerpt is Chapter 4, Section 4.2, of Portfolio Theory and Performance Analysis, *by Noel Amenc and Veronique Le Sourd.*

APPLYING THE CAPM TO PERFORMANCE MEASUREMENT: SINGLE-INDEX PERFORMANCE MEASUREMENT INDICATORS[1]

When we presented the methods for calculating the return on a portfolio or investment fund, we noted that the return value on its own was not a sufficient criterion for appreciating the performance and that it was necessary to associate a measure of the risk taken. Risk is an essential part of the investment. It can differ considerably from one portfolio to another. In addition, it is liable to evolve over time. Modern portfolio theory and the CAPM have established the link that exists between the risk and return of an investment quantitatively. More specifically, these theories highlighted the notion of rewarding risk. Therefore, we now possess the elements necessary for calculating indicators while taking both risk and return into account.

The first indicators developed came from portfolio theory and the CAPM. They are therefore more specifically related to equity portfolios. They enable a risk-adjusted performance value to be calculated. It is thus possible to compare the performance of funds with different levels of risk, while the return alone only enabled comparisons between funds with the same level of risk.

This section describes the different indicators and specifies, for each, their area of use. It again involves elementary measures because the risk is considered globally. We will see later on that the risk can be broken down into several areas, enabling a more thorough analysis.

The Treynor Measure

The Treynor (1965) ratio is defined by

$$T_P = \frac{E(R_P) - R_F}{\beta_P}$$

where

    $E(R_P)$ denotes the expected return of the portfolio;

    R_F denotes the return on the risk-free asset; and

    β_P denotes the beta of the portfolio.

---

[1] On this subject, the interested reader could consult Broquet and van den Berg (1992), Elton and Gruber (1995), Fabozzi (1995), Grandin (1998), Jacquillat and Solnik (1997), and Gallais-Hamonno and Grandin (1999).

This indicator measures the relationship between the return on the portfolio, above the risk-free rate, and its systematic risk. This ratio is drawn directly from the CAPM. By rearranging the terms, the CAPM relationship for a portfolio is written as follows:

$$\frac{E(R_P) - R_F}{\beta_P} = E(R_M) - R_F$$

The term on the left is the Treynor ratio for the portfolio, and the term on the right can be seen as the Treynor ratio for the market portfolio, since the beta of the market portfolio is 1 by definition. Comparing the Treynor ratio for the portfolio with the Treynor ratio for the market portfolio enables us to check whether the portfolio risk is sufficiently rewarded.

The Treynor ratio is particularly appropriate for appreciating the performance of a well-diversified portfolio, since it only takes the systematic risk of the portfolio into account, i.e., the share of the risk that is not eliminated by diversification. It is also for that reason that the Treynor ratio is the most appropriate indicator for evaluating the performance of a portfolio that only constitutes a part of the investor's assets. Since the investor has diversified his investments, the systematic risk of his portfolio is all that matters.

Calculating this indicator requires a reference index to be chosen to estimate the beta of the portfolio. The results can then depend heavily on that choice, a fact that has been criticised by Roll. We shall return to this point at the end of the chapter.

The Sharpe Measure

Sharpe (1966) defined this ratio as the reward-to-variability ratio, but it was soon called the Sharpe ratio in articles that mentioned it. It is defined by

$$S_P = \frac{E(R_P) - R_F}{\sigma(R_P)}$$

where

    $E(R_P)$ denotes the expected return of the portfolio;

    R_F denotes the return on the risk-free asset; and

    $\sigma(R_P)$ denotes the standard deviation of the portfolio returns.

This ratio measures the excess return, or risk premium, of a portfolio compared with the risk-free rate, compared, this time, with the total risk of the portfolio, measured by its standard deviation. It is drawn from the capital market line. The equation of this line, which was presented at the beginning of the chapter, can be written as follows:

$$\frac{E(R_P) - R_F}{\sigma(R_P)} = \frac{E(R_M) - R_F}{\sigma(R_M)}$$

This relationship indicates that, at equilibrium, the Sharpe ratio of the portfolio to be evaluated and the Sharpe ratio of the market portfolio are equal. The Sharpe ratio actually corresponds to the slope of the market line. If the portfolio is well diversified, then its Sharpe ratio will be close to that of the market. By comparing the Sharpe ratio of the managed portfolio and the Sharpe ratio of the market portfolio, the manager can check whether the expected return on the portfolio is sufficient to compensate for the additional share of total risk that he is taking.

Since this measure is based on the total risk, it enables the relative performance of portfolios that are not very diversified to be evaluated, because the unsystematic risk taken by the manager is included in this measure. This measure is also suitable for evaluating the performance of a portfolio that represents an individual's total investment.

The Sharpe ratio is widely used by investment firms for measuring portfolio performance. The index is drawn from portfolio theory, and not the CAPM like the Treynor and Jensen indices. It does not refer to a market index and is not therefore subject to Roll's criticism.

This ratio has also been subject to generalisations since it was initially defined. It thus offers significant possibilities for evaluating portfolio performance, while remaining simple to calculate. Sharpe (1994) sums up the variations on this measure. One of the most common involves replacing the risk-free asset with a benchmark portfolio. The measure is then called the information ratio. We will describe it in more detail later in the chapter.

The Jensen Measure

Jensen's alpha (Jensen, 1968) is defined as the differential between the return on the portfolio in excess of the risk-free rate and the return explained by the market model, or

$$E(R_P) - R_F = \alpha_P + \beta_P(E(R_M) - R_F)$$

It is calculated by carrying out the following regression:

$$R_{Pt} - R_{Ft} = \alpha_P + \beta_P(R_{Mt} - R_{Ft}) + \epsilon_{Pt}$$

The Jensen measure is based on the CAPM. The term $\beta_P(E(R_M) - R_F)$ measures the return on the portfolio

forecast by the model. α_P measures the share of additional return that is due to the manager's choices.

In order to evaluate the statistical significance of alpha, we calculate the t-statistic of the regression, which is equal to the estimated value of the alpha divided by its standard deviation. This value is obtained from the results of the regression. If the alpha values are assumed to be normally distributed, then a t-statistic greater than 2 indicates that the probability of having obtained the result through luck, and not through skill, is strictly less than 5%. In this case, the average value of alpha is significantly different from zero.

Unlike the Sharpe and Treynor measures, the Jensen measure contains the benchmark. As for the Treynor measure, only the systematic risk is taken into account. This third method, unlike the first two, does not allow portfolios with different levels of risk to be compared. The value of alpha is actually proportional to the level of risk taken, measured by the beta. To compare portfolios with different levels of risk, we can calculate the Black–Treynor ratio[2] defined by

$$\frac{\alpha_P}{\beta_P}$$

The Jensen alpha can be used to rank portfolios within peer groups. They group together portfolios that are managed in a similar manner, and that therefore have comparable levels of risk.

The Jensen measure is subject to the same criticism as the Treynor measure: the result depends on the choice of reference index. In addition, when managers practise a market timing strategy, which involves varying the beta according to anticipated movements in the market, the Jensen alpha often becomes negative, and does not then reflect the real performance of the manager. In what follows we present methods that allow this problem to be corrected by taking variations in beta into account.

Relationships between the Different Indicators and Use of the Indicators

It is possible to formulate the relationships between the Treynor, Sharpe and Jensen indicators.

---

[2] This ratio is defined in Salvati (1997). See also Treynor and Black (1973).

Treynor and Jensen

If we take the equation defining the Jensen alpha, or

$$E(R_P) - R_F = \alpha_P + \beta_P(E(R_M) - R_F) \qquad \textbf{(10.1)}$$

and we divide on each side by β_P, then we obtain the following:

$$\frac{E(R_P) - R_F}{\beta_P} = \frac{\alpha_P}{\beta_P} + (E(R_M) - R_F)$$

We then recognise the Treynor indicator on the left-hand side of the equation. The Jensen indicator and the Treynor indicator are therefore linked by the following exact linear relationship:

$$T_P = \frac{\alpha_P}{\beta_P} + (E(R_M) - R_F)$$

Sharpe and Jensen

It is also possible to establish a relationship between the Sharpe indicator and the Jensen indicator, but this time using an approximation. To do that we replace beta with its definition, or

$$\beta_P = \frac{\rho_{PM}\sigma_P\sigma_M}{\sigma_M^2}$$

where ρ_{PM} denotes the correlation coefficient between the return on the portfolio and the return on the market index.

If the portfolio is well diversified, then the correlation coefficient ρ_{PM} is very close to 1. By replacing β_P with its approximate expression in Equation (10.1) and simplifying, we obtain:

$$E(R_P) - R_F \approx \alpha_P + \frac{\sigma_P}{\sigma_M}(E(R_M) - R_F)$$

By dividing each side by σ_P, we finally obtain:

$$\frac{E(R_P) - R_F}{\sigma_P} \approx \frac{\alpha_P}{\sigma_P} + \frac{(E(R_M) - R_F)}{\sigma_M}$$

The portfolio's Sharpe indicator appears on the left-hand side, so

$$S_P \approx \frac{\alpha_P}{\sigma_P} + \frac{(E(R_M) - R_F)}{\sigma_M}$$

Treynor and Sharpe

The formulas for these two indicators are very similar. If we consider the case of a well-diversified portfolio

again, we can still use the following approximation for beta:

$$\beta_P \approx \frac{\sigma_P}{\sigma_M}$$

The Treynor indicator is then written as follows:

$$T_P \approx \frac{E(R_P) - R_F}{\sigma_P}\sigma_M$$

Hence

$$S_P \approx \frac{T_P}{\sigma_M}$$

It should be noted that only the relationship between the Treynor indicator and the Jensen indicator is exact. The other two are approximations that are only valid for a well-diversified portfolio.

Using the Different Measures

The three indicators allow us to rank portfolios for a given period. The higher the value of the indicator, the more interesting the investment. The Sharpe ratio and the Treynor ratio are based on the same principle, but use a different definition of risk. The Sharpe ratio can be used for all portfolios. The use of the Treynor ratio must be limited to well-diversified portfolios. The Jensen measure is limited to the relative study of portfolios with the same beta.

In this group of indicators the Sharpe ratio is the one that is most widely used and has the simplest interpretation: the additional return obtained is compared with a risk indicator taking into account the additional risk taken to obtain it.

These indicators are more particularly related to equity portfolios. They are calculated by using the return on the portfolio calculated for the desired period. The return on the market is approximated by the return on a representative index for the same period. The beta of the portfolio is calculated as a linear combination of the betas of the assets that make up the portfolio, with these being calculated in relation to a reference index over the study period. The value of the indicators depends on the calculation period and performance results obtained in the past are no guarantee of future performance. Sharpe wrote that the Sharpe ratio gave a better evaluation of the past and the Treynor ratio was more suitable for anticipating future performance. Table 10-1 summarises the characteristics of the three indicators.

TABLE 10-1 Characteristics of the Sharpe, Treynor and Jensen Indicators

Name	Risk Used	Source	Criticised by Roll	Usage
Sharpe	Total (sigma)	Portfolio theory	No	Ranking portfolios with different levels of risk Not very well-diversified portfolios Portfolios that constitute an individual's total personal wealth
Treynor	Systematic (beta)	CAPM	Yes	Ranking portfolios with different levels of risk Well-diversified portfolios Portfolios that constitute part of an individual's personal wealth
Jensen	Systematic (beta)	CAPM	Yes	Ranking portfolios with the same beta

Extensions to the Jensen Measure

Elton and Gruber (1995) present an additional portfolio performance measurement indicator. The principle used is the same as that of the Jensen measure, namely measuring the differential between the managed portfolio and a theoretical reference portfolio. However, the risk considered is now the total risk and the reference portfolio is no longer a portfolio located on the security market line, but a portfolio on the capital market line, with the same total risk as the portfolio to be evaluated.

More specifically, this involves evaluating a manager who has to construct a portfolio with a total risk of σ_P. He can obtain this level of risk by splitting the investment between the market portfolio and the risk-free asset. Let A be the portfolio thereby obtained. This portfolio is situated on the capital market line. Its return and risk respect the following relationship:

$$E(R_A) = R_F + \left(\frac{E(R_M) - R_F}{\sigma_M} \right) \sigma_P$$

since $\sigma_A = \sigma_P$. This portfolio is the reference portfolio.

If the manager thinks that he possesses particular stock picking skills, he can attempt to construct a portfolio with a higher return for the fixed level of risk. Let P be his portfolio. The share of performance that results from the manager's choices is then given by

$$E(R_P) - E(R_A) = E(R_P) - R_F - \left(\frac{E(R_M) - R_F}{\sigma_M} \right) \sigma_P$$

The return differential between portfolio P and portfolio A measures the manager's stock picking skills. The result can be negative if the manager does not obtain the expected result.

The idea of measuring managers' selectivity can be found in the Fama decomposition. But Fama compares the performance of the portfolio with portfolios situated on the security market line, i.e., portfolios that respect the CAPM relationship.

The Jensen measure has been the object of a certain number of generalisations, which enable the management strategy used to be included in the evaluation of the manager's value-added. Among these extensions are the models that enable a market timing strategy to be evaluated.

Finally, the modified versions of the CAPM can be used instead of the traditional CAPM to calculate the Jensen alpha. The principle remains the same: the share of the return that is not explained by the model gives the value of the Jensen alpha.

With the Black model, the alpha is characterised by

$$E(R_P) = E(R_Z) = \alpha_P + \beta_P(E(R_M) - E(R_Z))$$

With the Brennan model, the alpha is characterised by

$$E(R_P) - R_F = \alpha_P + \beta_P(E(R_M) - R_F - T(D_M - R_F)) + T(D_P - R_F)$$

where D_P is equal to the weighted sum of the dividend yields of the assets in the portfolio, or

$$D_P = \sum_{i=1}^{n} x_i D_i$$

x_i denotes the weight of asset i in the portfolio. The other notations are those that were used earlier.

We can go through all the models cited in this way. For each case, the value of α_p is estimated through regression.

The Tracking-Error

The tracking-error is a risk indicator that is used in the analysis of benchmarked funds. Benchmarked management involves constructing portfolios with the same level of risk as an index, or a portfolio chosen as a benchmark, while giving the manager the chance to deviate from the benchmark composition, with the aim of obtaining a higher return. This assumes that the manager possesses particular stock picking skills. The tracking-error then allows the risk differentials between the managed portfolio and the benchmark portfolio to be measured. It is defined by the standard deviation of the difference in return between the portfolio and the benchmark it is replicating, or

$$TE = \sigma(R_p - R_B)$$

where R_B denotes the return on the benchmark portfolio.

The lower the value, the closer the risk of the portfolio to the risk of the benchmark. Benchmarked management requires the tracking-error to remain below a certain threshold, which is fixed in advance. To respect this constraint, the portfolio must be reallocated regularly as the market evolves. It is necessary however to find the right balance between the frequency of the reallocations and the transaction costs that they incur, which have a negative impact on portfolio performance. The additional return obtained, measured by alpha, must also be sufficient to make up for the additional risk taken on by the portfolio. To check this, we use another indicator: the information ratio.

The Information Ratio

The information ratio, which is sometimes called the appraisal ratio, is defined by the residual return of the portfolio compared with its residual risk. The residual return of a portfolio corresponds to the share of the return that is not explained by the benchmark. It results from the choices made by the manager to overweight securities that he hopes will have a return greater than that of the benchmark. The residual, or diversifiable, risk measures the residual return variations. Sharpe (1994) presents the information ratio as a generalisation of his ratio, in which the risk-free asset is replaced by a benchmark portfolio. The information ratio is defined through the following relationship:

$$IR = \frac{E(R_p) - E(R_B)}{\sigma(R_p - R_B)}$$

We recognise the tracking-error in the denominator. The ratio can also be written as follows:

$$IR = \frac{\alpha_p}{\sigma(e_p)}$$

where α_p denotes the residual portfolio return, as defined by Jensen, and $\sigma(e_p)$ denotes the standard deviation of this residual return.

As specified above, this ratio is used in the area of benchmarked management. It allows us to check that the risk taken by the manager, in deviating from the benchmark, is sufficiently rewarded. It constitutes a criterion for evaluating the manager. Managers seek to maximise its value, i.e., to reconcile a high residual return and a low tracking-error. It is important to look at the value of the information ratio and the value of the tracking-error together. For the same information ratio value, the lower the tracking-error the higher the chance that the manager's performance will persist over time.

The information ratio is therefore an indicator that allows us to evaluate the manager's level of information compared with the public information available, together with his skill in achieving a performance that is better than that of the average manager. Since this ratio does not take the systematic portfolio risk into account, it is not appropriate for comparing the performance of a well-diversified portfolio with that of a portfolio with a low degree of diversification.

The information ratio also allows us to estimate a suitable number of years for observing the performance, in order to obtain a certain confidence level for the result. To do so, we note that there is a link between the t-statistic of the regression, which provides the alpha value, and the information ratio. The t-statistic is equal to the quotient of alpha and its standard deviation, and the information ratio is equal to the same quotient, but this time using annualised values. We therefore have

$$IR \approx \frac{t_{stat}}{\sqrt{T}}$$

where T denotes the length of the period, expressed in years, during which we observed the returns. The number of years required for the result obtained to be significant, with a given level of probability, is therefore calculated by the following relationship:

$$T = \left[\frac{t_{stat}}{IR}\right]^2$$

For example, a manager who obtains an average alpha of 2.5% with a tracking-error of 4% has an information ratio equal to 0.625. If we wish the result to be significant to 95%, then the value of the t-statistic is 1.96, according to the normal distribution table, and the number of years it is necessary to observe the portfolio returns is

$$T = \left[\frac{1.96}{0.625}\right]^2 = 9.8 \text{ years}$$

This shows clearly that the results must persist over a long period to be truly significant. We should note, however, that the higher the manager's information ratio, the more the number of years decreases. The number of years also decreases if we consider a lower level of probability, by going down, for example, to 80%.

The calculation of the information ratio has been presented by assuming that the residual return came from the Jensen model. More generally, this return can come from a multi-index or multi-factor model.

The Sortino Ratio

An indicator such as the Sharpe ratio, based on the standard deviation, does not allow us to know whether the differentials compared with the mean were produced above or below the mean.

Earlier, we introduced the notion of semi-variance and its more general versions. This notion can then be used to calculate the risk-adjusted return indicators that are more specifically appropriate for asymmetrical return distributions. This allows us to evaluate the portfolios obtained through an optimisation algorithm using the semi-variance instead of the variance. The best known indicator is the Sortino ratio (cf. Sortino and Price, 1994). It is defined on

the same principle as the Sharpe ratio. However, the risk-free rate is replaced with the minimum acceptable return (MAR), i.e., the return below which the investor does not wish to drop, and the standard deviation of the returns is replaced with the standard deviation of the returns that are below the MAR, or

$$\text{Sortino ratio} = \frac{E(R_p) - MAR}{\sqrt{\dfrac{1}{T}\sum_{\substack{t=0 \\ R_{pt} < MAR}}^{T}(R_{pt} - MAR)^2}}$$

Recently Developed Risk-Adjusted Return Measures

Specialised firms that study investment fund performance develop variations on the traditional measures, essentially on the Sharpe ratio. These measures are used to rank the funds and attribute management quality labels. We can cite, for example, Morningstar's rankings.

The Morningstar Rating System[3]

The Morningstar measure, which is called a risk-adjusted rating (RAR), is very widely used in the United States. This ranking system was first developed in 1985 by the firm Morningstar. In July 2002, Morningstar introduced some modifications to improve its methodology. The measure differs significantly from more traditional measures such as the Sharpe ratio and its different forms. The evaluation of funds is based on a system of stars. Sharpe (1998) presents the method used by Morningstar and describes its properties. He compares it with other types of measure and describes the limitations of the ranking system.

The principle of the Morningstar measure is to rank different funds that belong to the same peer group. The RAR for a fund is calculated as the difference between its relative return and its relative risk, or

$$RAR_{Pi} = RR_{Pi} - RRisk_{Pi}$$

where RR_{Pi} denotes the relative return for fund P_i; and $RRisk_{Pi}$ denotes the relative risk for fund P_i.

---

[3] Cf. Melnikoff (1998) and see Sharpe's web site (http://www .stanford.edu/~wfsharpe/home.htm) for a series of articles describing the calculation methods.

The relative return and the relative risk for the fund are obtained by dividing, respectively, the return and the risk of the fund by a quantity, called the base, which is common to all the funds in the peer group, or

$$RR_{P_i} = \frac{R_{P_i}}{BR_g}$$

and

$$RRisk_{P_i} = \frac{Risk_{P_i}}{BRisk_g}$$

where g denotes the peer group containing the fund P_i;

R_{P_i} denotes the return on fund P_i, in excess of the risk-free rate;

$Risk_{P_i}$ denotes the risk of fund P_i;

BR_g denotes the base used to calculate the relative returns of all the funds in the group;

$BRisk_g$ denotes the base used to calculate the relative risks of all the funds in the group.

In the first version of the methodology, the risk of a fund was measured by calculating the average of the negative values of the fund's monthly returns in excess of the short-term risk-free rate and by taking the opposite sign to obtain a positive quantity:

$$Risk_{P_i} = -\frac{1}{T}\sum_{t=1}^{T} \min(R_{P_i t}, 0)$$

where T denotes the number of months in the period being studied; and $R_{P_i t}$ denotes the monthly return of fund P_i, in excess of the risk-free rate.

Risk calculation has been modified in the new version of the star rating. Risk is measured by monthly variations in fund returns and now takes not only downside risk but also upside volatility into account, but with more emphasis on downward volatility. Funds with highly volatile returns are penalised, whether the volatility is upside or downside. The advantages of this improvement can be understood by looking at Internet funds. These funds were not considered risky in 1999, as they only exhibited upside volatility. But their extreme gains indicated a serious potential for extreme losses, as has been demonstrated since. The new risk measure would have attributed a higher level of risk to those funds than the previous measure did. As a result, the possibility of strong short-term performance masking the inherent risk of a fund has now

been reduced and it is more difficult for high-risk funds to earn high star ratings.

The base that is used to calculate the relative return of the funds is obtained by calculating the average return of the funds in the group. If the value obtained is greater than the risk-free rate for the period, then we use the result obtained, otherwise we use the value of the risk-free rate. We therefore have

$$BR_g = \max\left(\frac{1}{n}\sum_{i=1}^{n} R_{P_i}, R_F\right)$$

where n denotes the number of funds contained in the peer group; and R_F denotes the risk-free rate.

The base used to calculate the relative risk is obtained by calculating the average of the risks of the funds in the peer group, or

$$BRisk_g = \frac{1}{n}\sum_{i=1}^{n} Risk_{P_i}$$

In 1985, Morningstar defined four peer groups to establish its rankings: domestic stock funds, international stock funds, taxable bond funds and tax-exempt municipal bond funds. However, these four categories appear to be too few to make truly adequate comparisons. The improved star rating methodology[4] now uses 48 specific equity and debt peer groups. For example, equity funds are classified according to their capitalisation (large-cap, mid-cap and small-cap) and whether they are growth, value or blend. International stock funds are now subdivided into different parts of the world. By only comparing funds with funds from the same well-defined category, those that are providing superior risk-adjusted performance will be more accurately identified. For example, during periods favourable to large-cap stocks, large-cap funds received a high percentage of five-star rankings when evaluated in the broad domestic equity group. With the new system, only the best funds will receive five stars, as large-cap funds will only be compared with large-cap funds.

The ranking is then produced as follows. Each fund is attached to a single peer group. The funds in a peer group

---

[4] For more details, see Morningstar's web site www.morningstar.com, from which it is possible to visit the specific web sites for each country.

are ranked in descending order of their *RAR*. A number of stars is then attributed to each fund according to its position in the distribution of *RAR* values. The funds in the top 10% of the distribution obtain five stars; those in the following 22.5% obtain four stars; those in the following 35% obtain three stars; those in the next 22.5% obtain two stars; and, finally, those in the bottom 10% obtain one star.

The Morningstar measure is based on an investment period of one month, although funds are in fact held for longer periods, and a decrease in one month can be compensated for by an increase in the following month. This measure is not therefore very appropriate for measuring the risk of funds that are held over a long period.

Actuarial Approach

In this approach (see Melnikoff, 1998) the investor's aversion to risk is characterised by a constant, *W*, which measures his gain–shortfall equilibrium, i.e., the relationship between the expected gain desired by the investor to make up for a fixed shortfall risk. The average annual risk-adjusted return is then given by

$$RAR = R - (W - 1)S$$

where

- *S*   denotes the average annual shortfall rate;
- *W*   denotes the weight of the gain–shortfall aversion; and
- *R*   denotes the average annual rate of return obtained by taking all the observed returns.

For an average individual, *W* is equal to two, which means that the individual will agree to invest if the expected amount of his gain is double the shortfall. In this case, we have simply

$$RAR = R - S$$

Analysis Based on the VaR

The VaR was defined earlier and the different methods for calculating it were briefly presented. As a reminder, the VaR measures the risk of a portfolio as the maximum amount of loss that the portfolio can sustain for a given level of confidence. We may then wish to use this definition of risk to calculate a risk-adjusted return indicator to evaluate the performance of a portfolio. In order to define a logical indicator, we divide the VaR by the initial value of the portfolio and

thus obtain a percentage loss compared with the total value of the portfolio. We then calculate a Sharpe-like type of indicator in which the standard deviation is replaced with a risk indicator based on the VaR, or

$$\frac{R_P - R_F}{\dfrac{VaR_P}{V_P^0}}$$

where

- R_P denotes the return on the portfolio;
- R_F denotes the return on the risk-free asset;
- VaR_P denotes the VaR of the portfolio;
- V_P^0 denotes the initial value of the portfolio.

This type of ratio can only be compared for different portfolios if the portfolios' VaR has been evaluated for the same confidence threshold.

Furthermore, Dowd (1999) proposes an approach based on the VaR to evaluate an investment decision. We consider the case of an investor who holds a portfolio that he is thinking of modifying, by introducing, for example, a new asset. He will study the risk and return possibilities linked to a modification of the portfolio and choose the situation for which the risk-return balance seems to be sufficiently favourable. To do that, he could decide to define the risk in terms of the increase in the portfolio's VaR. He will change the portfolio if the resulting incremental VaR (IVaR) is sufficiently low compared with the return that he can expect. This can be formalised as a decision rule based on Sharpe's decision rule.

Sharpe's rule states that the most interesting asset in a set of assets is the one that has the highest Sharpe ratio. By calculating the existing Sharpe ratio and the Sharpe ratio for the modified portfolio and comparing the results, we can then judge whether the planned modification of the portfolio is desirable.

By using the definition of the Sharpe ratio, we find that it is useful to modify the portfolio if the returns and standard deviations of the portfolio before and after the modification are linked by the following relationship:

$$\frac{R_P^{new}}{\sigma_{R_P^{new}}} \geq \frac{R_P^{old}}{\sigma_{R_P^{old}}}$$

where R_P^{old} and R_P^{new} denote, respectively, the return on the portfolio before and after the modification; and $\sigma_{R_P^{old}}$ and

$\sigma_{R_P^{new}}$ denote, respectively, the standard deviation of the portfolio before and after the modification.

We assume that part of the new portfolio is made up of the existing portfolio, in proportion $(1 - a)$, and the other part is made up of asset A in proportion a.

The return on this portfolio is written as follows:

$$R_P^{new} = aR_A + (1 - a)R_P^{old}$$

where R_A denotes the return on asset A.

By replacing R_P^{new} with its expression in the inequality between the Sharpe ratios, we obtain:

$$\frac{aR_A + (1 - a)R_P^{old}}{\sigma_{R_P^{new}}} \geq \frac{R_P^{old}}{\sigma_{R_P^{old}}}$$

which finally gives

$$R_A \geq R_P^{old} + \frac{R_P^{old}}{a}\left(\frac{\sigma_{R_P^{new}}}{\sigma_{R_P^{old}}} - 1\right)$$

This relationship indicates the inequality that the return on asset A must respect for it to be advantageous to introduce it into the portfolio. The relationship depends on proportion a. It shows that the return on asset A must be at least equal to the return on the portfolio before the modification, to which is added a factor that depends on the risk associated with the acquisition of asset A. The higher the risk, the higher the adjustment factor and the higher the return on asset A will have to be.

Under certain assumptions, this relationship can be expressed through the *VaR* instead of the standard deviation. If the portfolio returns are normally distributed, then the *VaR* of the portfolio is proportional to its standard deviation, or

$$VaR = -\alpha \sigma_{R_P} W$$

where

- α denotes the confidence parameter for which the VaR is estimated;
- W is a parameter that represents the size of the portfolio; and
- σ_{R_P} is the standard deviation of the portfolio returns.

By using this expression of the VaR, we can calculate

$$\frac{VaR^{new}}{VaR^{old}} = \frac{W^{new}\sigma_{R_P^{new}}}{W^{old}\sigma_{R_P^{old}}}$$

which enables us to obtain the following relationship:

$$\frac{\sigma_{R_P^{new}}}{\sigma_{R_P^{old}}} = \frac{VaR^{new}}{VaR^{old}}\frac{W^{old}}{W^{new}}$$

We assume that the size of the portfolio is conserved. We therefore have $W^{old} = W^{new}$.

We therefore obtain simply, after substituting into the return on A relationship:

$$R_A \geq R_P^{old} + \frac{R_P^{old}}{a}\left(\frac{VaR^{new}}{VaR^{old}} - 1\right)$$

The incremental VaR between the new portfolio and the old portfolio, denoted by IVaR, is equal to the difference between the old and new value, or $IVaR = VaR^{new} - VaR^{old}$.

By replacing in the inequality according to the IVaR, we obtain:

$$R_A \geq R_P^{old} + \frac{R_P^{old}}{a}\left(\frac{IVaR}{VaR^{old}}\right) = R_P^{old}\left(1 + \frac{1}{a}\frac{IVaR}{VaR^{old}}\right)$$

By defining the function η_A as

$$\eta_A(VaR) = \frac{1}{a}\frac{IVaR}{VaR^{old}}$$

we can write

$$R_A \geq (1 + \eta_A(VaR))R_P^{old}$$

where $\eta A(VaR)$ denotes the percentage increase in the VaR occasioned by the acquisition of asset A, divided by the proportion invested in asset A.

Measure Taking the Management Style into Account

The risk-adjusted performance measures enable a fund to be evaluated in comparison with the market portfolio, but do not take the manager's investment style into account. The style, however, may be imposed by the management mandate constraints rather than chosen by the manager. In this case it is more useful to compare management results with a benchmark that accurately represents the manager's style, rather than comparing them with a broad benchmark representing the market (cf. Lobosco, 1999). The idea of using tailored benchmarks that are adapted to the manager's investment style comes from the work of Sharpe (1992).

Lobosco (1999) proposes a measure called *SRAP* (Style/Risk-Adjusted Performance). This is a risk-adjusted performance measure that includes the management style as defined by Sharpe. It was inspired by the work of Modigliani and Modigliani (1997), who defined an equation that enabled the annualised risk-adjusted performance (*RAP*) of a fund to be measured in relation to the market benchmark, or

$$RAP_P = \frac{\sigma_M}{\sigma_P}(R_P - R_F) + R_F$$

where

σ_M denotes the annualised standard deviation of the market returns;

σ_P denotes the annualised standard deviation of the returns of fund *P*;

R_P denotes the annualised return of fund *P*; and

R_F denotes the risk-free rate.

This relationship is drawn directly from the capital market line. If we were at equilibrium, we would have $RAP_P = R_M$, where R_M denotes the annualised average market return.

The relationship therefore allows us to look at the performance of the fund in relation to that of the market. The most interesting funds are those with the highest *RAP* value. To obtain a relative measure, one just calculates the difference between the *RAP* for the fund and the *RAP* for the benchmark, with the benchmark's *RAP* measure being simply equal to its return.

The first step in measuring the performance of a fund, when taking the investment style into account, is to identify the combination of indices that best represents the manager's style. We then calculate the differential between the fund's *RAP* measure and the *RAP* measure of its Sharpe benchmark.

Lobosco gives the example of a fund with an annualised performance of −1.72% and a standard deviation of 17.48%. The market portfolio is represented by the Russell 3000 index, the performance of which for the same period is 16.54% with a standard deviation of 11.52%. The risk-free rate is 5.21%.

The risk-adjusted performance of this fund is therefore

$$RAP(Fund) = \frac{11.52}{17.48}(-1.72 - 5.21) + 5.21 = 0.64\%$$

Its performance in relation to the market portfolio is

$$RelativeRAP = RAP(Fund) - RAP(Market) = 0.64 - 16.54$$
$$= -15.90\%$$

If we now observe that the style of this fund corresponds to a benchmark, 61% of which is made up of the Russell 2000 index of growth stocks and 39% of the Russell 2000 index of growth stocks, the performance of this benchmark is now 2.73% with a standard deviation of 13.44%.

The risk-adjusted performance of this benchmark is given by

$$RAP(SharpeBenchmark) = \frac{11.52}{13.44}(2.73 - 5.21) + 5.21 = 3.08\%$$

and the relative performance of the portfolio compared to this benchmark is given by

$$RelativeRAP = RAP(Fund) - RAP(SharpeBenchmark)$$
$$= 0.64 - 3.08 = -2.44\%$$

The relative performance of the fund is again negative, but the differential is much lower than compared with the whole market. The management style-adjusted performance measure is therefore a useful additional measure.

Risk-adjusted Performance Measure in the Area of Multimanagement

Muralidhar (2001) has developed a new risk-adjusted performance measure that allows us to compare the performance of different managers within a group of funds with the same objectives (a peer group). This measure can be grouped with the existing information ratio, the Sharpe ratio and the Modigliani and Modigliani measure, but it does contribute new elements. It includes not only the standard deviations of each portfolio, but also the correlation of each portfolio with the benchmark and the correlations between the portfolios themselves. The method proposed by Muralidhar allows us to construct portfolios that are split optimally between a risk-free asset, a benchmark and several managers, while taking the investors' objectives into account, both in terms of risk and, above all, the relative risk compared with the benchmark.

The principle involves reducing the portfolios to those with the same risk in order to be able to compare their performance. This is the same idea as in Modigliani and Modigliani (1997) who compared the performance of a portfolio and its benchmark by defining transformations in such a way that the transformed portfolio and benchmark had the same standard deviation.

To create a correlation-adjusted performance measure, Muralidhar considers an investor who splits his portfolio between a risk-free asset, a benchmark and an investment fund. We assume that this investor accepts a certain level of annualised tracking-error compared with his benchmark, which we call the objective tracking-error. The investor wishes to obtain the highest risk-adjusted value of alpha for a given portfolio tracking-error and variance. We define as a, b and $(1 - a - b)$ the proportions invested respectively in the investment fund, the benchmark B and the risk-free asset F. The portfolio thereby obtained is said to be correlation-adjusted. It is denoted by the initials CAP (for correlation-adjusted portfolio). The return on this portfolio is given by

$$R(CAP) = aR(manager) + bR(B) + (1 - a - b)R(F)$$

The proportions to be held must be chosen in an appropriate manner so that the portfolio obtained has a tracking-error equal to the objective tracking-error and its standard deviation is equal to the standard deviation of the benchmark.

The search for the best return, in view of the constraints, leads to the calculation of optimal proportions that depend on the standard deviations and correlations of the different elements in the portfolio. The problem is considered here with a single fund, but it can be generalised to the case of several funds, to handle the case of portfolios split between several managers, and to find the optimal allocation between the different managers. The formulas that give the optimal weightings in the case of several managers have the same structure as those obtained in the case of a single manager, but they use the weightings attributed to each manager together with the correlations between the managers.

Once the optimal proportions have been calculated, the return on the CAP has been determined entirely. By carrying out the calculation for each fund being studied, we can rank the different funds.

The Muralidhar measure is certainly useful compared with the risk-adjusted performance measure that had been developed previously. We observe that the Sharpe ratio, the information ratio and the Modigliani and Modigliani measure turn out to be insufficient to allow investors to rank different funds and to construct their optimal portfolio. These risk-adjusted measures only include the standard deviations of the portfolios and the benchmark, even though it is also necessary to include the correlations between the portfolios and between the portfolios and the benchmark. The Muralidhar model therefore provides a more appropriate risk-adjusted performance measure because it takes into account both the differences in standard deviation and the differences in correlations between the portfolios. We see that it produces a ranking of funds that is different from that obtained with the other measures. In addition, neither the information ratio nor the Sharpe ratio indicates how to construct portfolios in order to produce the objective tracking-error, while the Muralidhar measure provides the composition of the portfolios that satisfy the investors' objectives.

The composition of the portfolio obtained through the Muralidhar method enables us to solve the problem of an institutional investor's optimal allocation between active and passive management, with the possible use of a leverage effect to improve the risk-adjusted performance.

All the measures described in this section enable different investment funds to be ranked based on past performance. The calculations can be carried out over several successive periods on the basis that the more stable the ranking, the easier it will be to anticipate consistent results in the future.

- proportions of fund to be allocated to different funds
- This is correlation adjusted performance
- solve allocation problem

(risk free rate, Tracking error of benchmark fund &

standard deviation of

Arbitrage Pricing Theory and Multifactor Models of Risk and Return

11

Learning Objectives

Candidates, after completing this reading, should be able to:

- Describe the inputs, including factor betas, to a multifactor model.
- Calculate the expected return of an asset using a single-factor and a multifactor model.
- Describe properties of well-diversified portfolios and explain the impact of diversification on the residual risk of a portfolio.

- Explain how to construct a portfolio to hedge exposure to multiple factors.
- Describe and apply the Fama-French three factor model in estimating asset returns.

Excerpt is Chapter 10 of Investments, *Tenth Edition, by Zvi Bodie, Alex Kane, and Alan Marcus.*

The exploitation of security mispricing in such a way that risk-free profits can be earned is called arbitrage. It involves the simultaneous purchase and sale of equivalent securities in order to profit from discrepancies in their prices. Perhaps the most basic principle of capital market theory is that equilibrium market prices are rational in that they rule out arbitrage opportunities. If actual security prices allow for arbitrage, the result will be strong pressure to restore equilibrium. Therefore, security markets ought to satisfy a "no-arbitrage condition." In this chapter, we show how such no-arbitrage conditions together with the factor model allow us to generalize the security market line of the CAPM to gain richer insight into the risk-return relationship.

We begin by showing how the decomposition of risk into market versus firm-specific influences can be extended to deal with the multifaceted nature of systematic risk. Multifactor models of security returns can be used to measure and manage exposure to each of many economywide factors such as business-cycle risk, interest or inflation rate risk, energy price risk, and so on. These models also lead us to a multifactor version of the security market line in which risk premiums derive from exposure to multiple risk sources, each with their own risk premium.

We show how factor models combined with a no-arbitrage condition lead to a simple relationship between expected return and risk. This approach to the risk–return trade-off is called arbitrage pricing theory, or APT. In a single-factor market where there are no extra-market risk factors, the APT leads to a mean return–beta equation identical to that of the CAPM. In a multifactor market with one or more extra-market risk factors, the APT delivers a mean-beta equation similar to Merton's intertemporal extension of the CAPM (his ICAPM). We ask next what factors are likely to be the most important sources of risk. These will be the factors generating substantial hedging demands that brought us to the multifactor CAPM. Both the APT and the CAPM therefore can lead to multiple-risk versions of the security market line, thereby enriching the insights we can derive about the risk–return relationship.

MULTIFACTOR MODELS: AN OVERVIEW

The index model gave us a way of decomposing stock variability into market or systematic risk, due largely to macroeconomic events, versus firm-specific or idiosyncratic effects that can be diversified in large portfolios.

In the single-index model, the return on a broad market-index portfolio summarized the impact of the macro factor. Asset-risk premiums may also depend on correlations with extra-market risk factors, such as inflation, or changes in the parameters describing future investment opportunities: interest rates, volatility, market-risk premiums, and betas. For example, returns on an asset whose return increases when inflation increases can be used to hedge uncertainty in the future inflation rate. Its risk premium may fall as a result of investors' extra demand for this asset.

Risk premiums of individual securities should reflect their sensitivities to changes in extra-market risk factors just as their betas on the market index determine their risk premiums in the simple CAPM. When securities can be used to hedge these factors, the resulting hedging demands will make the SML multifactor, with each risk source that can be hedged adding an additional factor to the SML. Risk factors can be represented either by returns on these hedge portfolios (just as the index portfolio represents the market factor), or more directly by changes in the risk factors themselves, for example, changes in interest rates or inflation.

Factor Models of Security Returns

We begin with a familiar single-factor model. Uncertainty in asset returns has two sources: a common or macroeconomic factor and firm specific events. The common factor is constructed to have zero expected value, because we use it to measure *new* information concerning the macroeconomy, which, by definition, has zero expected value.

If we call F the deviation of the common factor from its expected value, β_i the sensitivity of firm i to that factor, and e_i the firm-specific disturbance, the factor model states that the actual return on firm i will equal its initially expected value plus a (zero expected value) random amount attributable to unanticipated economywide events, plus another (zero expected value) random amount attributable to firm-specific events.

Formally, the **single-factor model** is described by Equation (11.1):

$$R_i = E(R_i) + \beta_i F + e_i \qquad \text{(11.1)}$$

where $E(R_i)$ is the expected return on stock i. Notice that if the macro factor has a value of 0 in any particular period (i.e., no macro surprises), the return on the security will equal its previously expected value, $E(R_i)$, plus the effect of firm-specific events only. The nonsystematic components of returns, the e_is, are assumed to be uncorrelated among themselves and uncorrelated with the factor F.

Example 11.1 Factor Models

To make the factor model more concrete, consider an example. Suppose that the macro factor, F, is taken to be news about the state of the business cycle, measured by the unexpected percentage change in gross domestic product (GDP), and that the consensus is that GDP will increase by 4% this year. Suppose also that a stock's β value is 1.2. If GDP increases by only 3%, then the value of F would be −1%, representing a 1% disappointment in actual growth versus expected growth. Given the stock's beta value, this disappointment would translate into a return on the stock that is 1.2% lower than previously expected. This macro surprise, together with the firm-specific disturbance, e_i, determines the total departure of the stock's return from its originally expected value.

Concept Check 11.1

Suppose you currently expect the stock in Example 11.1 to earn a 10% rate of return. Then some macroeconomic news suggests that GDP growth will come in at 5% instead of 4%. How will you revise your estimate of the stock's expected rate of return?

The factor model's decomposition of returns into systematic and firm-specific components is compelling, but confining systematic risk to a single factor is not. Indeed, when we motivated systematic risk as the source of risk premiums, we noted that extra market sources of risk may arise from a number of sources such as uncertainty about interest rates, inflation, and so on. The market return reflects macro factors as well as the average sensitivity of firms to those factors.

It stands to reason that a more explicit representation of systematic risk, allowing for different stocks to exhibit different sensitivities to its various components, would constitute a useful refinement of the single-factor model. It is easy to see that models that allow for several factors—**multifactor models**—can provide better descriptions of security returns.

Apart from their use in building models of equilibrium security pricing, multifactor models are useful in risk management applications. These models give us a simple way to measure investor exposure to various macroeconomic risks and construct portfolios to hedge those risks.

Let's start with a two-factor model. Suppose the two most important macroeconomic sources of risk are uncertainties surrounding the state of the business cycle, news of which we will again measure by unanticipated growth in GDP and changes in interest rates. We will denote by IR any unexpected change in interest rates. The return on any stock will respond both to sources of macro risk and to its own firm-specific influences. We can write a two-factor model describing the excess return on stock i in some time period as follows:

$$R_i = E(R_i) + \beta_{iGDP}\text{GDP} + \beta_{iIR}\text{IR} + e_i \qquad (11.2)$$

The two macro factors on the right-hand side of the equation comprise the systematic factors in the economy. As in the single-factor model, both of these macro factors have zero expectation: They represent changes in these variables that have not already been anticipated. The coefficients of each factor in Equation (11.2) measure the sensitivity of share returns to that factor. For this reason the coefficients are sometimes called **factor loadings** or, equivalently, **factor betas**. An increase in interest rates is bad news for most firms, so we would expect interest rate betas generally to be negative. As before, e_i reflects firm-specific influences.

To illustrate the advantages of multifactor models, consider two firms, one a regulated electric-power utility in a mostly residential area, the other an airline. Because residential demand for electricity is not very sensitive to the business cycle, the utility has a low beta on GDP. But the utility's stock price may have a relatively high sensitivity to interest rates. Because the cash flow generated by the utility is relatively stable, its present value behaves much like that of a bond, varying inversely with interest rates. Conversely, the performance of the airline is very sensitive to economic activity but is less sensitive to interest rates. It will have a high GDP beta and a lower interest rate beta. Suppose that on a particular day, a news item suggests that the economy will expand. GDP is expected to increase, but so are interest rates. Is the "macro news" on this day good or bad? For the utility, this is bad news: its dominant sensitivity is to rates. But for the airline, which responds more to GDP, this is good news. Clearly a one-factor or single-index model cannot capture such differential responses to varying sources of macroeconomic uncertainty.

Example 11.2 Risk Assessment Using Multifactor Models

Suppose we estimate the two-factor model in Equation (11.2) for Northeast Airlines and find the following result:

$$R = .133 + 1.2(\text{GPD}) - .3(\text{IR}) + e$$

This tells us that, based on currently available information, the expected excess rate of return for Northeast is 13.3%, but that for every percentage point increase in GDP beyond current expectations, the return on Northeast shares increases on average by 1.2%, while for every unanticipated percentage point that interest rates increases, Northeast's shares fall on average by .3%.

Factor betas can provide a framework for a hedging strategy. The idea for an investor who wishes to hedge a source of risk is to establish an opposite factor exposure to offset that particular source of risk. Often, futures contracts can be used to hedge particular factor exposures.

As it stands, however, the multifactor model is no more than a *description* of the factors that affect security returns. There is no "theory" in the equation. The obvious question left unanswered by a factor model like Equation (11.2) is where E(R) comes from, in other words, what determines a security's expected excess rate of return. This is where we need a theoretical model of equilibrium security returns. We therefore now turn to arbitrage pricing theory to help determine the expected value, E(R), in Equations (11.1) and (11.2).

ARBITRAGE PRICING THEORY

Stephen Ross developed the **arbitrage pricing theory** (APT) in 1976.[1] Like the CAPM, the APT predicts a security market line linking expected returns to risk, but the path it takes to the SML is quite different. Ross's APT relies on three key propositions: (1) security returns can be described by a factor model; (2) there are sufficient securities to diversify away idiosyncratic risk; and (3) well-functioning security markets do not allow for the persistence of arbitrage opportunities. We begin with a simple version of Ross's model, which assumes that only one systematic factor affects security returns.

Arbitrage, Risk Arbitrage, and Equilibrium

An **arbitrage** opportunity arises when an investor can earn riskless profits without making a net investment. A trivial example of an arbitrage opportunity would arise if

shares of a stock sold for different prices on two different exchanges. For example, suppose IBM sold for $195 on the NYSE but only $193 on NASDAQ. Then you could buy the shares on NASDAQ and simultaneously sell them on the NYSE, clearing a riskless profit of $2 per share without tying up any of your own capital. The **Law of One Price** states that if two assets are equivalent in all economically relevant respects, then they should have the same market price. The Law of One Price is enforced by arbitrageurs: If they observe a violation of the law, they will engage in *arbitrage activity*—simultaneously buying the asset where it is cheap and selling where it is expensive. In the process, they will bid up the price where it is low and force it down where it is high until the arbitrage opportunity is eliminated.

The idea that market prices will move to rule out arbitrage opportunities is perhaps the most fundamental concept in capital market theory. Violation of this restriction would indicate the grossest form of market irrationality.

The critical property of a risk-free arbitrage portfolio is that any investor, regardless of risk aversion or wealth, will want to take an infinite position in it. Because those large positions will quickly force prices up or down until the opportunity vanishes, security prices should satisfy a "no-arbitrage condition," that is, a condition that rules out the existence of arbitrage opportunities.

There is an important difference between arbitrage and risk–return dominance arguments in support of equilibrium price relationships. A dominance argument holds that when an equilibrium price relationship is violated, many investors will make limited portfolio changes, depending on their degree of risk aversion. Aggregation of these limited portfolio changes is required to create a large volume of buying and selling, which in turn restores equilibrium prices. By contrast, when arbitrage opportunities exist, each investor wants to take as large a position as possible; hence it will not take many investors to bring about the price pressures necessary to restore equilibrium. Therefore, implications for prices derived from no-arbitrage arguments are stronger than implications derived from a risk–return dominance argument.

The CAPM is an example of a dominance argument, implying that all investors hold mean-variance efficient portfolios. If a security is mispriced, then investors will tilt their portfolios toward the underpriced and away from the overpriced securities. Pressure on equilibrium prices results from many investors shifting their portfolios, each by a relatively small dollar amount. The assumption that

[1] Stephen A. Ross, "Return, Risk and Arbitrage." in I. Friend and J. Bicksler, eds., *Risk and Return in Finance* (Cambridge, MA: Ballinger, 1976).

a large number of investors are mean-variance optimizers is critical. In contrast, the implication of a no-arbitrage condition is that a few investors who identify an arbitrage opportunity will mobilize large dollar amounts and quickly restore equilibrium.

Practitioners often use the terms *arbitrage* and *arbitrageurs* more loosely than our strict definition. Arbitrageur often refers to a professional searching for mispriced securities in specific areas such as merger-target stocks, rather than to one who seeks strict (risk-free) arbitrage opportunities. Such activity is sometimes called **risk arbitrage** to distinguish it from pure arbitrage.

To leap ahead, we will discuss "derivative" securities such as futures and options, whose market values are determined by prices of other securities. For example, the value of a call option on a stock is determined by the price of the stock. For such securities, strict arbitrage is a practical possibility, and the condition of no-arbitrage leads to exact pricing. In the case of stocks and other "primitive" securities whose values are not determined strictly by another bundle of assets, no-arbitrage conditions must be obtained by appealing to diversification arguments.

Well-Diversified Portfolios

Consider the risk of a portfolio of stocks in a single-factor market. We first show that if a portfolio is well diversified, its firm-specific or nonfactor risk becomes negligible, so that only factor (or systematic) risk remains. The excess return on an n-stock portfolio with weights w_i, $\Sigma w_i = 1$, is

$$R_P = E(R_P) + \beta_P F + e_P \qquad \textbf{(11.3)}$$

where

$$B_P = \sum w_i \beta_i; \quad E(R_P) = \sum w_i E(R_i)$$

are the weighted averages of the β_i and risk premiums of the n securities. The portfolio nonsystematic component (which is uncorrelated with F) is $e_P = \Sigma w_i e_i$, which similarly is a weighted average of the e_i of the n securities.

We can divide the variance of this portfolio into systematic and nonsystematic sources:

$$\sigma_P^2 = \beta_P^2 \sigma_F^2 + \sigma^2(e_P)$$

where σ_F^2 is the variance of the factor F and $\sigma^2(e_P)$ is the nonsystematic risk of the portfolio, which is given by

$$\sigma^2(e_P) = \text{Variance}\left(\sum w_i e_i\right) = \sum w_i^2 \sigma^2(e_i)$$

Note that in deriving the nonsystematic variance of the portfolio, we depend on the fact that the firm-specific e_is are uncorrelated and hence that the variance of the "portfolio" of nonsystematic e_is is the weighted sum of the individual nonsystematic variances with the square of the investment proportions as weights.

If the portfolio were equally weighted, $w_i = 1/n$, then the nonsystematic variance would be

$$\sigma^2(e_P) = \text{Variance}\left(\sum w_i e_i\right) = \sum \left(\frac{1}{n}\right)^2 \sigma^2(e_i)$$

$$= \frac{1}{n} \sum \frac{\sigma^2(e^i)}{n} = \frac{1}{n} \sigma^2(e_i)$$

where the last term is the average value of nonsystematic variance across securities. In words, the nonsystematic variance of the portfolio equals the average nonsystematic variance divided by n. Therefore, when n is large, nonsystematic variance approaches zero. This is the effect of diversification.

This property is true of portfolios other than the equally weighted one. *Any* portfolio for which each w_i becomes consistently smaller as n gets large (more precisely, for which each w_i^2 approaches zero as n increases) will satisfy the condition that the portfolio nonsystematic risk will approach zero. This property motivates us to define a **well-diversified portfolio** as one with each weight, w_i, small enough that for practical purposes the nonsystematic variance, $\sigma^2(e_P)$, is negligible.

Concept Check 11.2

1. A portfolio is invested in a very large number of shares (n is large). However, one-half of the portfolio is invested in stock 1, and the rest of the portfolio is equally divided among the other $n - 1$ shares. Is this portfolio well diversified?

2. Another portfolio also is invested in the same n shares, where n is very large. Instead of equally weighting with portfolio weights of $1/n$ in each stock, the weights in half the securities are $1.5/n$ while the weights in the other shares are $.5/n$. Is this portfolio well diversified?

Because the expected value of e_P for any well-diversified portfolio is zero, and its variance also is effectively zero, we can conclude that any realized value of e_P will be virtually zero. Rewriting Equation (11.1), we conclude that, for a well-diversified portfolio, for all practical purposes

$$R_P = E(R_P) + \beta_P F$$

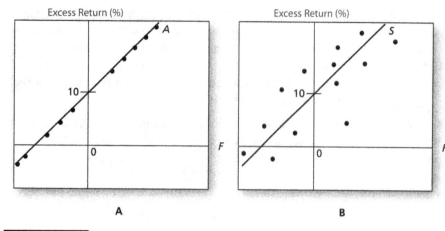

Excess Return (%) Excess Return (%)

A

B

FIGURE 11-1 Excess returns as a function of the systematic factor. *Panel A,* Well-diversified portfolio A. *Panel B,* Single stock (S).

The solid line in Figure 11-1, panel A plots the excess return of a well-diversified portfolio A with $E(R_A) = 10\%$ and $\beta_A = 1$ for various realizations of the systematic factor. The expected return of portfolio A is 10%; this is where the solid line crosses the vertical axis. At this point the systematic factor is zero, implying no macro surprises. If the macro factor is positive, the portfolio's return exceeds its expected value; if it is negative, the portfolio's return falls short of its mean. The excess return on the portfolio is therefore

$$E(R_A) + \beta_A F = 10\% + 1.0 \times F$$

Compare panel A in Figure 11-1 with panel B, which is a similar graph for a single stock (S) with $\beta_S = 1$. The undiversified stock is subject to nonsystematic risk, which is seen in a scatter of points around the line. The well-diversified portfolio's return, in contrast, is determined completely by the systematic factor.

In a single-factor world, all pairs of well-diversified portfolios are perfectly correlated: Their risk is fully determined by the same systematic factor. Consider a second well-diversified portfolio, Portfolio Q, with $R_Q = E(R_Q) + \beta_Q F$. We can compute the standard deviations of P and Q, as well as the covariance and correlation between them:

$$\sigma_P = B_P \sigma_F; \ \sigma_Q = \beta_Q \sigma_F$$
$$\text{Cov}(R_P, R_Q) = \text{Cov}(\beta_P F, \beta_Q F) = \beta_P \beta_Q \sigma_F^2$$
$$\rho_{PQ} = \frac{\text{Cov}(R_P, R_Q)}{\sigma_P \sigma_Q} = 1$$

Perfect correlation means that in a plot of expected return versus standard deviation, any two well-diversified portfolios lie on a straight line. We will see later that this common line is the CML.

Diversification and Residual Risk in Practice

What is the effect of diversification on portfolio residual SD *in practice,* where portfolio size is not unlimited? In reality, we may find (annualized) residual SDs as high as 50% for large stocks and even 100% for small stocks. To illustrate the impact of diversification, we examine portfolios of two configurations. One portfolio is equally weighted; this achieves the highest benefits of diversification with equal-SD stocks. For comparison, we form the other portfolio using far-from-equal weights. We select stocks in groups of four, with relative weights in each group of 70%, 15%, 10%, and 5%. The highest weight is 14 times greater than the lowest, which will severely reduce potential benefits of diversification. However, extended diversification in which we add to the portfolio more and more groups of four stocks with the same relative weights will overcome this problem because the highest portfolio weight still falls with additional diversification. In an equally weighted 1,000-stock portfolio, each weight is 0.1%; in the unequally weighted portfolio, with 1,000/4 = 250 groups of four stocks, the highest and lowest weights are 70%/250 = 0.28% and 5%/250 = 0.02%, respectively.

What is a large portfolio? Many widely held ETFs each include hundreds of stocks, and some funds such as the Wilshire 5000 hold thousands. These portfolios are accessible to the public since the annual expense ratios of investment companies that offer such funds are of the order of only 10 basis points. Thus a portfolio of 1,000 stocks is not unheard of, but a portfolio of 10,000 stocks is.

Table 11-1 shows portfolio residual SD as a function of the number of stocks. Equally weighted, 1,000-stock portfolios achieve small but not negligible standard deviations of 1.58% when residual risk is 50% and 3.16% when residual risk is 100%. The SDs for the unbalanced portfolios are about double these values. For 10,000-stock portfolios, the SDs are negligible, verifying that diversification can eliminate risk even in very unbalanced portfolios, at least in principle, if the investment universe is large enough.

(handwritten at top: $\alpha_M \geq 0$)

TABLE 11-1 — Residual Variance with Even and Uneven Portfolio Weights

Residual SD of Each Stock = 50%		Residual SD of Each Stock = 100%	
N	SD(e_p)	N	SD(e_p)
Equal weights: $w_i = 1/N$			
4	25.00	4	50.00
60	6.45	60	12.91
200	3.54	200	7.07
1,000	1.58	1,000	3.16
10,000	0.50	10,000	1.00
Sets of four relative weights: $w_1 = 0.65$, $w_2 = 0.2$, $w_3 = 0.1$, $w_4 = 0.05$			
4	36.23	4	72.46
60	9.35	60	18.71
200	5.12	200	10.25
1,000	2.29	1,000	4.58
10,000	0.72	10,000	1.45

Executing Arbitrage

Imagine a single-factor market where the well-diversified portfolio, M, represents the market factor, F, of Equation (11.1). The excess return on any security is given by $R_i = \alpha_i + \beta_i R_M + e_i$, and that of a well-diversified (therefore zero residual) portfolio, P, is

$$R_p = \alpha_p + \beta_p R_M \qquad \textbf{(11.4)}$$

$$E(R_p) = \alpha_p + \beta_p E(R_M) \qquad \textbf{(11.5)}$$

Now suppose that security analysis reveals that portfolio P has a positive alpha.[2] We also estimate the risk premium of the index portfolio, M, from macro analysis.

Since neither M nor portfolio P have residual risk, the only risk to the returns of the two portfolios is systematic, derived from their betas on the common factor (the beta of the index is 1.0). Therefore, you can eliminate the risk of P altogether: Construct a zero-beta portfolio, called Z,

(handwritten: $\beta : w_p \beta_p$)

(handwritten above right column: $\beta_Z = w_p \beta_{p} + w_M \beta_M$)

from P and M by appropriately selecting weights w_p and $w_M = 1 - w_p$ on each portfolio:

$$\beta_Z = w_p \beta_p + (1 - w_p)\beta_M = 0$$
$$\beta_M = 1$$
$$w_p = \frac{1}{1 - \beta_p}; \; w_M = 1 - w_p = \frac{-\beta_p}{1 - \beta_p} \qquad \textbf{(11.6)}$$

Therefore, portfolio Z is riskless, and its alpha is

$$\alpha_Z = w_p \alpha_p + (1 - w_p)\alpha_M = w_p \alpha_p \qquad \textbf{(11.7)}$$

The risk premium on Z must be zero because the risk of Z is zero. If its risk premium were not zero, you could earn arbitrage profits. Here is how:

Since the beta of Z is zero, Equation (11.5) implies that its risk premium is just its alpha. Using Equation (11.7), its alpha is $w_p \alpha_p$, so

$$E(R_Z) = w_p \alpha_p = \frac{1}{1 - B_p} \alpha_p \qquad \textbf{(11.8)}$$

You now form a zero-net-investment arbitrage portfolio: If $\beta_p < 1$ and the risk premium of Z is positive (implying that Z returns more than the risk-free rate), borrow and invest the proceeds in Z. For every borrowed dollar invested in Z, you get a net return (i.e., net of paying the interest on

---

[2] If the portfolio alpha is negative, we can still pursue the following strategy. We would simply switch to a short position in P, which would have a positive alpha of the same absolute value as P's, and a beta that is the negative of P's.

your loan) of $\frac{1}{1-B_p}\alpha_p$. This is a money machine, which you would work as hard as you can.[3] Similarly if $\beta_p > 1$, Equation (11.8) tells us that the risk premium is negative; therefore, sell Z short and invest the proceeds at the risk-free rate. Once again, a money machine has been created. Neither situation can persist, as the large volume of trades from arbitrageurs pursuing these strategies will push prices until the arbitrage opportunity disappears (i.e., until the risk premium of portfolio Z equals zero).

The No-Arbitrage Equation of the APT

We've seen that arbitrage activity will quickly pin the risk premium of any zero-beta well-diversified portfolio to zero.[4] Setting the expression in Equation (11.8) to zero implies that the alpha of *any* well-diversified portfolio must also be zero. From Equation (11.5), this means that for any well-diversified P,

$$E(R_P) = \beta_P E(R_M)$$ **(11.9)**

In other words, the risk premium (expected excess return) on portfolio P is the product of its beta and the market-index risk premium. Equation (11.9) thus establishes that the SML of the CAPM applies to well-diversified portfolios simply by virtue of the "no-arbitrage" requirement of the APT.

Another demonstration that the APT results in the same SML as the CAPM is more graphical in nature. First we show why all well-diversified portfolios with the same beta must have the same expected return. Figure 11-2 plots the returns on two such portfolios, A and B, both with betas of 1, but with differing expected returns: $E(r_A) = 10\%$ and $E(r_B) = 8\%$. Could portfolios A and B coexist with the return pattern depicted? Clearly not: No matter what the systematic factor turns out to be, portfolio A outperforms portfolio B, leading to an arbitrage opportunity.

If you sell short \$1 million of B and buy \$1 million of A, a zero-net-investment strategy, you would have a riskless payoff of \$20,000, as follows:

$(.10 + 1.0 \times F) \times \$1$ million	from long position in A
$-(.08 + 1.0 \times F) \times \$1$ million	from long position in B
$0.2 \times \$1$ million = \$20,000	net proceeds

Your profit is risk-free because the factor risk cancels out across the long and short positions. Moreover, the strategy requires zero-net-investment. You should pursue it on an infinitely large scale until the return discrepancy between the two portfolios disappears. Well-diversified portfolios with equal betas must have equal expected returns in market equilibrium, or arbitrage opportunities exist.

What about portfolios with different betas? Their risk premiums must be proportional to beta. To see why, consider Figure 11-3. Suppose that the risk-free rate is 4% and that a well-diversified portfolio, C, with a beta of .5, has an expected return of 6%. Portfolio C plots below the line from the risk-free asset to portfolio A. Consider, therefore, a new portfolio, D, composed of half of portfolio A and half of the risk-free asset. Portfolio D's beta will be $(.5 \times 0 + .5 \times 1.0) = .5$, and its expected return will be $(.5 \times 4 + .5 \times 10) = 7\%$. Now portfolio D has an equal beta but a greater expected return than portfolio C. From our analysis in the previous paragraph we know that this constitutes an arbitrage opportunity. We conclude that, to preclude arbitrage opportunities, the expected return on all well-diversified portfolios must lie on the straight line from the risk-free asset in Figure 11-3.

Notice in Figure 11-3 that risk premiums are indeed proportional to portfolio betas. The risk premium is depicted by the vertical arrow, which measures the distance between the risk-free rate and the expected return on the

---

[3] The function in Equation (11.8) becomes unstable at $\beta_p = 1$. For values of β_p near 1, it becomes infinitely large with the sign of α_p. This isn't an economic absurdity. since in that case, the sizes of your long position in P and short position in M will be almost identical, and the arbitrage profit you earn *per dollar invested* will be nearly infinite.

[4] As an exercise, show that when $\alpha_p < 0$ you reverse the position of P in Z, and the arbitrage portfolio will still earn a riskless excess return.

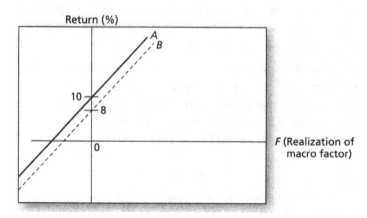

FIGURE 11-2 Returns as a function of the systematic factor: an arbitrage opportunity.

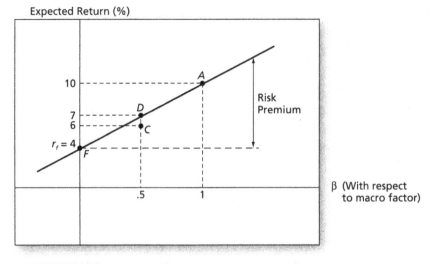

Expected Return (%)

FIGURE 11-3 An arbitrage opportunity.

portfolio. As in the simple CAPM, the risk premium is zero for $\beta = 0$ and rises in direct proportion to β.

THE APT, THE CAPM, AND THE INDEX MODEL

Equation (11.9) raises three questions:

1. Does the APT also apply to less-than-well-diversified portfolios?

2. Is the APT as a model of risk and return superior or inferior to the CAPM? Do we need both models?

3. Suppose a security analyst identifies a positive-alpha portfolio with some remaining residual risk. Don't we already have a prescription for this case from the Treynor-Black (T-B) procedure applied to the index model? Is this framework preferred to the APT?

The APT and the CAPM

The APT is built on the foundation of well-diversified portfolios. However, we've seen, for example in Table 11-1, that even large portfolios may have non-negligible residual risk. Some indexed portfolios may have hundreds or thousands of stocks, but active portfolios generally cannot, as there is a limit to how many stocks can be actively analyzed in search of alpha. How does the APT stand up to these limitations?

Suppose we order all portfolios in the universe by residual risk. Think of Level 0 portfolios as having zero residual

risk; in other words, they are the theoretically well-diversified portfolios of the APT. Level 1 portfolios have very small residual risk, say up to 0.5%. Level 2 portfolios have yet greater residual SD, say up to 1%, and so on.

If the SML described by Equation (11.9) applies to all well-diversified Level 0 portfolios, it must at least approximate the risk premiums of Level 1 portfolios. Even more important, while Level 1 risk premiums may deviate slightly from Equation (11.9), such deviations should be unbiased, with alphas equally likely to be positive or negative. Deviations should be uncorrelated with beta or residual SD and should average to zero.

We can apply the same logic to portfolios of slightly higher Level 2 residual risk. Since all Level 1 portfolios are still well approximated by Equation (11.9), so must be risk premiums of Level 2 portfolios, albeit with slightly less accuracy. Here too, we may take comfort in the lack of bias and zero average deviations from the risk premiums predicted by Equation (11.9). But still, the precision of predictions of risk premiums from Equation (11.9) consistently deteriorates with increasing residual risk. (One might ask why we don't transform Level 2 portfolios into Level 1 or even Level 0 portfolios by further diversifying, but as we've pointed out, this may not be feasible in practice for assets with considerable residual risk when active portfolio size or the size of the investment universe is limited.) If residual risk is sufficiently high and the impediments to complete diversification are too onerous, we cannot have full confidence in the APT and the arbitrage activities that underpin it.

Despite this shortcoming, the APT is valuable. First, recall that the CAPM requires that almost all investors be mean-variance optimizers. We may well suspect that they are not. The APT frees us of this assumption. It is sufficient that a small number of sophisticated arbitrageurs scour the market for arbitrage opportunities. This alone produces an SML, Equation (11.9). that is a good and unbiased approximation for all assets but those with significant residual risk.

Perhaps even more important is the fact that the APT is anchored by observable portfolios such as the market index. The CAPM is not even testable because it relies on an unobserved, all-inclusive portfolio. The reason that the APT is not fully superior to the CAPM is that at the level of individual assets and high residual risk, pure arbitrage may be insufficient to enforce Equation (11.9). Therefore, we need to turn to the CAPM as a complementary theoretical construct behind equilibrium risk premiums.

It should be noted, however, that when we replace the unobserved market portfolio of the CAPM with an observed, broad index portfolio that may not be efficient, we no longer can be sure that the CAPM predicts risk premiums of all assets with no bias. Neither model therefore is free of limitations. Comparing the APT arbitrage strategy to maximization of the Sharpe ratio in the context of an index model may well be the more useful framework for analysis.

The APT and Portfolio Optimization in a Single-Index Market

The APT is couched in a single-factor market[5] and applies with perfect accuracy to *well-diversified* portfolios. It shows arbitrageurs how to generate infinite profits if the risk premium of a well-diversified portfolio deviates from Equation (11.9). The trades executed by these arbitrageurs are the enforcers of the accuracy of this equation.

In effect, the APT shows how to take advantage of security mispricing when diversification opportunities are abundant. When you lock in and scale up an arbitrage opportunity you're sure to be rich as Croesus regardless of the composition of the rest of your portfolio, but only if the arbitrage portfolio is truly risk-free! However, if the arbitrage position is not perfectly well diversified, an increase in its scale (borrowing cash, or borrowing shares to go short) will increase the risk of the arbitrage position, potentially without bound. The APT ignores this complication.

Now consider an investor who confronts the same single factor market, and whose security analysis reveals an underpriced asset (or portfolio), that is, one whose risk premium implies a positive alpha. This investor can follow the advice to construct an optimal risky portfolio. The optimization process will consider both the potential profit from a position in the mispriced asset, as well as the risk of the overall portfolio and efficient diversification.

The Treynor-Black (T-B) procedure can be summarized as follows.[6]

1. Estimate the risk premium and standard deviation of the benchmark (index) portfolio, RP_M and σ_M.

2. Place all the assets that are mispriced into an active portfolio. Call the alpha of the active portfolio α_A, its systematic-risk coefficient β_A, and its residual risk $\sigma(e_A)$. Your optimal risky portfolio will allocate to the active portfolio a weight, w_A^*:

$$w_A^0 = \frac{\alpha_A / \sigma^2(e_A)}{E(R_M) / \sigma_M^2}; \; w_A^* = \frac{w_A^0}{1 + w_A^0(1 - \beta_A)}$$

The allocation to the passive portfolio is then, $w_M^* = 1 - w_A^*$. With this allocation, the increase in the Sharpe ratio of the optimal portfolio, S_P, over that of the passive portfolio, S_M, depends on the size of the information ratio of the active portfolio, $IR_A = \alpha_A / \sigma(e_A)$. The optimized portfolio can attain a Sharpe ratio of $S_P = \sqrt{S_M^2 + IR_A^2}$.

3. To maximize the Sharpe ratio of the risky portfolio, you maximize the IR of the active portfolio. This is achieved by allocating to each asset in the active portfolio a portfolio weight proportional to: $w_{Ai} = \alpha_i / \sigma^2(e_i)$, When this is done, the square of the information ratio of the active portfolio will be the sum of the squared individual information ratios: $IR_A^2 = \sum IR_i^2$.

Now see what happens in the T-B model when the residual risk of the active portfolio is zero. This is essentially the assumption of the APT, that a well-diversified portfolio (with zero residual risk) can be formed. When the residual risk of the active portfolio goes to zero, the position in it goes to infinity. This is precisely the same implication as the APT: When portfolios are well-diversified, you will scale up an arbitrage position without bound. Similarly, when the residual risk of an asset in the active T-B portfolio is zero, it will displace all other assets from that

---

[5] The APT is easily extended to a multifactor market as we show later.

[6] The tediousness of some of the expressions involved in the T-B method should not deter anyone. The calculations are pretty straightforward, especially in a spreadsheet. The estimation of the risk parameters also is a relatively straightforward statistical task. The real difficulty is to uncover security alphas and the macro-factor risk premium, RP_M.

portfolio, and thus the residual risk of the active portfolio will be zero and elicit the same extreme portfolio response.

When residual risks are nonzero, the T-B procedure produces the optimal risky portfolio, which is a compromise between seeking alpha and shunning potentially diversifiable risk. The APT ignores residual risk altogether, assuming it has been diversified away. Obviously, we have no use for the APT in this context. When residual risk can be made small through diversification, the T-B model prescribes very aggressive (large) positions in mispriced securities that exert great pressure on equilibrium risk premiums to eliminate nonzero alpha values. The T-B model does what the APT is meant to do but with more flexibility in terms of accommodating the practical limits to diversification. In this sense, Treynor and Black anticipated the development of the APT.

Example 11.3 Exploiting Alpha

Table 11-2 summarizes a rudimentary experiment that compares the prescriptions and predictions of the APT and T-B model in the presence of realistic values of residual risk. We use relatively small alpha values (1 and 3%), three levels of residual risk consistent with values in Table 11-1 (2, 3, and 4%), and two levels of beta (0.5 and 2) to span the likely range of reasonable parameters.

The first set of columns in Table 11-2, titled Active Portfolio, show the parameter values in each example. The second set of columns, titled Zero-Net-Investment, Arbitrage (Zero-Beta), shows the weight in the active portfolio and resultant information ratio of the active portfolio. This would be the Sharpe ratio if the arbitrage position (the positive-alpha, zero-beta portfolio) made up the entire risky portfolio (as would be prescribed by the APT). The

TABLE 11-2 Performance of APT vs. Index Model When Diversification of Residual SD Is Incomplete

Index Risk Premium = 7			Index SD = 20		Index Sharpe Ratio = 0.35			
Active Portfolio			**Zero-Net-Investment, Arbitrage (Zero-Beta) Portfolio**		**Treynor-Black Procedure**			
Alpha (%)	Residual SD	Beta	*w* in Active	Info Ratio	*w*(beta = 0)	*w*(beta)	Sharpe Ratio	Incremental Sharpe Ratio
1	4	0.5	2	0.25	3.57	1.28	0.43	0.18
1	4	2	1	0.25	3.57	1.00	0.43	0.18
1	3	0.5	2	0.33	6.35	1.52	0.48	0.15
1	3	2	1	0.33	6.35	1.00	0.48	0.15
1	2	0.5	2	0.50	14.29	1.75	0.61	0.11
1	2	2	1	0.50	14.29	1.00	0.61	0.11
3	4	0.5	2	0.75	10.71	1.69	0.83	0.08
3	4	2	1	0.75	10.71	1.00	0.83	0.08
3	3	0.5	2	1.00	19.05	1.81	1.06	0.06
3	3	2	1	1.00	19.05	1.00	1.06	0.06
3	2	0.5	2	1.50	42.86	1.91	1.54	0.04
3	2	2	1	1.50	42.86	1.00	1.54	0.04

last set of columns shows the T-B position in the active portfolio that maximizes the Sharpe ratio of the overall risky portfolio. The final column shows the increment to the Sharpe ratio of the T-B portfolio relative to the APT portfolio.

Keep in mind that even when the two models call for a similar weight in the active portfolio (compare *w* in Active for the APT model to *w*(beta) for the T-B model), they nevertheless prescribe a different overall risky portfolio. The APT assumes zero investment beyond what is necessary to hedge out the market risk of the active portfolio. In contrast, the T-B procedure chooses a mix of active and index portfolios to maximize the Sharpe ratio. With identical investment in the active portfolio, the T-B portfolio can still include additional investment in the index portfolio.

To obtain the Sharpe ratio of the risky portfolio, we need the Sharpe ratio of the index portfolio. As an estimate, we use the average return and standard deviation of the broad market index (NYSE + AMEX + NASDAQ) over the period 1926–2012. The top row (over the column titles) of Table 11-2 shows an annual Sharpe ratio of 0.35. The rows of the table are ordered by the information ratio of the active portfolio.

Table 11-2 shows that the T-B procedure noticeably improves the Sharpe ratio beyond the information ratio of the APT (for which the IR is also the Sharpe ratio). However, as the information ratio of the active portfolio increases, the difference in the T-B and APT active portfolio positions declines, as does the difference between their Sharpe ratios. Put differently, the higher the information ratio, the closer we are to a risk-free arbitrage opportunity, and the closer are the prescriptions of the APT and T-B models.

A MULTIFACTOR APT

We have assumed so far that only one systematic factor affects stock returns. This simplifying assumption is in fact too simplistic. We've noted that it is easy to think of several factors driven by the business cycle that might affect stock returns: interest rate fluctuations, inflation rates, and so on. Presumably, exposure to any of these factors will affect a stock's risk and hence its expected return. We can derive a multifactor version of the APT to accommodate these multiple sources of risk.

Suppose that we generalize the single-factor model expressed in Equation (11.1) to a two-factor model:

$$R_i = E(R_i) + \beta_{i1}F_1 + \beta_{i2}F_2 + e_i \qquad \textbf{(11.10)}$$

In Example 11.2, factor 1 was the departure of GDP growth from expectations, and factor 2 was the unanticipated change in interest rates. Each factor has zero expected value because each measures the *surprise* in the systematic variable rather than the level of the variable. Similarly, the firm-specific component of unexpected return. e_i, also has zero expected value. Extending such a two-factor model to any number of factors is straightforward.

We can now generalize the simple APT to a more general multifactor version. But first we must introduce the concept of a **factor portfolio**, which is a well-diversified portfolio constructed to have a beta of 1 on one of the factors and a beta of zero on any other factor. We can think of a factor portfolio as a *tracking portfolio.* That is, the returns on such a portfolio track the evolution of particular sources of macroeconomic risk but are uncorrelated with other sources of risk. It is possible to form such factor portfolios because we have a large number of securities to choose from, and a relatively small number of factors. Factor portfolios will serve as the benchmark portfolios for a multifactor security market line. The multidimensional SML predicts that exposure to each risk factor contributes to the security's total risk premium by an amount equal to the factor beta times the risk premium of the factor portfolio tracking that source of risk. We illustrate with an example.

Example 11.4 Multifactor SML

Suppose that the two factor portfolios, portfolios 1 and 2, have expected returns $E(r_1) = 10\%$ and $E(r_2) = 12\%$. Suppose further that the risk-free rate is 4%. The risk premium on the first factor portfolio is 10% − 4% = 6%, whereas that on the second factor portfolio is 12% − 4% = 8%.

Now consider a well-diversified portfolio, portfolio A, with beta on the first factor, $\beta_{A1} = .5$, and beta on the second factor, $\beta_{A2} = .75$. The multifactor APT states that the overall risk premium on this portfolio must equal the sum of the risk premiums required as compensation for each source of systematic risk. The risk premium attributable to risk factor 1 should be the portfolio's exposure to factor 1, β_{A1}, multiplied by the risk premium earned on the first factor portfolio, $E(r_1) - r_f$. Therefore, the portion of portfolio A's risk premium that is compensation for its exposure to the first factor is $\beta_{A1}[E(r_1) - r_f] = .5(10\% - 4\%) = 3\%$, whereas the risk premium attributable to risk factor 2 is

$\beta_{A2}[E(r_2) - r_f] = .75(12\% - 4\%) = 6\%$. The total risk premium on the portfolio should be $3\% + 6\% = 9\%$ and the total return on the portfolio should be $4\% + 9\% = 13\%$.

To generalize the argument in Example 11.4, note that the factor exposures of any portfolio, P, are given by its betas, β_{P1} and β_{P2}. A competing portfolio, Q, can be formed by investing in factor portfolios with the following weights: β_{P1} in the first factor portfolio, β_{P2} in the second factor portfolio, and $1 - \beta_{P1} - \beta_{P2}$ in T-bills. By construction, portfolio Q will have betas equal to those of portfolio P and expected return of

$$E(r_Q) = \beta_{P1}E(r_1) + \beta_{P2}E(r_2) + (1 - \beta_{P1} - \beta_{P2})r_f$$
$$= r_f + \beta_{P1}[E(r_1) - r_f] + \beta_{P2}[E(r_2) - r_f] \quad \textbf{(11.11)}$$

Using the numbers in Example 11.4:

$$E(r_Q) = 4 + .5 \times (10 - 4) + .75 \times (12 - 4) = 13\%$$

Example 11.5 Mispricing and Arbitrage

Suppose that the expected return on portfolio A from Example 11.4 were 12% rather than 13%. This return would give rise to an arbitrage opportunity. Form a portfolio from the factor portfolios with the same betas as portfolio A. This requires weights of .5 on the first factor portfolio, .75 on the second factor portfolio, and −.25 on the risk-free asset. This portfolio has exactly the same factor betas as portfolio A: It has a beta of .5 on the first factor because of its .5 weight on the first factor portfolio, and a beta of .75 on the second factor. (The weight of −.25 on risk-free T-bills does not affect the sensitivity to either factor.)

Now invest $1 in portfolio Q and sell (short) $1 in portfolio A. Your net investment is zero, but your expected dollar profit is positive and equal to

$$\$1 \times E(r_Q) - \$1 \times E(r_A) = \$1 \times .13 - \$1 \times .12 = \$.01$$

Moreover, your net position is riskless. Your exposure to each risk factor cancels out because you are long $1 in portfolio Q and short $1 in portfolio A, and both of these well-diversified portfolios have exactly the same factor betas. Thus, if portfolio A's expected return differs from that of portfolio Q's, you can earn positive risk-free profits on a zero-net-investment position. This is an arbitrage opportunity.

Because portfolio Q in Example 11.5 has precisely the same exposures as portfolio A to the two sources of risk, their expected returns also ought to be equal. So

portfolio A also ought to have an expected return of 13%. If it does not, then there will be an arbitrage opportunity.[7]

We conclude that any well-diversified portfolio with betas β_{P1} and β_{P2} must have the return given in Equation (11.11) if arbitrage opportunities are to be precluded. Equation (11.11) simply generalizes the one-factor SML.

Finally, the extension of the multifactor SML of Equation (11.11) to individual assets is precisely the same as for the one-factor APT. Equation (11.11) cannot be satisfied by every well-diversified portfolio unless it is satisfied approximately by individual securities. Equation (11.11) thus represents the multifactor SML for an economy with multiple sources of risk.

We pointed out earlier that one application of the CAPM is to provide "fair" rates of return for regulated utilities. The multifactor APT can be used to the same ends. Box 11-1 summarizes a study in which the APT was applied to find the cost of capital for regulated electric companies. Notice that empirical estimates for interest rate and inflation risk premiums in the box are negative, as we argued was reasonable in our discussion of Example 11.2.

Concept Check 11.3

Using the factor portfolios of Example 11.4, find the equilibrium rate of return on a portfolio with $\beta_1 = .2$ and $2 = 1.4$.

THE FAMA-FRENCH (FF) THREE-FACTOR MODEL

The currently dominant approach to specifying factors as candidates for relevant sources of systematic risk uses firm characteristics that seem on empirical grounds to proxy for exposure to systematic risk. The factors chosen are variables that on past evidence seem to predict average returns well and therefore may be capturing risk premiums. One example of this approach is the Fama and French three-factor model and its variants, which

---

[7] The risk premium on portfolio A is 9% (more than the historical risk premium of the S&P 500) despite the fact that its betas, which are both below 1, might *seem* defensive. This highlights another distinction between multifactor and single-factor models. Whereas a beta greater than 1 in a single-factor market is aggressive, we cannot say in advance what would be aggressive or defensive in a multifactor economy where risk premiums depend on the sum of the contributions of several factors.

BOX 11-1 Using the APT to Find Cost of Capital

Elton, Gruber, and Mei* use the APT to derive the cost of capital for electric utilities. They assume that the relevant risk factors are unanticipated developments in the term structure of interest rates, the level of interest rates, inflation rates, the business cycle (measured by GDP), foreign exchange rates, and a summary measure they devise to measure other macro factors.

Their first step is to estimate the risk premium associated with exposure to each risk source. They accomplish this in a two-step strategy:

1. *Estimate "factor loadings" (i.e., betas) of a large sample of firms.* Regress returns of 100 randomly selected stocks against the systematic risk factors. They use a time-series regression for each stock (e.g., 60 months of data), therefore estimating 100 regressions, one for each stock.

2. *Estimate the reward earned per unit of exposure to each risk factor.* For each month, regress the return of each stock against the five betas estimated. The coefficient on each beta is the extra average return earned as beta increases, i.e., it is an estimate of the risk premium for that risk factor from that month's data. These estimates are of course subject to sampling error. Therefore, average the risk premium estimates across the 12 months in each year. The average response of return to risk is less subject to sampling error.

The risk premiums are in the middle column of the table at the top of the next column.

Notice that some risk premiums are negative. The interpretation of this result is that risk premium should be positive for risk factors you don't want exposure to, but *negative* for factors you *do* want exposure to. For example, you should desire securities that have higher returns when inflation increases and be willing to accept lower expected returns on such securities; this shows up as a negative risk premium.

Factor	Factor Risk Premium	Factor Betas for Niagara Mohawk
Term structure	.425	1.0615
Interest rates	−.051	−2.4167
Exchange rates	−.049	1.3235
Business cycle	.041	.1292
Inflation	−.069	−.5220
Other macro factors	.530	.3046

Therefore, the expected return on any security should be related to its factor betas as follows:

$$r_f + .425\,\beta_{\text{term struc}} - .051\,\beta_{\text{int rate}}$$
$$-.049\,\beta_{\text{ex rate}} + .041\,\beta_{\text{bus cycle}} - .069\,\beta_{\text{inflation}} + .530\,\beta_{\text{other}}$$

Finally, to obtain the cost of capital for a particular firm, the authors estimate the firm's betas against each source of risk, multiply each factor beta by the "cost of factor risk" from the table above, sum over all risk sources to obtain the total risk premium, and add the risk-free rate.

For example, the beta estimates for Niagara Mohawk appear in the last column of the table above. Therefore, its cost of capital is

$$\text{Cost of capital} = r_f + .425 \times 1.0615 - .051(-2.4167)$$
$$-.049(1.3235) + .041(.1292)$$
$$-.069(-.5220) + .530(.3046)$$
$$= r_f + .72$$

In other words, the monthly cost of capital for Niagara Mohawk is .72% above the monthly risk-free rate. Its annualized risk premium is therefore .72% x 12 = 8.64%.

---

*Edwin J. Elton, Martin J. Gruber, and Jianping Mei, "Cost of Capital Using Arbitrage Pricing Theory: A Case Study of Nine New York Utilities," *Financial Markets, Institutions, and Instruments* 3 (August 1994), pp. 46–68.

---

have come to dominate empirical research and industry applications:[8]

$$R_{it} = \alpha_i + \beta_{iM}R_{Mt} + \beta_{iSMB}SMB_t + \beta_{iHML}HML_t + e_{it} \quad \textbf{(11.12)}$$

where

SMB = Small Minus Big, i.e., the return of a portfolio of small stocks in excess of the return on a portfolio of large stocks.

HML = High Minus Low, i.e., the return of a portfolio of stocks with a high book-to-market ratio in excess of the return on a portfolio of stocks with a low book-to-market ratio.

Note that in this model the market index does play a role and is expected to capture systematic risk originating from macroeconomic factors.

These two firm-characteristic variables are chosen because of long-standing observations that corporate capitalization (firm size) and book-to-market ratio predict deviations of average stock returns from levels

---

[8] Eugene F. Fama and Kenneth R. French, "Multifactor Explanations of Asset Pricing Anomalies," *Journal of Finance* 51 (1996), pp. 55–84.

consistent with the CAPM. Fama and French justify this model on empirical grounds: While SMB and HML are not themselves obvious candidates for relevant risk factors, the argument is that these variables may proxy for yet-unknown more-fundamental variables. For example, Fama and French point out that firms with high ratios of book-to-market value are more likely to be in financial distress and that small stocks may be more sensitive to changes in business conditions. Thus, these variables may capture sensitivity to risk factors in the macroeconomy.

The problem with empirical approaches such as the Fama-French model, which use proxies for extramarket sources of risk, is that none of the factors in the proposed models can be clearly identified as hedging a significant source of uncertainty. Black[9] points out that when researchers scan and rescan the database of security returns in search of explanatory factors (an activity often called data-snooping), they may eventually uncover past "patterns" that are due purely to chance. Black observes that return premiums to factors such as firm size have proven to be inconsistent since first discovered. However, Fama and French have shown that size and book-to-market ratios have predicted average returns in various time periods and in markets all over the world, thus mitigating potential effects of data-snooping.

The firm-characteristic basis of the Fama-French factors raises the question of whether they reflect a multi-index ICAPM based on extra-market hedging demands or just represent yet-unexplained anomalies, where firm characteristics are correlated with alpha values. This is an important distinction for the debate over the proper interpretation of the model, because the validity of FF-style models may signify either a deviation from rational equilibrium (as there is no rational reason to prefer one or another of these firm characteristics per se), or that firm characteristics identified as empirically associated with average returns are correlated with other (yet unknown) risk factors.

The issue is still unresolved.

SUMMARY

1. Multifactor models seek to improve the explanatory power of single-factor models by explicitly accounting for the various systematic components of security

risk. These models use indicators intended to capture a wide range of macroeconomic risk factors.

2. Once we allow for multiple risk factors, we conclude that the security market line also ought to be multidimensional, with exposure to each risk factor contributing to the total risk premium of the security.

3. A (risk-free) arbitrage opportunity arises when two or more security prices enable investors to construct a zero-net-investment portfolio that will yield a sure profit. The presence of arbitrage opportunities will generate a large volume of trades that puts pressure on security prices. This pressure will continue until prices reach levels that preclude such arbitrage.

4. When securities are priced so that there are no risk-free arbitrage opportunities, we say that they satisfy the no-arbitrage condition. Price relationships that satisfy the no-arbitrage condition are important because we expect them to hold in real-world markets.

5. Portfolios are called "well-diversified" if they include a large number of securities and the investment proportion in each is sufficiently small. The proportion of a security in a well-diversified portfolio is small enough so that for all practical purposes a reasonable change in that security's rate of return will have a negligible effect on the portfolio's rate of return.

6. In a single-factor security market, all well-diversified portfolios have to satisfy the expected return–beta relationship of the CAPM to satisfy the no-arbitrage condition. If all well-diversified portfolios satisfy the expected return–beta relationship, then individual securities also must satisfy this relationship, at least approximately.

7. The APT does not require the restrictive assumptions of the CAPM and its (unobservable) market portfolio. The price of this generality is that the APT does not guarantee this relationship for all securities at all times.

8. A multifactor APT generalizes the single-factor model to accommodate several sources of systematic risk. The multidimensional security market line predicts that exposure to each risk factor contributes to the security's total risk premium by an amount equal to the factor beta times the risk premium of the factor portfolio that tracks that source of risk.

9. A multifactor extension of the single-factor CAPM, the ICAPM, is a model of the risk–return trade-off that

---

[9] Fischer Black, "Beta and Return," *Journal of Portfolio Management* 20 (1993), pp. 8-18.

predicts the same multidimensional security market line as the APT. The ICAPM suggests that priced risk factors will be those sources of risk that lead to significant hedging demand by a substantial fraction of investors.

Key Terms

single-factor model

multifactor model

factor loading

factor beta

arbitrage pricing theory

arbitrage

Law of One Price

risk arbitrage

well-diversified portfolio

factor portfolio

Key Equations

Single factor model: $R_i = E(R_i) + \beta_i F + e_i$

Multifactor model (here, 2 factors, F_1 and F_2):
$R_i = E(R_i) + \beta_1 F_1 + \beta_2 F_2 + e_i$

Single-index model: $R_i = \alpha_i + \beta_i R_M + e_i$

Multifactor SML (here, 2 factors, labeled 1 and 2)
$$E(r_i) = r_f + \beta_1 \left[E(r_1) - r_f \right] + \beta_2 \left[E(r_2) - r_f \right]$$
$$= r_f + \beta_1 E(R_1) + \beta_2 E(R_2)$$

where the risk premiums on the two factor portfolios are $E(R_1)$ and $E(R_2)$.

Information Risk and Data Quality Management

12

Learning Objectives

Candidates, after completing this reading, should be able to:

- Identify the most common issues that result in data errors.
- Explain how a firm can set expectations for its data quality and describe some key dimensions of data quality used in this process.

- Describe the operational data governance process, including the use of scorecards in managing information risk.

Excerpt is Chapter 3 of Risk Management in Finance: Six Sigma and Other Next Generation Techniques, *by Anthony Tarantino and Deborah Cernauskas.*

It would not be a stretch of the imagination to claim that most organizations today are heavily dependent on the use of information to both *run* and *improve* the ways that they achieve their business objectives. That being said, the reliance on dependable information introduces risks to the ability of a business to achieve its business goals, and this means that no enterprise risk management program is complete without instituting processes for assessing, measuring, reporting, reacting to, and controlling the risks associated with poor data quality.

However, the consideration of information as a fluid asset, created and used across many different operational and analytic applications, makes it difficult to envision ways to assess the risks related to data failures as well as ways to monitor conformance to business user expectations. This requires some exploration into types of risks relating to the use of information, ways to specify data quality expectations, and developing a data quality scorecard as a management tool for instituting data governance and data quality control.

In this chapter we look at the types of risks that are attributable to poor data quality as well as an approach to correlating business impacts to data flaws. Data governance (DG) processes can contribute to the description of data quality expectations and the definition of relevant metrics and acceptability thresholds for monitoring conformance to those expectations. Combining the raw metrics scores with measured staff performance in observing data service-level agreements contributes to the creation of a data quality scorecard for managing risks.

ORGANIZATIONAL RISK, BUSINESS IMPACTS, AND DATA QUALITY

If successful business operations rely on high-quality data, then the opposite is likely to be true as well: flawed data will delay or obstruct the successful completion of business processes. Determining the specific impacts that are related to the different data issues that emerge is a challenging process, but assessing impact is simplified through the characterization of impacts within a business impact taxonomy. Categories in this taxonomy relate to aspects of the business's financial, confidence, and compliance activities, yet all business impact categories deal with enterprise risk. There are two aspects

of looking at information and risk; the first looks at how flawed information impacts organizational risk, while the other looks at the types of data failures that create the exposure.

Business Impacts of Poor Data Quality

Many data quality issues may occur within different business processes, and a data quality analysis process should incorporate a business impact assessment to identify and prioritize risks. To simplify the analysis, the business impacts associated with data errors can be categorized within a classification scheme intended to support the data quality analysis process and help in distinguishing between data issues that lead to material business impact and those that do not. This classification scheme defines six primary categories for assessing either the negative impacts incurred as a result of a flaw, or the potential opportunities for improvement resulting from improved data quality:

1. Financial impacts, such as increased operating costs, decreased revenues, missed opportunities, reduction or delays in cash flow, or increased penalties, fines, or other charges.

2. Confidence-based impacts, such as decreased organizational trust, low confidence in forecasting, inconsistent operational and management reporting, and delayed or improper decisions.

3. Satisfaction impacts such as customer, employee, or supplier satisfaction, as well as general market satisfaction.

4. Productivity impacts such as increased workloads, decreased throughput, increased processing time, or decreased end-product quality.

5. Risk impacts associated with credit assessment, investment risks, competitive risk, capital investment and/or development, fraud, and leakage.

6. Compliance is jeopardized, whether that compliance is with government regulations, industry expectations, or self-imposed policies (such as privacy policies).

Despite the natural tendency to focus on financial impacts, in many environments the risk and compliance impacts are largely compromised by data quality issues. Some examples to which financial institutions are particularly sensitive include:

- Anti-money laundering aspects of the Bank Secrecy Act and the USA PATRIOT Act have mandated private organizations to take steps in identifying and preventing money laundering activities that could be used in financing terrorist activities.
- Sarbanes-Oxley, in which section 302 mandates that the principal executive officer or officers and the principal financial officer or officers certify the accuracy and correctness of financial reports.
- Basel II Accords provide guidelines for defining the regulations as well as guiding the quantification of operational and credit risk as a way to determine the amount of capital financial institutions are required to maintain as a guard against those risks.
- The Graham-Leach-Bliley Act of 1999 mandates financial institutions with the obligation to "respect the privacy of its customers and to protect the security and confidentiality of those customers' nonpublic personal information."
- Credit risk assessment, which requires accurate documentation to evaluate an individual's or organization's abilities to repay loans.
- System development risks associated with capital investment in deploying new application systems emerge when moving those systems into production is delayed due to lack of trust in the application's underlying data assets.

While the sources of these areas of risk differ, an interesting similarity emerges: not only do these mandate the use or presentation of high-quality information, they also require means of demonstrating the adequacy of internal controls overseeing that quality to external parties such as auditors. This means that not only must financial institutions manage the quality of organizational information, they must also have governance processes in place that are transparent and auditable.

Information Flaws

The root causes for the business impacts are related to flaws in the critical data elements upon which the successful completion of the business processes depend. There are many types of erred data, although these common issues lead to increased risk:

- Data entry errors
- Missing data
- Duplicate records
- Inconsistent data
- Nonstandard formats
- Complex data transformations
- Failed identity management processes
- Undocumented, incorrect, or misleading metadata

All of these types of errors can lead to inconsistent reporting, inaccurate aggregation, invalid data mappings, incorrect product pricing, and failures in trade settlement, among other process failures.

EXAMPLES

The general approach to correlating business impacts to data quality issues is not new, and in fact there are some interesting examples that demonstrate different types of risks that are attributable to flaws (both inadvertent and deliberate) in data.

Employee Fraud and Abuse

In 1997, the Department of Defense Guidelines on Data Quality categorized costs into four areas: prevention, appraisal, internal failure, and external failure. In turn, the impacts were evaluated to assess costs to correct data problems as opposed to costs incurred by ignoring them. Further assessment looked at direct costs (such as costs for appraisal, correction, or support) versus indirect costs (such as customer satisfaction). That report documents examples of how poor data quality impacts specific business processes: ". . . the inability to match payroll records to the official employment record can cost millions in payroll overpayments to deserters, prisoners, and 'ghost' soldiers. In addition, the inability to correlate purchase orders to invoices is a major problem in unmatched disbursements."[1]

The 2006 Association of Certified Fraud Examiners Report to the Nation[2] details a number of methods that

---

[1] U.S. Dept. of Defense, "DoD Guidelines on Data Quality Management," 1997, accessible via www.tricare.mil/ocfo/_docs/DoDGuidelinesOnDataQualityManagement.pdf.

[2] "2006 ACFE Report to the Nation on Occupational Fraud and Abuse," www.acfe.com/documents/2006-rttn.pdf.

unethical employees can use to modify existing data to commit fraudulent payments. Invalid data is demonstrated to have significant business impacts, and the report details median costs associated with these different types of improper disbursements.

Underbilling and Revenue Assurance

NTL, a cable operator in the United Kingdom, anticipated business benefits in improving the efficiency and value of an operator's network through data quality improvement. Invalid data translated into discrepancies between services provided and services invoiced, resulting in a waste of unknown excess capacity. Their data quality improvement program was, to some extent, self-funded through the analysis of "revenue assurance to detect under billing. For example, . . . results indicated leakage of just over 3 percent of total revenue."[3]

Credit Risk

In 2002, a PricewaterhouseCoopers study on credit risk data indicated that a significant percentage of the top banks were deficient in credit risk data management, especially in the areas of counterparty data repositories, counterparty hierarchy data, common counterparty identifiers, and consistent data standards.[4]

Insurance Exposure

A 2008 Ernst & Young survey on catastrophe exposure data quality highlighted that "shortcomings in exposure data quality are common," and that "not many insurers are doing enough to correct these shortcomings," which included missing or inaccurate values associated with insured values, locations, building class, occupancy class, as well as additional characteristics.[5]

---

[3] Herbert, Brian, "Data Quality Management—A Key to Operator Profitability," *Billing and OSS World,* March 2006, accessible at www.billingworld.com/articles/feature/Data-Quality-Management-A-Key-to-Operator.html.

[4] Inserro, Richard J., "Credit Risk Data Challenges Underlying the New Basel Capital Accord," *RMA Journal,* April 2002, accessible at www.pwc.com/tr/eng/about/svcs/abas/frm/creditrisk/articles/pwc_baselcreditdata-rma.pdf.

[5] Ernst & Young, "Raising the Bar on Catastrophe Data," 2008, accessible via www.ey.com/Global/assets.nsf/US/Actuarial_Raising_the_bar_catastrophe_data/ $file/Actuarial_Raising_the_bar_catastrophe_data.pdf.

Development Risk

Experience with our clients has indicated a common pattern in which significant investment in capital acquisitions and accompanying software development has been made in the creation of new business application systems, yet the deployment of those systems is delayed (or perhaps even canceled) due to organizational mistrust of the application data. Such delayed application development puts investments at risk.

Compliance Risk

Pharmaceutical companies are bound to abide by the federal Anti-Kickback Statute, which restricts companies from offering or paying remuneration in return for arranging for the furnishing of items or services for which payment may be made under Medicare or a state health care program. Pharmaceutical companies fund research using their developed products as well as market those same products to potentially the same pool of practitioners and providers, so there is a need for stringent control and segregation of the data associated with both research grants and marketing.

Our experience with some of our clients has shown that an assessment of party information contained within master data sets indicated some providers within the same practice working under research grants while others within the same practice subjected to marketing. Despite the fact that no individual appeared within both sets of data, the fact that individuals rolled up within the same organizational hierarchy exposed the organization to potential violation of the Anti-Kickback Statute.

DATA QUALITY EXPECTATIONS

These examples are not unique, but instead demonstrate patterns that commonly emerge across all types of organizations. Knowledge of the business impacts related to data quality issues is the catalyst to instituting data governance practices that can oversee the control and assurance of data validity. The first step toward managing the risks associated with the introduction of flawed data into the environment is articulating the business user expectations for data quality and asserting specifications that can be used to monitor organizational conformance to those expectations. These expectations are defined in the context of "data quality dimensions," high-level categorizations of assertions that lend themselves to quantification, measurement, and reporting.

The intention is to provide an ability to characterize business user expectations in terms of acceptability thresholds applied to quantifiers for data quality that are correlated to the different types of business impacts, particularly the different types of risk. And although the academic literature in data quality enumerates many different dimensions of data quality, an initial development of a data quality scorecard can rely on a subset of those dimensions, namely, accuracy, completeness, consistency, reasonableness, currency, and identifiability.

Accuracy

The dimension of accuracy measures the degree with which data instances compare to the "real-life" entities they are intended to model. Often, accuracy is measured in terms of agreement with an identified reference source of correct information such as a "system of record," a similar corroborative set of data values from another table, comparisons with dynamically computed values, or the results of manually checking value accuracy.

Completeness

The completeness dimension specifies the expectations regarding the population of data attributes. Completeness expectations can be measured using rules relating to varying levels of constraint—mandatory attributes that require a value, data elements with conditionally optional values, and inapplicable attribute values.

Consistency

Consistency refers to measuring reasonable comparison of values in one data set to those in another data. Consistency is relatively broad, and can encompass an expectation that two data values drawn from separate data sets must not conflict with each other, or define more complex comparators with a set of predefined constraints. More formal consistency constraints can be encapsulated as a set of rules that specify relationships between values of attributes, either across a record or message, or along all values of a single attribute.

However, be careful not to confuse consistency with accuracy or correctness. Consistency may be defined between one set of attribute values and another attribute set within

the same record (record-level consistency), between one set of attribute values and another attribute set in different records (cross-record consistency), or between one set of attribute values and the same attribute set within the same record at different points in time (temporal consistency).

Reasonableness

This dimension is used to measure conformance to consistency expectations relevant within specific operational contexts. For example, one might expect that the total sales value of all the transactions each day is not expected to exceed 105 percent of the running average total sales for the previous 30 days.

Currency

This dimension measures the degree to which information is current with the world that it models. Currency measures whether data is considered to be "fresh," and its correctness in the face of possible time-related changes. Data currency may be measured as a function of the expected frequency rate at which different data elements are expected to be refreshed, as well as verifying that the data is up to date. Currency rules may be defined to assert the "lifetime" of a data value before it needs to be checked and possibly refreshed.

Uniqueness

This dimension measures the number of inadvertent duplicate records that exist within a data set or across data sets. Asserting uniqueness of the entities within a data set implies that no entity exists more than once within the data set and that there is a key that can be used to uniquely access each entity (and only that specific entity) within the data set.

Other Dimensions of Data Quality

This list is by no means complete—there are many other aspects of expressing the expectations for data quality, such as semantic consistency (dealing with the consistency of meanings of data elements), structural format conformance, timeliness, and valid ranges, valid within defined data domains, among many others. The principal concept is that the selected dimensions characterize aspects of the business user expectations and that they can be quantified using a reasonable measurement process.

MAPPING BUSINESS POLICIES TO DATA RULES

Having identified the dimensions of data quality that are relevant to the business processes, we can map the information policies and their corresponding business rules to those dimensions. For example, consider a business policy that specifies that personal data collected over the web may be shared only if the user has not opted out of that sharing process. This business policy defines information policies: the data model must have a data attribute specifying whether a user has opted out of information sharing, and that attribute must be checked before any records may be shared. This also provides us with a measurable metric: the count of shared records for those users who have opted out of sharing.

The same successive refinement can be applied to almost every business policy and its corresponding information policies. As we distill out the information requirements, we also capture assertions about the business user expectations for the result of the operational processes. Many of these assertions can be expressed as rules for determining whether a record does or does not conform to the expectations. The assertion is a quantifiable measurement when it results in a count of nonconforming records, and therefore monitoring data against that assertion provides the necessary data control.

Once we have reviewed methods for inspecting and measuring against those dimensions in a quantifiable manner, the next step is to interview the business users to determine the acceptability thresholds. Scoring below the acceptability threshold indicates that the data does not meet business expectations, and highlights the boundary at which noncompliance with expectations may lead to material impact to the downstream business functions. Integrating these thresholds with the methods for measurement completes the construction of the data quality control. Missing the desired threshold will trigger a data quality event, notifying the data steward and possibly even recommending specific actions for mitigating the discovered issue.

DATA QUALITY INSPECTION, CONTROL, AND OVERSIGHT: OPERATIONAL DATA GOVERNANCE

In this section we highlight the relationship between data issues and their downstream impacts, and note that being able to control the quality of data throughout the information processing flow will enable immediate assessment, initiation of remediation, and an audit trail demonstrating the levels of data quality as well as the governance processes intended to ensure data quality.

Operational data governance is the manifestation of the processes and protocols necessary to ensure that an acceptable level of confidence in the data effectively satisfies the organization's business needs. A data governance program defines the roles, responsibilities, and accountabilities associated with managing data quality. Rewarding those individuals who are successful at their roles and responsibilities can ensure the success of the data governance program. To measure this, a "data quality scorecard" provides an effective management tool for monitoring organizational performance with respect to data quality control.

Operational data governance combines the ability to identify data errors as early as possible with the process of initiating the activities necessary to address those errors to avoid or minimize any downstream impacts. This essentially includes notifying the right individuals to address the issue and determining if the issue can be resolved appropriately within an agreed-to time frame. Data inspection processes are instituted to measure and monitor compliance with data quality rules, while service-level agreements (SLAs) specify the reasonable expectations for response and remediation.

Note that data quality inspection differs from data validation. While the data validation process reviews and measures conformance of data with a set of defined business rules, inspection is an ongoing process to:

- Reduce the number of errors to a reasonable and manageable level.

- Enable the identification of data flaws along with a protocol for interactively making adjustments to enable the completion of the processing stream.

- Institute a mitigation or remediation of the root cause within an agreed-to time frame.

The value of data quality inspection as part of operational data governance is in establishing trust on behalf of downstream users that any issue likely to cause a significant business impact is caught early enough to avoid any significant impact on operations. Without this inspection process, poor-quality data pervades every system, complicating practically any operational or analytical process.

MANAGING INFORMATION RISK VIA A DATA QUALITY SCORECARD

While there are practices in place for measuring and monitoring certain aspects of organizational data quality, there is an opportunity to evaluate the relationship between the business impacts of noncompliant data as indicated by the business clients and the defined thresholds for data quality acceptability. The degree of acceptability becomes the standard against which the data is measured, with operational data governance instituted within the context of measuring performance in relation to the data governance procedures. This measurement essentially covers conformance to the defined standards, as well as monitoring staff agility in taking specific actions when the data sets do not conform. Given the set of data quality rules, methods for measuring conformance, the acceptability thresholds defined by the business clients, and the SLAs, we can monitor data governance by observing not only compliance of the data to the business rules, but of the data stewards to observing the processes associated with data risks and failures.

The dimensions of data quality provide a framework for defining metrics that are relevant within the business context while providing a view into controllable aspects of data quality management. The degree of reportability and controllability may differ depending on one's role within the organization, and correspondingly, so will the level of detail reported in a data quality scorecard. Data stewards may focus on continuous monitoring in order to resolve issues according to defined SLAs, while senior managers may be interested in observing the degree to which poor data quality introduces enterprise risk.

Essentially, the need to present higher-level data quality scores introduces a distinction between two types of metrics. The simple metrics based on measuring against defined dimensions of data quality can be referred to as "base-level" metrics, and they quantify specific observance of acceptable levels of defined data quality rules. A higher-level concept would be the "complex" metric representing a rolled-up score computed as a function (such as a sum) of applying specific weights to a collection of existing metrics, both base-level and complex. The rolled-up metric provides a qualitative overview of how data quality impacts the organization in different ways, since the scorecard can be populated with metrics rolled up across different dimensions depending on the audience. Complex data quality metrics can be accumulated for reporting in a scorecard in one of three different views: by **issue**, by **business process,** or by **business impact.**

Data Quality Issues View

Evaluating the impacts of a specific data quality issue across multiple business processes demonstrates the diffusion of pain across the enterprise caused by specific data flaws. This scorecard scheme, which is suited to data analysts attempting to prioritize tasks for diagnosis and remediation, provides a rolled-up view of the impacts attributed to each data issue. Drilling down through this view sheds light on the root causes of impacts of poor data quality, as well as identifying "rogue processes" that require greater focus for instituting monitoring and control processes.

Business Process View

Operational managers overseeing business processes may be interested in a scorecard view by business process. In this view, the operational manager can examine the risks and failures preventing the business process's achievement of the expected results. For each business process, this scorecard scheme consists of complex metrics representing the impacts associated with each issue. The drill-down in this view can be used for isolating the source of the introduction of data issues at specific stages of the business process as well as informing the data stewards in diagnosis and remediation.

Business Impact View

Business impacts may have been incurred as a result of a number of different data quality issues originating in a number of different business processes. This reporting scheme displays the aggregation of business impacts rolled up from the different issues across different process flows. For example, one scorecard could report rolled-up metrics documenting the accumulated impacts associated with credit risk, compliance with privacy protection, and decreased sales. Drilling down through the metrics will point to the business processes from which the issues originate; deeper review will point to the specific issues within each of the business processes. This view is suited to a more senior manager seeking a high-level overview of the risks associated with data quality issues, and how that risk is introduced across the enterprise.

Managing Scorecard Views

Essentially, each of these views composing a data quality scorecard require the construction and management of a hierarchy of metrics related to various levels of accountability for support the organization's business objectives. But no matter which scheme is employed, each is supported by describing, defining, and managing base-level and complex metrics such that:

- Scorecards reflecting business relevance are driven by a hierarchical rollup of metrics.

- The definition of metrics is separated from its contextual use, thereby allowing the same measurement to be used in different contexts with different acceptability thresholds and weights.

- The appropriate level of presentation can be materialized based on the level of detail expected for the data consumer's specific data governance role and accountability.

SUMMARY

Scorecards are effective management tools when they can summarize important organizational knowledge as well as alerting the appropriate staff members when diagnostic or remedial actions need to be taken. Part of an information risk management program would incorporate a data quality scorecard that supports an organizational data governance program; this program is based on defining metrics within a business context that correlate the metric score to acceptable levels of business performance. This means that the metrics should reflect the business processes' (and applications') dependence on acceptable data, and that the data quality rules being observed and monitored as part of the governance program are aligned with the achievement of business goals.

These processes simplify the approach to evaluating risks to achievement of business objectives, how those risks are associated with poor data quality and how one can define metrics that capture data quality expectations and acceptability thresholds. The impact taxonomy can be used to narrow the scope of describing the business impacts, while the dimensions of data quality guide the analyst in defining quantifiable measures that can be correlated to business impacts. Applying these processes will result in a set of metrics that can be combined into different scorecard schemes that effectively address senior-level manager, operational manager, and data steward responsibilities to monitor information risk as well as support organizational data governance.

Principles for Effective Risk Data Aggregation and Risk Reporting

13

Candidates, after completing this reading, should be able to:

- Explain the potential benefits of having effective risk data aggregation and reporting.
- Describe key governance principles related to risk data aggregation and risk reporting practices.
- Identify the data architecture and IT infrastructure features that can contribute to effective risk data aggregation and risk reporting practices.

- Describe characteristics of a strong risk data aggregation capability and demonstrate how these characteristics interact with one another.
- Describe characteristics of effective risk reporting practices.

Excerpt is courtesy of Basel Committee on Banking Supervision.

Where is the wisdom we have lost in knowledge? Where is the knowledge we have lost in information?

T. S. Eliot. *The Rock* (1934)

INTRODUCTION

1. One of the most significant lessons learned from the global financial crisis that began in 2007 was that banks' information technology (IT) and data architectures were inadequate to support the broad management of financial risks. Many banks lacked the ability to aggregate risk exposures and identify concentrations quickly and accurately at the bank group level, across business lines and between legal entities. Some banks were unable to manage their risks properly because of weak risk data aggregation capabilities and risk reporting practices. This had severe consequences to the banks themselves and to the stability of the financial system as a whole.

2. In response, the Basel Committee issued supplemental Pillar 2 (supervisory review process) guidance[1] to enhance banks' ability to identify and manage bankwide risks. In particular, the Committee emphasised that a sound risk management system should have appropriate management information systems (MIS)[2] at the business and bank-wide level. The Basel Committee also included references to data aggregation as part of its guidance on corporate governance.[3]

3. Improving banks' ability to aggregate risk data will improve their resolvability. For global systemically important banks (G-SIBs) in particular, it is essential that resolution authorities have access to aggregate risk data that complies with the FSB's Key Attributes of Effective Resolution Regimes for Financial Institutions[4] as well as the principles set out below. For recovery, a robust data framework will help banks and supervisors anticipate problems ahead. It will also improve the prospects of finding alternative options to restore financial strength and viability when the firm comes under severe stress. For example, it could improve the prospects of finding a suitable merger partner.

4. Many in the banking industry[5] recognise the benefits of improving their risk data aggregation capabilities and are working towards this goal. They see the improvements in terms of strengthening the capability and the status of the risk function to make judgments. This leads to gains in efficiency, reduced probability of losses and enhanced strategic decision-making, and ultimately increased profitability.

5. Supervisors observe that making improvements in risk data aggregation capabilities and risk reporting practices remains a challenge for banks, and supervisors would like to see more progress, in particular, at G-SIBs. Moreover, as the memories of the crisis fade over time, there is a danger that the enhancement of banks' capabilities in these areas may receive a slower-track treatment. This is because IT systems, data and reporting processes require significant investments of financial and human resources with benefits that may only be realised over the long-term.

6. The Financial Stability Board (FSB) has several international initiatives underway to ensure continued progress is made in strengthening firms' risk data aggregation capabilities and risk reporting practices, which is essential to support financial stability. These include:

- The development of the *Principles for effective risk data aggregation and risk reporting* included in this report. This work stems from a recommendation in the FSB's *Progress report on implementing the recommendations on enhanced supervision,* issued on 4 November 2011:

  "The FSB, in collaboration with the standard setters, will develop a set of supervisory expectations to move firms', particularly SIFIs, data aggregation capabilities to a level where supervisors, firms, and other users (e.g., resolution authorities) of the data are confident that the MIS reports accurately capture the risks. A timeline should be set for all SIFIs to meet supervisory expectations; the deadline for G-SIBs to meet these expectations should be the beginning of 2016, which is the date when the

[1] Basel Committee, *Enhancements to the Basel II framework* (July 2009) at www.bis.org/publ/bcbs158.pdf.
[2] MIS in this context refers to *risk* management information.
[3] Basel Committee, *Principles for enhancing corporate governance* (October 2010) at www.bis.org/publ/bcbs176.pdf.
[4] Financial Stability Board, *Key Attributes of Effective Resolution Regimes for Financial Institutions* (October 2011) at www.financial stabilityboard.org/publications/r_111104dd.pdf.

[5] See Institute of International Finance report, *Risk IT and Operations: Strengthening capabilities* (June 2011).

added loss absorbency requirement begins to be phased in for G-SIBs."

- The development of a new common data template for global systemically important financial institutions (G-SIFIs) in order to address key information gaps identified during the crisis, such as bi-lateral exposures and exposures to countries/sectors/instruments. This should provide the authorities with a stronger framework for assessing potential systemic risks.

- A public-private sector initiative to develop a Legal Entity Identifier (LEI) system. The LEI system will identify unique parties to financial transactions across the globe and is designed to be a key building block for improvements in the quality of financial data across the globe.

7. There are also other initiatives and requirements relating to data that will have to be implemented in the following years.[6] The Committee considers that upgraded risk data aggregation and risk reporting practices will allow banks to comply effectively with those initiatives.

DEFINITION

8. For the purpose of this paper, the term "risk data aggregation" means defining, gathering, and processing risk data according to the bank's risk reporting requirements to enable the bank to measure its performance against its risk tolerance/appetite.[7] This includes sorting, merging or breaking down sets of data.

OBJECTIVES

9. This paper presents a set of principles to strengthen banks' risk data aggregation capabilities and internal

---

[6] For instance, data reporting requirements arising from Basel III and the Solvency II rules; recovery and resolution plans; revisions to the supervisory reporting frameworks of financial reporting (FINREP) and common reporting (COREP) as well as to the international financial reporting standards (IFRS) and to the Foreign Account Tax Compliance Act (FATCA).

[7] "Risk appetite is the level and type of risk a firm is able and willing to assume in its exposures and business activities, given its business objectives and obligations to stakeholders" as defined by the Senior Supervisors Group report, *Observations on Developments in Risk Appetite Frameworks and IT Infrastructure* (December 2010).

risk reporting practices (the Principles). In turn, effective implementation of the Principles is expected to enhance risk management and decision-making processes at banks.

10. The adoption of these Principles will enable fundamental improvements to the management of banks. The Principles are expected to support a bank's efforts to:

- Enhance the infrastructure for reporting key information, particularly that used by the board and senior management to identify, monitor and manage risks;

- Improve the decision-making process throughout the banking organisation;

- Enhance the management of information across legal entities, while facilitating a comprehensive assessment of risk exposures at the global consolidated level;

- Reduce the probability and severity of losses resulting from risk management weaknesses;

- Improve the speed at which information is available and hence decisions can be made; and

- Improve the organisation's quality of strategic planning and the ability to manage the risk of new products and services.

11. Strong risk management capabilities are an integral part of the franchise value of a bank. Effective implementation of the Principles should increase the value of the bank. The Committee believes that the long-term benefits of improved risk data aggregation capabilities and risk reporting practices will outweigh the investment costs incurred by banks.

12. For bank supervisors, these Principles will complement other efforts to improve the intensity and effectiveness of bank supervision. For resolution authorities, improved risk data aggregation should enable smoother bank resolution, thereby reducing the potential recourse to taxpayers.

SCOPE AND INITIAL CONSIDERATIONS

13. These Principles are initially addressed to SIBs and apply at both the banking group and on a solo basis. Common and clearly stated supervisory expectations regarding risk data aggregation and risk reporting are necessary for these institutions. National supervisors may nevertheless choose to apply the Principles to

a wider range of banks, in a way that is proportionate to the size, nature and complexity of these banks' operations.

14. Banks identified as G-SIBs by the FSB in November 2011[8] or November 2012[9] must meet these Principles by January 2016; G-SIBs designated in subsequent annual updates will need to meet the Principles within three years of their designation.[10] G-SIBs subject to the 2016 timeline are expected to start making progress towards effectively implementing the Principles from early 2013. National supervisors and the Basel Committee will monitor and assess this progress in accordance with Section V of this document.

15. It is strongly suggested that national supervisors also apply these Principles to banks identified as D-SIBs by their national supervisors three years after their designation as D-SIBs.[11]

16. The Principles and supervisory expectations contained in this paper apply to a bank's risk management data. This includes data that is critical to enabling the bank to manage the risks it faces. Risk data and reports should provide management with the ability to monitor and track risks relative to the bank's risk tolerance/appetite.

17. These Principles also apply to all key internal risk management models, including but not limited to, Pillar 1 regulatory capital models (e.g., internal ratings-based approaches for credit risk and advanced measurement approaches for operational risk), Pillar 2 capital models and other key risk management models (e.g., value-at-risk).

18. The Principles apply to a bank's group risk management processes. However, banks may also benefit from applying the Principles to other processes, such as financial and operational processes, as well as supervisory reporting.

19. All the Principles included in this paper are also applicable to processes that have been outsourced to third parties.

20. The Principles cover four closely related topics:
    - Overarching governance and infrastructure
    - Risk data aggregation capabilities
    - Risk reporting practices
    - Supervisory review, tools and cooperation

21. Risk data aggregation capabilities and risk reporting practices are considered separately in this paper, but they are clearly inter-linked and cannot exist in isolation. High quality risk management reports rely on the existence of strong risk data aggregation capabilities, and sound infrastructure and governance ensures the information flow from one to the other.

22. Banks should meet all risk data aggregation and risk reporting principles simultaneously. However, trade-offs among Principles could be accepted in exceptional circumstances such as urgent/ad hoc requests of information on new or unknown areas of risk. There should be no trade-offs that materially impact risk management decisions. Decision-makers at banks, in particular the board and senior management, should be aware of these trade-offs and the limitations or shortcomings associated with them.

Supervisors expect banks to have policies and processes in place regarding the application of trade-offs. Banks should be able to explain the impact of these trade-offs on their decision-making process through qualitative reports and, to the extent possible, quantitative measures.

23. The concept of materiality used in this paper means that data and reports can exceptionally exclude information only if it does not affect the decision-making process in a bank (i.e., decision-makers, in particular the board and senior management, would have been influenced by the omitted information or made a different judgment if the correct information had been known).

In applying the materiality concept, banks will take into account considerations that go beyond the number or size of the exposures not included, such as the

---

[8] See the FSB, *Policy Measures to Address to Systemically Important Financial Institutions* (4 November 2011) at www.financialstabilityboard.org/publications/r_111104bb.pdf

[9] See the FSB, *Update of group of global systemically important banks—G-SIBs* (1 November 2012) at www.financialstabilityboard.org/publications/r_121031ac.pdf

[10] This is in line with the FSB's *Update of group of global systemically important banks—G-SIBs* (1 November 2012).

[11] See Basel Committee, *A framework for dealing with domestic systemically important banks* (October 2012) at www.bis.org/publ/bcbs233.pdf

type of risks involved, or the evolving and dynamic nature of the banking business. Banks should also take into account the potential future impact of the information excluded on the decision-making process at their institutions. Supervisors expect banks to be able to explain the omissions of information as a result of applying the materiality concept.

24. Banks should develop forward-looking reporting capabilities to provide early warnings of any potential breaches of risk limits that may exceed the bank's risk tolerance/appetite. These risk reporting capabilities should also allow banks to conduct a flexible and effective stress testing which is capable of providing forward-looking risk assessments. Supervisors expect risk management reports to enable banks to anticipate problems and provide a forward looking assessment of risk.

25. Expert judgment may occasionally be applied to incomplete data to facilitate the aggregation process, as well as the interpretation of results within the risk reporting process. Reliance on expert judgment in place of complete and accurate data should occur only on an exception basis, and should not materially impact the bank's compliance with the Principles. When expert judgment is applied, supervisors expect that the process be clearly documented and transparent so as to allow for an independent review of the process followed and the criteria used in the decision-making process.

I. OVERARCHING GOVERNANCE AND INFRASTRUCTURE

26. A bank should have in place a strong governance framework, risk data architecture and IT infrastructure. These are preconditions to ensure compliance with the other Principles included in this document. In particular, a bank's board should oversee senior management's ownership of implementing all the risk data aggregation and risk reporting principles and the strategy to meet them within a timeframe agreed with their supervisors.

Principle 1

Governance—A bank's risk data aggregation capabilities and risk reporting practices should be subject to strong

governance arrangements consistent with other principles and guidance established by the Basel Committee.[12]

27. A bank's board and senior management should promote the identification, assessment and management of data quality risks as part of its overall risk management framework. The framework should include agreed service level standards for both outsourced and in-house risk data-related processes, and a firm's policies on data confidentiality, integrity and availability, as well as risk management policies.

28. A bank's board and senior management should review and approve the bank's group risk data aggregation and risk reporting framework and ensure that adequate resources are deployed.

29. A bank's risk data aggregation capabilities and risk reporting practices should be:

    a. Fully documented and subject to high standards of validation. This validation should be independent and review the bank's compliance with the Principles in this document. The primary purpose of the independent validation is to ensure that a bank's risk data aggregation and reporting processes are functioning as intended and are appropriate for the bank's risk profile. Independent validation activities should be aligned and integrated with the other independent review activities within the bank's risk management program,[13] and encompass all components of the bank's risk data aggregation and reporting processes. Common practices suggest that the independent validation of risk data aggregation and risk reporting practices should be conducted using staff with specific IT, data and reporting expertise.[14]

    b. Considered as part of any new initiatives, including acquisitions and/or divestitures, new product development, as well as broader process and IT change initiatives. When considering a material acquisition, a bank's due diligence process should

---

[12] For instance, the Basel Committee's *Principles for Enhancing Corporate Governance* (October 2010) and *Enhancements to the Basel II framework* (July 2009).
[13] In particular the so-called "second line of defence" within the bank's internal control system.
[14] Furthermore, validation should be conducted separately from audit work to ensure full adherence to the distinction between the second and third *lines of defence*, within a bank's internal control system. See, *inter alia*, Principles 2 and 13 in the Basel Committee's *Internal Audit Function in Banks* (June 2012).

assess the risk data aggregation capabilities and risk reporting practices of the acquired entity, as well as the impact on its own risk data aggregation capabilities and risk reporting practices. The impact on risk data aggregation should be considered explicitly by the board and inform the decision to proceed. The bank should establish a timeframe to integrate and align the acquired risk data aggregation capabilities and risk reporting practices within its own framework.

c. Unaffected by the bank's group structure. The group structure should not hinder risk data aggregation capabilities at a consolidated level or at any relevant level within the organisation (e.g., sub-consolidated level, jurisdiction of operation level). In particular, risk data aggregation capabilities should be independent from the choices a bank makes regarding its legal organisation and geographical presence.[15]

30. A bank's senior management should be fully aware of and understand the limitations that prevent full risk data aggregation, in terms of coverage (e.g., risks not captured or subsidiaries not included), in technical terms (e.g., model performance indicators or degree of reliance on manual processes) or in legal terms (legal impediments to data sharing across jurisdictions). Senior management should ensure that the bank's IT strategy includes ways to improve risk data aggregation capabilities and risk reporting practices and to remedy any shortcomings against the Principles set forth in this document taking into account the evolving needs of the business. Senior management should also identify data critical to risk data aggregation and IT infrastructure initiatives through its strategic IT planning process, and support these initiatives through the allocation of appropriate levels of financial and human resources.

31. A bank's board is responsible for determining its own risk reporting requirements and should be aware of limitations that prevent full risk data aggregation in the reports it receives. The board should also be aware of the bank's implementation of, and ongoing compliance with the Principles set out in this document.

Principle 2

Data architecture and IT infrastructure—A bank should design, build and maintain data architecture and IT infrastructure which fully supports its risk data aggregation capabilities and risk reporting practices not only in normal times but also during times of stress or crisis, while still meeting the other Principles.

32. Risk data aggregation capabilities and risk reporting practices should be given direct consideration as part of a bank's business continuity planning processes and be subject to a business impact analysis.

33. A bank should establish integrated[16] data taxonomies and architecture across the banking group, which includes information on the characteristics of the data (metadata), as well as use of single identifiers and/or unified naming conventions for data including legal entities, counterparties, customers and accounts.

34. Roles and responsibilities should be established as they relate to the ownership and quality of risk data and information for both the business and IT functions. The owners (business and IT functions), in partnership with risk managers, should ensure there are adequate controls throughout the lifecycle of the data and for all aspects of the technology infrastructure. The role of the business owner includes ensuring data is correctly entered by the relevant front office unit, kept current and aligned with the data definitions, and also ensuring that risk data aggregation capabilities and risk reporting practices are consistent with firms' policies.

II. RISK DATA AGGREGATION CAPABILITIES

35. Banks should develop and maintain strong risk data aggregation capabilities to ensure that risk management reports reflect the risks in a reliable way (i.e., meeting data aggregation expectations is necessary to meet reporting expectations). Compliance with these Principles should not be at the expense of each other. These risk data aggregation capabilities

---

[15] While taking into account any legal impediments to sharing data across jurisdictions.

[16] Banks do not necessarily need to have one data model; rather, there should be robust automated reconciliation procedures where multiple models are in use.

should meet all Principles below simultaneously in accordance with paragraph 22 of this document.

Principle 3

Accuracy and Integrity—A bank should be able to generate accurate and reliable risk data to meet normal and stress/crisis reporting accuracy requirements. Data should be aggregated on a largely automated basis so as to minimise the probability of errors.

36. A bank should aggregate risk data in a way that is accurate and reliable.

   a. Controls surrounding risk data should be as robust as those applicable to accounting data.
   b. Where a bank relies on manual processes and desktop applications (e.g., spreadsheets, databases) and has specific risk units that use these applications for software development, it should have effective mitigants in place (e.g., end-user computing policies and procedures) and other effective controls that are consistently applied across the bank's processes.
   c. Risk data should be reconciled with bank's sources, including accounting data where appropriate, to ensure that the risk data is accurate.[17]
   d. A bank should strive towards a single authoritative source for risk data per each type of risk.
   e. A bank's risk personnel should have sufficient access to risk data to ensure they can appropriately aggregate, validate and reconcile the data to risk reports.

37. As a precondition, a bank should have a "dictionary" of the concepts used, such that data is defined consistently across an organisation.

38. There should be an appropriate balance between automated and manual systems. Where professional judgments are required, human intervention may be appropriate. For many other processes, a higher degree of automation is desirable to reduce the risk of errors.

39. Supervisors expect banks to document and explain all of their risk data aggregation processes whether automated or manual (judgment based or otherwise). Documentation should include an explanation

of the appropriateness of any manual workarounds, a description of their criticality to the accuracy of risk data aggregation and proposed actions to reduce the impact.

40. Supervisors expect banks to measure and monitor the accuracy of data and to develop appropriate escalation channels and action plans to be in place to rectify poor data quality.

Principle 4

Completeness—A bank should be able to capture and aggregate all material risk data across the banking group. Data should be available by business line, legal entity, asset type, industry, region and other groupings, as relevant for the risk in question, that permit identifying and reporting risk exposures, concentrations and emerging risks.

41. A bank's risk data aggregation capabilities should include all material risk exposures, including those that are off-balance sheet.

42. A banking organisation is not required to express all forms of risk in a common metric or basis, but risk data aggregation capabilities should be the same regardless of the choice of risk aggregation systems implemented. However, each system should make clear the specific approach used to aggregate exposures for any given risk measure, in order to allow the board and senior management to assess the results properly.

43. Supervisors expect banks to produce aggregated risk data that is complete and to measure and monitor the completeness of their risk data. Where risk data is not entirely complete, the impact should not be critical to the bank's ability to manage its risks effectively. Supervisors expect banks' data to be materially complete, with any exceptions identified and explained.

Principle 5

Timeliness—A bank should be able to generate aggregate and up-to-date risk data in a timely manner while also meeting the principles relating to accuracy and integrity, completeness and adaptability. The precise timing will depend upon the nature and potential volatility of the risk being measured as well as its criticality to the overall risk profile of the bank. The precise timing will also depend on the bank-specific frequency requirements for risk

---

[17] For the purposes of this paper, reconciliation means the process of comparing items or outcomes and explaining the differences.

management reporting, under both normal and stress/crisis situations, set based on the characteristics and overall risk profile of the bank.

44. A bank's risk data aggregation capabilities should ensure that it is able to produce aggregate risk information on a timely basis to meet all risk management reporting requirements.

45. The Basel Committee acknowledges that different types of data will be required at different speeds, depending on the type of risk, and that certain risk data may be needed faster in a stress/crisis situation. Banks need to build their risk systems to be capable of producing aggregated risk data rapidly during times of stress/crisis for all critical risks.

46. Critical risks include but are not limited to:

a. The aggregated credit exposure to a large corporate borrower. By comparison, groups of retail exposures may not change as critically in a short period of time but may still include significant concentrations;

b. Counterparty credit risk exposures, including, for example, derivatives;

c. Trading exposures, positions, operating limits, and market concentrations by sector and region data;

d. Liquidity risk indicators such as cash flows/settlements and funding; and

e. Operational risk indicators that are time-critical (e.g., systems availability, unauthorised access).

47. Supervisors will review that the bank specific frequency requirements, for both normal and stress/crisis situations, generate aggregate and up-to-date risk data in a timely manner.

Principle 6

Adaptability—A bank should be able to generate aggregate risk data to meet a broad range of on-demand, ad hoc risk management reporting requests, including requests during stress/crisis situations, requests due to changing internal needs and requests to meet supervisory queries.

48. A bank's risk data aggregation capabilities should be flexible and adaptable to meet ad hoc data requests, as needed, and to assess emerging risks. Adaptability will enable banks to conduct better risk management, including forecasting information, as well as to support stress testing and scenario analyses.

49. Adaptability includes:

a. Data aggregation processes that are flexible and enable risk data to be aggregated for assessment and quick decision-making;

b. Capabilities for data customisation to users' needs (e.g., dashboards, key takeaways, anomalies), to drill down as needed, and to produce quick summary reports;

c. Capabilities to incorporate new developments on the organisation of the business and/or external factors that influence the bank's risk profile; and

d. Capabilities to incorporate changes in the regulatory framework.

50. Supervisors expect banks to be able to generate subsets of data based on requested scenarios or resulting from economic events. For example, a bank should be able to aggregate risk data quickly on country credit exposures[18] as of a specified date based on a list of countries, as well as industry credit exposures as of a specified date based on a list of industry types across all business lines and geographic areas.

III. RISK REPORTING PRACTICES

51. Accurate, complete and timely data is a foundation for effective risk management. However, data alone does not guarantee that the board and senior management will receive appropriate information to make effective decisions about risk. To manage risk effectively, the right information needs to be presented to the right people at the right time. Risk reports based on risk data should be accurate, clear and complete. They should contain the correct content and be presented to the appropriate decision-makers in a time that allows for an appropriate response. To effectively achieve their objectives, risk reports should comply with the following principles. Compliance with these principles should not be at the expense of each other in accordance with paragraph 22 of this document.

Principle 7

Accuracy—Risk management reports should accurately and precisely convey aggregated risk data and reflect risk in an exact manner. Reports should be reconciled and validated.

---

[18] Including, for instance, sovereign, bank, corporate and retail exposures.

52. Risk management reports should be accurate and precise to ensure a bank's board and senior management can rely with confidence on the aggregated information to make critical decisions about risk.

53. To ensure the accuracy of the reports, a bank should maintain, at a minimum, the following:

   a. Defined requirements and processes to reconcile reports to risk data;

   b. Automated and manual edit and reasonableness checks, including an inventory of the validation rules that are applied to quantitative information. The inventory should include explanations of the conventions used to describe any mathematical or logical relationships that should be verified through these validations or checks; and

   c. Integrated procedures for identifying, reporting and explaining data errors or weaknesses in data integrity via exceptions reports.

54. Approximations are an integral part of risk reporting and risk management. Results from models, scenario analyses, and stress testing are examples of approximations that provide critical information for managing risk. While the expectations for approximations may be different than for other types of risk reporting, banks should follow the reporting principles in this document and establish expectations for the reliability of approximations (accuracy, timeliness, etc.) to ensure that management can rely with confidence on the information to make critical decisions about risk. This includes principles regarding data used to drive these approximations.

55. Supervisors expect that a bank's senior management should establish accuracy and precision requirements for both regular and stress/crisis reporting, including critical position and exposure information. These requirements should reflect the criticality of decisions that will be based on this information.

56. Supervisors expect banks to consider accuracy requirements analogous to accounting materiality. For example, if omission or misstatement could influence the risk decisions of users, this may be considered material. A bank should be able to support the rationale for accuracy requirements. Supervisors expect a bank to consider precision requirements based on validation, testing or reconciliation processes and results.

Principle 8

Comprehensiveness—Risk management reports should cover all material risk areas within the organisation. The depth and scope of these reports should be consistent with the size and complexity of the bank's operations and risk profile, as well as the requirements of the recipients.

57. Risk management reports should include exposure and position information for all significant risk areas (e.g., credit risk, market risk, liquidity risk, operational risk) and all significant components of those risk areas (e.g., single name, country and industry sector for credit risk). Risk management reports should also cover risk-related measures (e.g., regulatory and economic capital).

58. Reports should identify emerging risk concentrations, provide information in the context of limits and risk appetite/tolerance and propose recommendations for action where appropriate. Risk reports should include the current status of measures agreed by the board or senior management to reduce risk or deal with specific risk situations. This includes providing the ability to monitor emerging trends through forward-looking forecasts and stress tests.

59. Supervisors expect banks to determine risk reporting requirements that best suit their own business models and risk profiles. Supervisors will need to be satisfied with the choices a bank makes in terms of risk coverage, analysis and interpretation, scalability and comparability across group institutions. For example, an aggregated risk report should include, but not be limited to, the following information: capital adequacy, regulatory capital, capital and liquidity ratio projections, credit risk, market risk, operational risk, liquidity risk, stress testing results, inter- and intra-risk concentrations, and funding positions and plans.

60. Supervisors expect that risk management reports to the board and senior management provide a forward-looking assessment of risk and should not just rely on current and past data. The reports should contain forecasts or scenarios for key market variables and the effects on the bank so as to inform the board and senior management of the likely trajectory of the bank's capital and risk profile in the future.

Principle 9

Clarity and usefulness—Risk management reports should communicate information in a clear and concise manner. Reports should be easy to understand yet comprehensive enough to facilitate informed decision-making. Reports should include meaningful information tailored to the needs of the recipients.

61. A bank's risk reports should contribute to sound risk management and decision-making by their relevant recipients, including, in particular, the board and senior management. Risk reports should ensure that information is meaningful and tailored to the needs of the recipients.

62. Reports should include an appropriate balance between risk data, analysis and interpretation, and qualitative explanations. The balance of qualitative versus quantitative information will vary at different levels within the organisation and will also depend on the level of aggregation that is applied to the reports. Higher up in the organisation, more aggregation is expected and therefore a greater degree of qualitative interpretation will be necessary.

63. Reporting policies and procedures should recognise the differing information needs of the board, senior management, and the other levels of the organisation (for example risk committees).

64. As one of the key recipients of risk management reports, the bank's board is responsible for determining its own risk reporting requirements and complying with its obligations to shareholders and other relevant stakeholders. The board should ensure that it is asking for and receiving relevant information that will allow it to fulfil its governance mandate relating to the bank and the risks to which it is exposed. This will allow the board to ensure it is operating within its risk tolerance/appetite.

65. The board should alert senior management when risk reports do not meet its requirements and do not provide the right level and type of information to set and monitor adherence to the bank's risk tolerance/appetite. The board should indicate whether it is receiving the right balance of detail and quantitative versus qualitative information.

66. Senior management is also a key recipient of risk reports and it is responsible for determining its own risk reporting requirements. Senior management should ensure that it is receiving relevant information that will allow it to fulfil its management mandate relative to the bank and the risks to which it is exposed.

67. A bank should develop an inventory and classification of risk data items which includes a reference to the concepts used to elaborate the reports.

68. Supervisors expect that reports will be clear and useful. Reports should reflect an appropriate balance between detailed data, qualitative discussion, explanation and recommended conclusions. Interpretation and explanations of the data, including observed trends, should be clear.

69. Supervisors expect a bank to confirm periodically with recipients that the information aggregated and reported is relevant and appropriate, in terms of both amount and quality, to the governance and decision-making process.

Principle 10

Frequency—The board and senior management (or other recipients as appropriate) should set the frequency of risk management report production and distribution. Frequency requirements should reflect the needs of the recipients, the nature of the risk reported, and the speed, at which the risk can change, as well as the importance of reports in contributing to sound risk management and effective and efficient decision-making across the bank. The frequency of reports should be increased during times of stress/crisis.

70. The frequency of risk reports will vary according to the type of risk, purpose and recipients. A bank should assess periodically the purpose of each report and set requirements for how quickly the reports need to be produced in both normal and stress/crisis situations. A bank should routinely test its ability to produce accurate reports within established timeframes, particularly in stress/crisis situations.

71. Supervisors expect that in times of stress/crisis all relevant and critical credit, market and liquidity position/exposure reports are available within a very short period of time to react effectively to evolving risks. Some position/exposure information may be needed immediately (intraday) to allow for timely and effective reactions.

Principle 11

Distribution—Risk management reports should be distributed to the relevant parties while ensuring confidentiality is maintained.

72. Procedures should be in place to allow for rapid collection and analysis of risk data and timely dissemination of reports to all appropriate recipients. This should be balanced with the need to ensure confidentiality as appropriate.

73. Supervisors expect a bank to confirm periodically that the relevant recipients receive timely reports.

IV. SUPERVISORY REVIEW, TOOLS AND COOPERATION

74. Supervisors will have an important role to play in monitoring and providing incentives for a bank's implementation of, and ongoing compliance with the Principles. They should also review compliance with the Principles across banks to determine whether the Principles themselves are achieving their desired outcome and whether further enhancements are required.

Principle 12

Review—Supervisors should periodically review and evaluate a bank's compliance with the eleven Principles above.

75. Supervisors should review a bank's compliance with the Principles in the preceding sections. Reviews should be incorporated into the regular programme of supervisory reviews and may be supplemented by thematic reviews covering multiple banks with respect to a single or selected issue. Supervisors may test a bank's compliance with the Principles through occasional requests for information to be provided on selected risk issues (for example, exposures to certain risk factors) within short deadlines, thereby testing the capacity of a bank to aggregate risk data rapidly and produce risk reports. Supervisors should have access to the appropriate reports to be able to perform this review.

76. Supervisors should draw on reviews conducted by the internal or external auditors to inform their assessments of compliance with the Principles. Supervisors may require work to be carried out by a bank's

internal audit functions or by experts independent from the bank. Supervisors must have access to all appropriate documents such as internal validation and audit reports, and should be able to meet with and discuss risk data aggregation capabilities with the external auditors or independent experts from the bank, when appropriate.

77. Supervisors should test a bank's capabilities to aggregate data and produce reports in both stress/crisis and steady-state environments, including sudden sharp increases in business volumes.

Principle 13

Remedial actions and supervisory measures—Supervisors should have and use the appropriate tools and resources to require effective and timely remedial action by a bank to address deficiencies in its risk data aggregation capabilities and risk reporting practices. Supervisors should have the ability to use a range of tools, including Pillar 2.

78. Supervisors should require effective and timely remedial action by a bank to address deficiencies in its risk data aggregation capabilities and risk reporting practices and internal controls.

79. Supervisors should have a range of tools at their disposal to address material deficiencies in a bank's risk data aggregation and reporting capabilities. Such tools may include, but are not limited to, requiring a bank to take remedial action; increasing the intensity of supervision; requiring an independent review by a third party, such as external auditors; and the possible use of capital add-ons as both a risk mitigant and incentive under Pillar 2.[19]

80. Supervisors should be able to set limits on a bank's risks or the growth in their activities where deficiencies in risk data aggregation and reporting are assessed as causing significant weaknesses in risk management capabilities.

81. For new business initiatives, supervisors may require that banks' implementation plans ensure that robust risk data aggregation is possible before allowing a new business venture or acquisition to proceed.

---

[19] Basel Committee, *Enhancements to the Basel II framework* (July 2009).

82. When a supervisor requires a bank to take remedial action, the supervisor should set a timetable for completion of the action. Supervisors should have escalation procedures in place to require more stringent or accelerated remedial action in the event that a bank does not adequately address the deficiencies identified, or in the case that supervisors deem further action is warranted.

Principle 14

Home/host cooperation—Supervisors should cooperate with relevant supervisors in other jurisdictions regarding the supervision and review of the Principles, and the implementation of any remedial action if necessary.

83. Effective cooperation and appropriate information sharing between the home and host supervisory authorities should contribute to the robustness of a bank's risk management practices across a bank's operations in multiple jurisdictions. Wherever possible, supervisors should avoid performing redundant and uncoordinated reviews related to risk data aggregation and risk reporting.

84. Cooperation can take the form of sharing of information within the constraints of applicable laws, as well as discussion between supervisors on a bilateral or multilateral basis (e.g., through colleges of supervisors), including, but not limited to, regular meetings. Communication by conference call and email may be particularly useful in tracking required remedial actions. Cooperation through colleges should be in line with the Basel Committee's *Good practice principles on supervisory colleges*.[20]

85. Supervisors should discuss their experiences regarding the quality of risk data aggregation capabilities and risk reporting practices in different parts of the group. This should include any impediments to risk data aggregation and risk reporting arising from cross-border issues and also whether risk data is distributed appropriately across the group. Such exchanges will enable supervisors to identify significant concerns at an early stage and to respond promptly and effectively.

V. IMPLEMENTATION TIMELINE AND TRANSITIONAL ARRANGEMENTS

86. Supervisors expect that a bank's data and IT infrastructures will be enhanced in the coming years to ensure that its risk data aggregation capabilities and risk reporting practices are sufficiently robust and flexible enough to address their potential needs in normal times and particularly during times of stress/crisis.

87. National banking supervisors will start discussing implementation of the Principles with G-SIB's senior management in early 2013. This will ensure that banks develop a strategy to meet the Principles by 2016.

88. In order for G-SIBs to meet the Principles in accordance with the 2016 timeline, national banking supervisors will discuss banks' analysis of risk data aggregation capabilities with their senior management and agree to timelines for required improvements. Supervisory approaches are likely to include requiring self-assessments by G-SIBs against these expectations in early 2013, with the goal of closing significant gaps before 2016. Supervisors may also engage technical experts to support their assessments of banks' plans in respect of the 2016 deadline.[21]

89. The Basel Committee will track G-SIBs progress towards complying with the Principles through its Standards Implementation Group (SIG) from 2013 onwards. This will include any observations on the effectiveness of the Principles themselves and whether any enhancements or other revisions of the Principles are necessary in order to achieve the desired outcomes. The Basel Committee will share its findings with the FSB at least annually starting from the end of 2013.

---

[20] Basel Committee, *Good practice principles on supervisory colleges* (October 2010) www.bis.org/publ/bcbs177. pdf

[21] The Basel Committee recognises that under very specific and exceptional circumstances, national supervisors might have to apply some degree of flexibility in implementing the 2016 deadline. For instance, in cases where processes have been outsourced to third parties, there could be impacts on implementation timelines as some outsourcing contracts may have terms extending beyond 2016.

GARP Code of Conduct

Learning Objectives

Candidates, after completing this reading, should be able to:

- Describe the responsibility of each GARP member with respect to professional integrity, ethical conduct, conflicts of interest, confidentiality of information, and adherence to generally accepted practices in risk management.

- Describe the potential consequences of violating the GARP Code of Conduct.

Excerpt is GARP Code of Conduct, *by GARP.*

INTRODUCTION

The GARP Code of Conduct ("Code") sets forth principles of professional conduct for Global Association of Risk Professional ("GARP") Financial Risk Management program (FRM®) certification and other GARP certification and diploma holders and candidates, GARP's Board of Trustees, its Regional Directors, GARP Committee Members and GARP's staff (hereinafter collectively referred to as "GARP Members") in support of the advancement of the financial risk management profession. These principles promote the highest levels of ethical conduct and disclosure and provide direction and support for both the individual practitioner and the risk management profession.

The pursuit of high ethical standards goes beyond following the letter of applicable rules and regulations and behaving in accordance with the intentions of those laws and regulations, it is about pursuing a universal ethical culture.

All individuals, firms and associations have an ethical character. Some of the biggest risks faced by firms today do not involve legal or compliance violations but rest on decisions involving ethical considerations and the application of appropriate standards of conduct to business decision making.

There is no single prescriptive ethical standard that can be globally applied. We can only expect that GARP Members will continuously consider ethical issues and adjust their conduct accordingly as they engage in their daily activities.

This document makes references to professional standards and generally accepted risk management practices. Risk practitioners should understand these as concepts that reflect an evolving shared body of professional standards and practices. In considering the issues this raises ethical behavior must weigh the circumstances and the culture of the applicable global community in which the practitioner resides.

CODE OF CONDUCT

The Code is comprised of the following Principles, Professional Standards and Rules of Conduct which GARP Members agree to uphold and implement.

Principles

Professional Integrity and Ethical Conduct

GARP Members shall act with honesty, integrity, and competence to fulfill the risk professional's responsibilities and to uphold the reputation of the risk management profession. GARP Members must avoid disguised contrivances in assessments, measurements and processes that are intended to provide business advantage at the expense of honesty and truthfulness.

Conflicts of Interest

GARP Members have a responsibility to promote the interests of all relevant constituencies and will not knowingly perform risk management services directly or indirectly involving an actual or potential conflict of interest unless full disclosure has been provided to all affected parties of any actual or apparent conflict of interest. Where conflicts are unavoidable GARP Members commit to their full disclosure and management.

Confidentiality

GARP Members will take all reasonable precautionary measures to prevent intentional and unintentional disclosure of confidential information.

Professional Standards

Fundamental Responsibilities

- GARP Members must endeavor, and encourage others, to operate at the highest level of professional skill.
- GARP Members should always continue to perfect their expertise.
- GARP Members have a personal ethical responsibility and cannot out-source or delegate that responsibility to others.

Best Practices

- GARP Members will promote and adhere to applicable 'best practice standards', and will ensure that risk management activities performed under his/her direct supervision or management satisfies these applicable standards.
- GARP Members recognize that risk management does not exist in a vacuum.

- GARP Members commit to considering the wider impact of their assessments and actions on their colleagues and the wider community and environment in which they work.

Communication and Disclosure

GARP Members issuing any communications on behalf of their firm will ensure that the communications are clear, appropriate to the circumstances and their intended audience, and satisfy applicable standards of conduct.

RULES OF CONDUCT

Professional Integrity and Ethical Conduct

GARP Members

1. Shall act professionally, ethically and with integrity in all dealings with employers, existing or potential clients, the public, and other practitioners in the financial services industry.

2. Shall exercise reasonable judgment in the provision of risk services while maintaining independence of thought and direction. GARP Members must not offer, solicit, or accept any gift, benefit, compensation, or consideration that could be reasonably expected to compromise their own or another's independence and objectivity.

3. Must take reasonable precautions to ensure that the Member's services are not used for improper, fraudulent or illegal purposes.

4. Shall not knowingly misrepresent details relating to analysis, recommendations, actions, or other professional activities.

5. Shall not engage in any professional conduct involving dishonesty or deception or engage in any act that reflects negatively on their integrity, character, trustworthiness, or professional ability or on the risk management profession.

6. Shall not engage in any conduct or commit any act that compromises the integrity of the GARP, the (Financial Risk Manager) FRM® designation or the integrity or validity of the examinations leading to the award of the right to use the FRM designation or any other credentials that may be offered by GARP.

7. Shall endeavor to be mindful of cultural differences regarding ethical behavior and customs, and to avoid any actions that are, or may have the appearance of being unethical according to local customs. If there appears to be a conflict or overlap of standards, the GARP member should always seek to apply the higher standard.

Conflict of Interest

GARP Members Shall

1. Act fairly in all situations and must fully disclose any actual or potential conflict to all affected parties.

2. Make full and fair disclosure of all matters that could reasonably be expected to impair their independence and objectivity or interfere with their respective duties to their employer, clients, and prospective clients.

Confidentiality

GARP Members

1. Shall not make use of confidential information for inappropriate purposes and unless having received prior consent shall maintain the confidentiality of their work, their employer or client.

2. Must not use confidential information to benefit personally.

Fundamental Responsibilities

GARP Members Shall

1. Comply with all applicable laws, rules, and regulations (including this Code) governing the GARP Members' professional activities and shall not knowingly participate or assist in any violation of such laws, rules, or regulations.

2. Have ethical responsibilities and cannot out-source or delegate those responsibilities to others.

3. Understand the needs and complexity of their employer or client, and should provide appropriate and suitable risk management services and advice.

4. Be diligent about not overstating the accuracy or certainty of results or conclusions.

5. Clearly disclose the relevant limits of their specific knowledge and expertise concerning risk assessment, industry practices and applicable laws and regulations.

General Accepted Practices

GARP Members Shall

1. Execute all services with diligence and perform all work in a manner that is independent from interested parties. GARP Members should collect, analyze and distribute risk information with the highest level of professional objectivity.

2. Shall be familiar with current generally accepted risk management practices and shall clearly indicate any departure from their use.

3. Shall ensure that communications include factual data and do not contain false information.

4. Shall make a distinction between fact and opinion in the presentation of analysis and recommendations.

APPLICABILITY AND ENFORCEMENT

Every GARP Member should know and abide by this Code. Local laws and regulations may also impose obligations on GARP Members. Where local requirements conflict with the Code, such requirements will have precedence.

Violation(s) of this Code may result in, among other things, the temporary suspension or permanent removal of the GARP Member from GARP's Membership roles, and may also include temporarily or permanently removing from the violator the right to use or refer to having earned the FRM designation or any other GARP granted designation, following a formal determination that such a violation has occurred.

SAMPLE EXAM QUESTIONS—FOUNDATIONS OF RISK MANAGEMENT

1. The efficient frontier is defined by the set of portfolios that, for each volatility level, maximizes the expected return. According to the capital asset pricing model (CAPM), which of the following statements are correct with respect to the efficient frontier?

   A. The capital market line always has a positive slope and its steepness depends on the market risk premium and the volatility of the market portfolio.

   B. The capital market line is the straight line connecting the risk-free asset with the zero beta minimum variance portfolio.

   C. Investors with the lowest risk aversion will typically hold the portfolio of risky assets that has the lowest standard deviation on the efficient frontier.

   D. The efficient frontier allows different individuals to have different portfolios of risky assets based upon their individual forecasts for asset returns.

2. A high net worth investor is monitoring the performance of an index tracking fund in which she has invested. The performance figures of the fund and the benchmark portfolio are summarized in the table below:

Year	Benchmark Return	Fund Return
2005	9.00%	1.00%
2006	7.00%	3.00%
2007	7.00%	5.00%
2008	5.00%	4.00%
2009	2.00%	1.50%

   What is the tracking error of the fund over this period?

   A. 0.09%

   B. 1.10%

   C. 3.05%

   D. 4.09%

3. Suppose that the correlation of the return of a portfolio with the return of its benchmark is 0.8, the volatility of the return of the portfolio is 5%, and the volatility of the return of the benchmark is 4%. What is the beta of the portfolio?

   A. 1.00

   B. 0.64

   C. 0.80

   D. −1.00

4. In characterizing various dimensions of a bank's data, the Basel Committee has suggested several principles to promote strong and effective risk data aggregation capabilities. Which statement correctly describes a recommendation which the bank should follow in accordance with the given principle?

   A. The integrity principle recommends that data aggregation should be completely automated without any manual intervention.

   B. The completeness principle recommends that a financial institution should capture data on its entire universe of material risk exposures.

   C. The adaptability principle recommends that a bank should frequently update its risk reporting systems to incorporate changes in best practices.

   D. The accuracy principle recommends that the risk data be reconciled with management's estimates of risk exposure prior to aggregation.

5. Which of the following is not necessarily considered a failure of risk management?

   A. Incorrect measurement of known risks

   B. Failure in communicating risk issues to top management

   C. Failure to minimize losses on credit portfolios

   D. Failure to use appropriate risk metrics

6. Which of the following is a common attribute of the collapse at both Metallgesellschaft and Long-Term Capital Management (LTCM)?

   A. Cash flow problems caused by large mark to market losses

   B. High leverage

   C. Fraud

   D. There are no similarities between the causes of the collapse at Metallgesellschaft and LTCM.

7. Portfolio A has an expected return of 8%, volatility of 20%, and beta of 0.5. Assume that the market has an expected return of 10% and volatility of 25%. Also, assume a risk-free rate of 5%. What is Jensen's alpha for portfolio A?

   A. 0.5%

   B. 1.0%

   C. 10%

   D. 15%

8. According to the Capital Asset Pricing Model (CAPM), over a single time period, investors seek to maximize their:

   A. wealth and are concerned about the tails of return distributions.

   B. wealth and are not concerned about the tails of return distributions.

   C. expected utility and are concerned about the tails of return distributions.

   D. expected utility and are not concerned about the tails of return distributions.

9. Gregory is analyzing the historical performance of two commodity funds tracking the Reuters/Jefferies-CRB® Index (CRB) as benchmark. He collated the data on the monthly returns and decided to use the information ratio (IR) to assess which fund achieved higher returns more efficiently and presented his findings.

	Fund I	Fund II	Benchmark Returns
Average monthly returns	1.488%	1.468%	1.415%
Average excess return	0.073%	0.053%	0.000%
Standard deviation of returns	0.294%	0.237%	0.238%
Tracking error	0.344%	0.341%	0.000%

What is the information ratio for each fund, and what conclusion can be drawn?

A. IR for Fund I = 0.212, IR for Fund II = 0.155; Fund II performed better as it has a lower IR.

B. IR for Fund I = 0.212, IR for Fund II = 0.155; Fund I performed better as it has a higher IR.

C. IR for Fund I = 0.248, IR for Fund II = 0.224; Fund I performed better as it has a higher IR.

D. IR for Fund I = 0.248, IR for Fund II = 0.224; Fund II performed better as it has a lower IR.

10. An analyst is estimating the sensitivity of the return of stock A to different macroeconomic factors. He prepares the following estimates for the factor betas:

$$\beta_{\text{Industrial production}} = 1.3 \qquad \beta_{\text{interest rate}} = -0.75$$

Under baseline expectations, with industrial production growth of 3% and an interest rate of 1.5%, the expected return for Stock A is estimated to be 5%.

The economic research department is forecasting an acceleration of economic activity for the following year, with GDP forecast to grow 4.2% and interest rates increasing 25 basis points to 1.75%.

What return of Stock A can be expected for next year according to this forecast?

A. 4.8%

B. 6.4%

C. 6.8%

D. 7.8%

SAMPLE EXAM ANSWERS AND EXPLANATIONS— FOUNDATIONS OF RISK MANAGEMENT

1. **Answer: A**

   Explanation: The capital market line connects the risk-free asset with the market portfolio, which is the efficient portfolio at which the capital market line is tangent to the efficient frontier. The equation of the capital market line is as follows:

   $$\bar{R}_e = R_F + \frac{\bar{R}_M - R_F}{\sigma_M}\sigma_e$$

   where the subscript e denotes an efficient portfolio. Since the shape of the efficient frontier is dictated by the market risk premium, $(\bar{R}_M - R_F)$, and the volatility of the market, the slope of the capital market line will also be dependent on these two factors.

2. **Answer: C**

   Explanation: Relative risk measures risk relative to a benchmark index and measures it in terms of tracking error or deviation from the index.

   We need to calculate the standard deviation (square root of the variance) of the series:

   $$\{0.08, 0.04, 0.02, 0.01, 0.005\}.$$

   Perform the calculation by computing the difference of each data point from the mean, square the result of each, take the average of those values, and then take the square root. This is equal to 3.04%.

3. **Answer: A**

   Explanation: The following equation is used to calculate beta:

   $$\beta = \rho\frac{\sigma(portfolio)}{\sigma(benchmark)} = 0.8 * \frac{0.05}{0.04} = 1.00.$$

   where ρ represents the correlation coefficient and σ the volatility.

4. **Answer: B**

   Explanation: The completeness principle recommends that a bank be able to capture and aggregate all data on the material risks to which it is exposed across the organization. This will allow it to identify and report risk exposures, concentrations, and set exposure limits.

5. **Answer: C**

   Explanation: A failure to minimize losses on credit portfolios is not necessarily a failure of risk management. The firm may have used prudent risk management and decided that the potential rewards from entering into the credit agreements adequately compensated the firm for the risks taken. It could also have ignored the advice of its risk managers to attempt to minimize its credit losses. Either way, this is not necessarily a failure of risk management.

6. **Answer: A**

   Explanation: Metallgesellschaft and Long Term Capital Management (LTCM) dealt in the derivatives market in huge quantities, and both experienced a cash flow crisis due to the change in economic conditions. This led to huge mark-to-market losses and margin calls.

7. **Answer: A**

   Explanation: The Jensen measure of a portfolio, or Jensen's alpha, can be calculated using the following equation:

   $$\alpha_p = E(R_p) - R_F - \beta[E(R_M) - R_F]$$

   In this example, $\alpha_p = 8\% - 5\% - 0.5 * (10\% - 5\%)$, or 0.5%.

8. **Answer: D**

   Explanation: CAPM assumes investors seek to maximize the expected utility of their wealth at the end of the period, and that when choosing their portfolios, investors only consider the first two moments of the return distribution: the expected return and the variance. Hence, investors are not concerned with the tails of the return distribution.

9. **Answer: B**

   Explanation: The information ratio may be calculated by either a comparison of the residual return to residual risk or the excess return to tracking error. The higher the IR, the better 'informed' the manager is at picking assets to invest in. Since neither residual return nor risk is given, only the latter is an option.

   $IR = E(R_p - R_b)/\text{Tracking Error}$

   For Fund I: IR = 0.00073/0.00344 = 0.212; For Fund II: IR = 0.00053/0.00341 = 0.155

10. **Answer: B**

    Explanation: The expected return for Stock A equals the expected return for the stock under the baseline scenario, plus the impact of "shocks," or excess returns of, both factors. Since the baseline scenario incorporates 3% industrial production growth and a 1.5% interest rate, the "shocks" are 1.2% for the GDP factor and 0.25% for the interest rate factor.

    Therefore the expected return for the new scenario = Baseline scenario expected return + $\beta_{\text{Industrial production}}$ * Industrial production shock + $\beta_{\text{interest rate}}$ * Interest rate shock

    or 5% + (1.3 * 1.2%) + (−0.75 * 0.25%) = 6.37%.

Index

business impacts, of poor data quality, 180-181
business performance, ERM and, 62-63
business process view, 185
business risk, 19, 21, 22
business risk committee, 51-52

Cabiallavetta, Mathis, 92
capital asset pricing model (CAPM), 28
    applying to performance measurement, 147-158
    APT and, 169-170
    overview, 134
    prices and, 140-141
    rigorous approach to, 139-140
    simple approach to, 135-139
    underlying assumptions, 134-135
capital market line, 136
capital markets activities, 22
Capital One Financial, 76
Cernauskas, Deborah, 179-186
Chase Manhattan Bank/Drysdale Securities, 87-88
Chicago Board of Trade (CBOT), 35-36
Chicago Board Options Exchange (CBOE), 35
Chicago Mercantile Exchange (CME), 36
chief executive officer (CEO), 52
chief risk officer (CRO), 45, 50-51, 52, 61, 63-65
Citigroup, 102-103, 114
clarity, risk reporting and, 198
cliff risk, 114
Code of Conduct, GARP, 204-205
collateralized debt obligations (CDOs), 111-113
Committee of Sponsoring Organizations of the Treadway
    Commission (COSO), 61
commodity price risk, 16
communication failures, 126
compensation committee, 43, 44, 49-50
completeness
    data quality and, 183
    risk data aggregation and, 195
compliance, 180
compliance costs, 29
compliance risk, 182
comprehensiveness, risk reporting and, 197
concentration risks, 18
confidence levels, 8
confidence-based impacts, 180
Conseco, 17
consistency, data quality and, 183
contango markets, 37
corporate governance
    committees and risk limits, 46-50
    ERM and, 65, 66
    limits and limit standards policies, 52-53
    overview, 42-45
    risk management and, 43-45
    role of audit function, 54-56
    roles and responsibilities, 50-52
    Sarbanes-Oxley Act (SOX), 42
    standards for monitoring risk, 53-54
    true risk governance, 45-46

corporate risk management
    constructing and implementing a strategy, 36-37
    determining the objective, 31, 33-34
    dynamic strategies that failed, 37
    hedging operations vs. hedging financial positions, 30-31
    instruments for, 34-36
    mapping the risks, 34
    overview, 28
    performance evaluation, 37-38
    reasons not to manage risk, 28-29
    reasons to manage risk, 29-30
correlation-adjusted portfolio (CAP), 158
cost of capital, finding with APT, 174
covariance, 6
credit cards, 22
credit default swaps (CDS), 17
credit derivatives, 17
credit events, 17
credit risk, 10, 16-18, 182
credit risk assessment, 181
credit spread, 114
Crosby, James, 64
Crouhy, Michel, 4-57
currency, data quality and, 183
currency risks, 34

Daiwa Bank, 95
data architecture, risk data aggregation and, 194
data quality
    compliance risk, 182
    credit risk, 182
    development risk, 182
    employee fraud and abuse, 181-182
    expectations, 182-183
    information flaws, 181
    inspection, control, and oversight, 184
    insurance exposure, 182
    issues view, 185
    managing via data quality scorecard, 185-186
    mapping business policies to data rules, 184
    other dimensions of, 183
    overview, 180
    poor, business impacts of, 180-181
    underbilling and revenue assurance, 182
data quality scorecard, 184, 185-186
data resources, for ERM, 66, 67
De Angelis, Anthony, 87
default risk, 16
default-rate risk, 7
delegation process, for market risk authorities, 51
Deloitte, 11, 64
Department of Defense Guidelines on Data Quality, 181
derivatives, 127
Deutsche Bank, 64, 93
development risk, 182
Dey Report, 66
distribution, risk reporting and, 199
diversification, 165-166
Dodd-Frank, 23-24, 114